UNIVERSITY OF
GLOUCESTERSHIRE
at Cheltenham and Gloucester

Negotiate the Best Deal

Negotiate the Best Deal

Techniques that really work

GERALD ATKINSON

Published in association with the Institute of Directors

DIRECTOR BOOKS

Published by Director Books,
an imprint of Fitzwilliam Publishing Limited,
Simon & Schuster International Group,
Fitzwilliam House, 32 Trumpington Street,
Cambridge CB2 1QY, England

First published 1990

© Gerald Atkinson, 1990

British Library Cataloguing in Publication Data

Atkinson, Gerald *1938*–
   Negotiate the best deal.
   1. Business negotiation
   I. Title
   658.45

   ISBN 1–870555–19–8

Designed by Geoff Green
Typeset by Goodfellow & Egan Limited, Cambridge
Printed in Great Britain by BPCC Wheatons Ltd, Exeter

To my parents whose love of God and their fellow man was so gloriously infectious.

To my family who have given me so much happiness.

Thank you.

Contents

viii   Contents

Acknowledgements

I would like to thank three parties in particular.

First, the experienced negotiators who, as we spent the hours together, gave so willingly of their time and experience. Among them I am indebted in particular to Geoff Armstrong, Dennis Boyd, Chris Carter, George Chadfield, John Cummins, John Dewhurst, Bob Farrands, Derrick Frost, Colin Gosnell, Derek Holbrook, Terry Janes, Geoff Keeys, Steve Oram, David Palmer, Edward Robinson and Tony Simmonds.

Second, those, especially my wife, who typed the manuscript and who, even with the benefit of word processors, accepted long revisions to short deadlines with such good grace.

Third, my publishers who, though accustomed to authors who fail to meet deadlines, put up with the excuses of this one very well.

Introduction

The outcome of negotiation can be spectacular. There are few other areas in which the investment of time and effort can yield so immediate and profitable a return.

Gone are the days when negotiation was seen as a secondary activity that somehow should not be necessary. Swift business opportunities and stronger, sharper market forces have seen to that. But negotiation is still viewed with suspicion by many, and feelings of deep anxiety are generated by it. Both are understandable. For of all business activities, it is probably the one that is least understood. Certainly it is the one most susceptible to opinion and value judgement.

Negotiate the Best Deal will dispel mystique:

1. It will give crystal clear insight into the processes of negotiation. Part I deals with what we call 'the inner game of negotiation' and shows you how to control it.
2. It will demonstrate how systematic preparation generates the optimum strategy. Part II gives the techniques that make for incisive preparation.
3. It will give advice and guidance on sound negotiating technique. Part III deals with the negotiating tactics and behaviour that make for productive negotiation.

Negotiate the Best Deal has been written with four parties very much in mind: the *director* who has overall responsibility for the outcome – but probably is not there; the *lead negotiator* who has the opportunity to negotiate a better deal than ever before; the *negotiating team* which, dependent on its insight, discipline and empathy, is a valuable asset or a heavy liability; and the *other party* who despite possible appearances to the contrary has an interest in settlement too! As we will see, the relationships between these four play a crucial part.

This book goes deeper into negotiation than most others. Yet managers are busier than ever before. So while the text gives considerable detail, I have used sub-headings extensively and there are summary points at the end of each chapter. The outcome of this is a work that will meet both general and specific needs.

My contacts with companies over the years lead me to the conclusion that female executives are putting their natural persuasive talents to even better use by getting more involved in negotiation, particularly contract negotiation. My reason for mentioning this is that when writing a book such as this, I had to decide whether to refer to the other party as him, her or them – or a mix of these. In fact because the majority of my audience is still likely to be male, I have decided on the first and last options, and I trust that female expertise will be neither flattered nor offended!

I have enjoyed writing the book for a number of reasons. I would like to mention two.

First, I find negotiation stimulating. It is one of those activities in which technique and understanding really do pay off. In what to some may seem an unpredictable, even uncontrollable exchange, there is indeed logic, system and technique. Use them and they give insight, and power to control the outcome. Expertise makes all the difference. So to write about them is rewarding.

Second, while the book is based on my own experience over the last thirty years as negotiator, consultant and trainer of some very senior executives, I have gone out of my way to ask on a systematic basis a number of our top specialist negotiators – some thirty in all – in both the commercial and labour fields for the insight and experience they can give. I refer to them in the book as the 'experienced negotiators' that they undoubtedly are. I have found my discussions with them stimulating, and have enjoyed every minute. I thank them wholeheartedly. But more to the point as you will see, the book is infinitely richer for their thought and comment.

One final point. On occasion I refer to negotiation as 'a game'. Indeed, I have already spoken of 'the inner game'. And negotiation has its moves, tactics, teams, ploys – yes, and rules, except we call them conventions! Of course in this sense it is a game because it has all of these. But again, of course, it is not, because it is not trivial. At times it is desperately important. So if any reader feels that I view it as an amusement, as light and of little consequence, they could not be more mistaken.

So here it is: *Negotiate the Best Deal*. I trust that the guidance it offers will give you success in negotiation as never before.

Gerald Atkinson
Inkpen Great Common, Berkshire, England
September 1990

1
The components of success

The hopes that surround negotiation are immense. They are greater than ever before. Obviously, the requirement to negotiate successful business contracts, ventures and deals continues with increasing intensity on an ever-wider scale. But at the time of writing, the outcome of the immense changes taking place in Eastern Europe, within the Soviet Union and in South Africa is being determined by negotiation. Again as the member countries of the European Community are redefining its purpose and reviewing their relationships, they are doing so through negotiation. Another breakthrough in arms limitation has just taken place, and further international trade agreements have recently been made. And these are just some of the higher-profile issues. Then, lower down the scale, in every society or organisation in which the right of dissent is upheld, negotiation is going on, day in, day out, on a myriad of topics at the work-place, in the community and between individuals as they live and deal with each other.

What then can we say? Quite simply this. Starting at the level of the individual, most of us negotiate more frequently ourselves and are more affected by the agreements negotiated by others than we probably ever dreamed of. Then, moving to the level of the institution, those who negotiate on its behalf are playing a major part in its survival and growth. And finally, moving to the level of nation, those who negotiate are carrying an awesome responsibility – to those in that nation certainly, but also, as negotiations to control world pollution and to safeguard our environment are added to nuclear arms reduction and control, to the human race.

Negotiation then is a supremely important activity. Increasingly, more is expected of it and of those who are involved in it.

Different types of negotiation

At this moment we must pause, briefly, to define our terms since the word 'negotiation' is an umbrella term which hides the fact that it loosely describes what are in fact three very different approaches. A lack of understanding of the difference between them can be the source of much confusion, frustration and, on occasion, of spectacular failure.

The first approach or type of negotiation we can call *mainstream negotiation*. It covers most negotiating activity and relates to the situation in which two or more parties come together to find settlement on one or a series of negotiating items. Each party gives himself room for manoeuvre since he knows that the best way to get movement by the other is to be able to give it himself. But the terms on which he can settle are not open. Each negotiator has his constraints, each operates within a mandate. His limits are set, and he will probably be unable to exceed them. Nevertheless, both parties come to negotiate with the full intention of finding a deal.

Second is what we call *pressure bargaining*. Its nature speaks for itself, and the fundamental difference between it and mainstream negotiation is that one or maybe both parties wish to achieve an outcome, but seek it through coercion rather than compromise. Labour negotiations can start as pressure bargaining or can all too easily slip into it.

Finally there is *joint problem solving*. It is very different from the other two since its purpose is to enable the parties to create new solutions to jointly agreed problems rather than to find a compromise within their respective mandates. It is very appealing. Among its recent advocates are Roger Fisher and Bill Ury, who in their book *Getting to Yes*[1] call it 'principled negotiation'.

For it to work, it requires a high level of trust between the parties, a strong commitment by them to find the best rather than their preferred solution to their jointly agreed objective within jointly agreed constraints, and a very considerable degree of flexibility within their respective mandates which will allow them to do so. When these requirements are related to the practicabilities of most negotiating situations, it becomes clear that joint problem solving is far from the norm. Trust there may well be. But it is the inability of the parties to depart sufficiently from their mandates that make it an exceptional activity, and the harsh reality is that a party which persists in the problem solving mode when the other is using either mainstream negotiation or, worse still, pressure bargaining will lose, and lose heavily.

Three very different situations therefore. All called negotiation, but each with a very different purpose and with very different strategies, tactics and behaviour.

This book concentrates on mainstream negotiation for two very good reasons. First, because it accounts for 90 per cent or more of negotiating activity. Publicity is given to pressure bargaining, conflict and breakdown, but the norm is that most negotiations avoid these extremes. And we have seen that because of the immense constraints that secular self-interest puts on it, pure joint problem solving is rare indeed. So since mainstream negotiation is the norm, it is our concern.

But there is a second reason: if 90 per cent of negotiation is 'beginning-to-end' mainstream negotiation, I would suggest that both pressure bargaining and joint problem solving tend to start as mainstream negotiation but then polarise to either extreme. So if after the opening moves of probing and conditioning the parties believe they are far from each other, they will move to pressure bargaining. If on the other hand they find they are close, or are now discussing, for example, how they might overcome the problem of implementing something they have already agreed, they may move into joint problem solving. So the second reason for concentrating on mainstream negotiation is that either it precedes pressure bargaining, or it paves the way, as parties negotiate on what the problem or objective is, and what the constraints are, for joint problem solving.

So with mainstream negotiation now firmly established as the scope of this book, we can move on to look in this chapter at what makes for successful negotiation.

The four components of success

What constitutes success in negotiation? I have no doubt that it is achieving a negotiated agreement that both parties will honour on the most favourable terms you can achieve within your mandate. But what are the key factors that enable you to do this? What are the components of success? There will be many, including chance, fortune and a stroke of luck! But after thirty years of deep involvement in all aspects of negotiation, after wide reading and considerable research, and after detailed discussion with some of our most experienced negotiators, I suggest that there are four components that assume a level of importance above all the others.

An understanding of the inner game

Negotiation is a complex activity. To determine a negotiating objective requires clear analysis. To generate useful strategy requires insight and technique. To negotiate well requires skill in many areas. But all require an understanding of the processes and the forces that are at work in negotiation as the party is moved from a position of rational or emotional opposition to one of agreement or accommodation. These are the forces of what we call the inner game. In Part I we look at them and at how they can be managed. We will deal with such aspects as:

- Personal and positional credibility in negotiation.
- Positional needs and negotiating style.
- The rejection pattern.
- The natural sequence and rhythm of negotiation.
- The use of pressure in negotiation.
- The processes of movement, adjustment and accommodation.

When these are understood, the negotiating process can be controlled and the first component of success is in place.

A relevant negotiating objective

The need to know what you want from negotiation, the requirement to have a negotiating objective, is surely so obvious that it hardly deserves mention, let alone elevation to the status of a component of success! Perhaps. But it is in the word 'relevant' that its importance lies.

I would suggest that a negotiating objective must be 'relevant' in four ways. Clearly it should first and foremost meet your own needs – there is little point in negotiating if it does not. Second, it should address the needs of the other party. It should therefore take into account concessions. This being so it should, third, fall within a range of negotiation positions that runs from your first proposal to your at worst settlement point. And fourth, it should relate to the strength of your negotiating position. Little purpose is served on the one hand in attempting to negotiate a position that is bound to fail, or on the other in massively underplaying it. These four requirements are taken up again in Part II when we look at incisive preparation.

Systematic strategy development

The requirement to prepare for negotiation, as opposed to 'playing it by ear', is an absolute one. Indeed for the experienced negotiators with whom I spoke it was their top priority, and virtually every book on negotiation stresses its importance. Yet the advice available in them on how specifically to set about preparation to develop a game plan and to assess its viability is conspicuous by its absence. It is for this reason that in Part II I give detailed guidance and show how to develop strategy from start to finish. My method revolves around a series of techniques that are put into a four-stage sequence of systematic preparation that is given in outline in Figure 1.1.

Stage 1 consists of identifying the issues of negotiation and of determining how you will handle them. At Stage 2 the relationship between the negotiating objective and its power base is assessed, and strategies to enhance negotiating power are developed. In Stage 3 the strategies identified in the previous two stages are combined with the appropriate standard strategies of negotiation and an overall game plan is created. Finally at Stage 4 the detail that will be required in negotiation is checked and all parties are fully briefed.

Strategy is a function of requirement. There is little purpose in developing a sophisticated and detailed game plan for simple and straightforward negotiation. The techniques of systematic preparation that we will give can be used singly or in combination, and strategy can be detailed or general. But whether simple or

Stage 1:	Identify the issues of negotiation and determine how to handle them.
Stage 2:	Assess negotiating power and develop strategies to enhance it.
Stage 3:	Create the overall game plan.
Stage 4:	Check the negotiating position, strategy and detail.

Figure 1.1 Systematic preparation: the four-stage approach

complex, the four-stage approach of systematic preparation is a powerful means of developing a strategy that is both relevant and unique.

Perceptive negotiating technique

Negotiation has a natural sequence. The perceptive negotiator understands it and works with it. He departs from it only with good reason. It has four stages which are given in Figure 1.2.

In general terms, Stage 1 comprises the opening moves when the negotiator sets about the general task of conditioning and

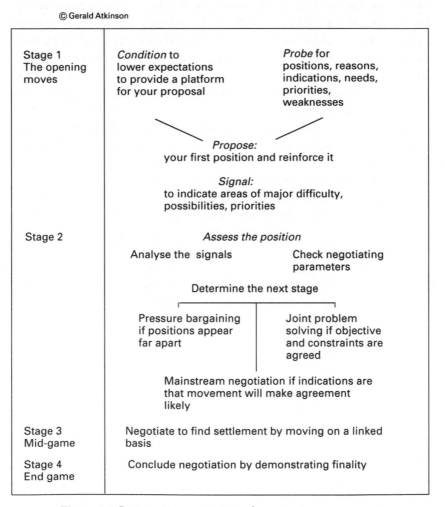

© Gerald Atkinson

Figure 1.2 Systematic negotiation: the mainstream sequence

probing to get the persuasion process underway, and to elicit the responses that will enable him to direct it. When he feels able to, he will propose his first position and will attempt to sustain it. However, depending on the level of resistance, he may find that as this stage comes to an end, he has to signal the basis on which movement by him could occur.

There is now a need, at Stage 2, to assess the position, and at best an adjournment should be taken. The negotiations so far should be assessed and, in particular, attention to signals should be given. On the basis of this analysis, a view should be taken of how negotiations are likely to develop, with strategy revised or sharpened if necessary. If it is considered that they are likely to move to the extremes of either pressure bargaining or joint problem solving, the implications of this – and particularly of pressure bargaining – for the next stage should be very seriously considered indeed.

But assuming that negotiation continues in the mainstream mode, Stage 3, the mid-game stage, is one of movement by both parties using the principles of mutual or linked movement with further probing and signalling taking place. It is here that the deal is either made or lost. Stage 4 is the end game of negotiation which consists of demonstrating finality and of closure.

To be aware of this natural sequence of negotiation is one aspect of perceptive negotiation. The other is to be able to mobilise the right sort of negotiating behaviour and the right tactic at the right time.

Every negotiator has his own style – and long live the difference! But to that I would add that for negotiation to be productive, the negotiator should be specially skilled in certain areas. We have identified these, and we call them the key tasks of negotiation. For the opening moves they include conditioning and proposing, probing, responding, summarising, handling rejection and signalling. For mid-game two more are added: getting movement and face-saving. For the end game there are two others: demonstrating finality and handling deadlock.

Productive negotiation is the subject of Part III of this book. Since they play a significant part, we also look at the conventions of negotiation and at the negotiating team as well as at the tactics and behaviour of individual performance.

I cannot leave this first chapter without returning to the point of relationships, mentioned in the Introduction. It is a point to which we continually return, and, like the four components we have just outlined, it has a major influence on success or failure.

Three key relationships

The lead negotiator and his director

Probably the most significant relationship of the three is the one that is least visible at the negotiating table. The responsibility of the director for setting negotiating objectives and monitoring the negotiation as it develops is a clear one. But perhaps what is less apparent is the vital part he plays in supporting his negotiator, particularly if the going gets tough. Negotiation is stressful enough for him in its own right. The last thing the negotiator needs is sniping or political manoeuvring from within.

Related to protection and support is empathy. If the lead negotiator feels that as negotiation proceeds he can look for and get sympathy, advice and encouragement, a major point of tension is at least eased. His performance will be more assured, the risks that are necessary will be more likely to be taken and, most important of all, if negotiations are going off the rails, he will not be afraid to admit it to his director in time for something to be done.

The lead negotiator and his team

Many negotiations are conducted by single negotiators. But when a team is present its members can be an asset or a liability – much will depend on the discipline they show in negotiation and the empathy they have with each other. This is very much affected by the degree of trust and the sense of unity that exist between the lead negotiator and his team. The experienced negotiators often referred to the value of a good team working well. They talked of the mechanics of team organisation such as the different roles of team members, and they agreed on the importance of the team acting in a coherent and credible manner. And they kept coming back to 'the strength and extra energy' for the negotiator that comes from 'knowing that the team is with you every inch of the way' and 'the tremendous value of trust and empathy'. In short, the effect which team members can have on their leader is considerable.

The lead negotiator and his opponent

Much will be said about this relationship as we progress. But there is one feature which I suggest plays a very significant part in how it develops. The experienced negotiators were in no doubt at all. It relates to respect. 'Have a level of respect for the other negotiator. He's got a job to do.' 'Don't be superficial in your treatment of the other team or their arguments. That amounts to an insult!' 'Don't feel that in order to win that you have to dominate him personally. That way lies disaster.' Obviously the relationship has many features. But if negotiation is to be truly productive, this is the one on which the others depend. If the relationship is founded on mutual respect, then business can and almost certainly will be done.

These then are the four components of successful negotiation and the three relationships that really matter. In the pages that follow we will see how they are used and developed to the best effect.

Summary

1. There are three very different types of negotiation:
    (a) *Mainstream negotiation* in which the purpose of the parties is to find settlement of conflicting positions using the principles of *movement* and *compromise*.
    (b) *Pressure bargaining* in which parties with very different positions attempt to achieve a settlement favourable to themselves with a preference for *coercion* rather than *compromise*.
    (c) *Joint problem solving* in which the parties seek the best solution to an agreed problem within agreed constraints on a jointly created basis.
2. Mainstream negotiation accounts for 90 per cent or more of all negotiation. Both pressure bargaining and joint problem solving often commence in the mainstream negotiation mode.
3. The three types of negotiation are very different. You must identify which game you are in and play it accordingly.
4. Four 'components of success' which have a major influence have been identified:

(a) an understanding of the inner game;
(b) a relevant negotiating objective;
(c) systematic strategy development;
(d) perceptive negotiating technique.
The first component is the subject of Part I, the second and third components form the basis of Part II, and the fourth component is dealt with in Part III.

5.   There are three key relationships. They are the lead negotiator with:
(a) his director;
(b) his team;
(c) his opponent.

Reference

1.   Fisher, R. and Ury, W. (1982) *Getting to Yes*, Hutchinson, London.

Part I
Understanding and managing the inner game

In the broadest sense, persuasion on the one hand and handling opposition and rejection on the other account for much of the time and effort spent in negotiation. They dominate the opening moves and persist into the midgame even though the emphasis by then should have changed to a pattern of movement, adjustment and accommodation. As we look at the inner game we try to see what is going on behind the words in each of these areas.

In Part I we start by dealing with the three main components of the persuasion process in negotiation. In Chapter 2 we discuss the personal credibility that is all important when one negotiator deals with another. In Chapter 3 we look at what lies behind the positional credibility that each will try to develop. And in Chapter 4 we discuss how the positional needs and negotiating style, particularly of the other party, affect negotiation. Then in Chapter 5 we look closely at an unwelcome but inevitable element of negotiation, rejection, and we consider how best to view and then deal with it. Finally, in Chapter 6, we look behind the processes of adjustment and accommodation. Both must occur if agreement is to be reached. Each of these chapters is in two parts: the inner game is first identified and discussed, and then suggestions are given on how it can best be managed and controlled.

Case study: A close run thing

The five year contract to supply had a further three years to run. But as always, it was subject to price which was negotiated annually. When you got the contract two years ago it was barely on a break-even basis. But you did achieve a major strategic objective – you are now the sole supplier, and this accounts for over 40 per cent of your total production. Last year you did all you could to make the contract profitable. You had some success but at the cost of considerable acrimony: a straight price increase which, though agreed, was much resented. This year looked as though it was going to be the same.

You started in the usual way by talking of the product – how good it was, and how well your being sole supplier had worked for him. He had got most of the modifications he had requested during the year and you were still working on the rest; his use of the national and international dealer network of your parent company had already clearly helped him a lot; both parties were very much committed to each other. This was the sort of preamble to discussion of price increase which you had planned and that you thought he would expect.

But it did not go as well as you hoped. He was indeed clearly resentful of last year's settlement. He kept carping about what were, in your eyes, minor points. He also seemed to be preoccupied with his own problems – loss of a substantial customer in the Middle East, and a high wage settlement that had been wrung out of the company by some aggressive union negotiation. All of these you already knew about. But he insisted on talking about them at length.

Then he pressed you for your price. So you gave it him. You did not beat about the bush. You gave it up front: high, no strings attached, no ifs and buts.

His first reaction was one of absolute incredulity. It did not seem to be play-acting; he just did not seem to be able to grasp what you said. But this rapidly changed to hostility and anger. It seemed as though all the acrimony from last year had been stored, recharged and then unleashed in a prolonged and bitter attack.

You defended as well as you could, but against that tirade, your proposals looked more and more unreasonable. He became increasingly aggressive and cynical and refused either to hear again the context in which your offer was made or to put his own proposal on the table. You went round and round with neither of you saying anything new. Then he talked of breaking off negotiation and of looking for another supplier even though you both knew that this was hardly an option that was open to him. But he seemed to mean it.

It was at this point that you proposed a break in negotiation of a week during which you suggested he looked again at your proposal. His response to that was that it was you that would have to do the looking. He talked of halving the increase you had proposed, and said that unless you did so, you would get no response from him. On that basis you adjourned.

Seemingly against the odds, the next meeting went a lot better. Still the same skirmishing, but the personal hostility seemed to have evaporated. And luck and good homework were on your side; you were able to remind him that during the break one of his major competitors in Europe had announced a substantial price increase. He acknowledged the fact, but still insisted that your demand was far too high and that you must reduce it before he would respond. You virtually ignored the point and instead gave some new examples of the benefits of the special relationship you had, concentrating on two valuable modifications you had given over the last year. His attitude started to change, so you decided to keep up the momentum and told him of the very favourable preliminary test-bed results for a major modification that you had been working on for some time – how they exceeded specification with even lower running temperatures than required.

He seemed particularly interested, so you asked him in what area of sales this would help most. As you anticipated, he said the Middle East. You agreed, and then you asked if it would give his product the edge elsewhere. He did not respond to that exactly, but he seemed to get the point.

You then said that you knew of his difficulties in Europe and that if he would respond to your proposal with a figure, you felt that a settlement could be reached – after all it was in your joint interests to find one.

After some summarising of arguments by both sides, he took the plunge, offered you 50 per cent of your original figure, and demanded that you now respond to it. You did not attack his offer directly. Nor did you reduce your demand. But you came in with some further detail which demonstrated how valuable your dealer network had been to him over the last year. He said that in fact it was not as good as you thought and that it could be improved. Instead of defending it you asked how.

Initially he was a bit vague but with some coaxing he gave you some of his ideas. You discussed them for a while, but you managed to stay non-committal. He then pressed you on price.

You now acknowledged that particularly in view of his difficulties in Europe and the Middle East, your demand must have come as a shock to him. You indicated that you could move on it but that it would then require further movement by him to reach a settlement. He did not disagree, so you proposed settlement at 80 per cent of your original figure.

After a fair amount of backtracking he increased his offer to 65 per cent of your asking price. You rejected it and returned to some of the points he had made about the service of your dealer network. You explored them further, said you would need to look at them in more detail, but that you were just about at the end of the line on price. On that basis you adjourned for three days.

When you met again you started by summarising how the previous meeting ended. You asked him whether he had any comments, to which he said he was interested to hear how you were going to improve the service of your dealer network. You said that some of his suggestions were possible, but that for each, if they were implemented, there was a cost, and that your last offer on price was now more than justified. He questioned this, but you were able to support your argument with figures. He said that if he were to move on his offer he would look for the improvements in dealer service as 'part of the package'.

You said that that would mean the 80 per cent figure. He rejected it, so you pressed him for his proposal, to which he made an offer of 70 per cent conditional on a series of improvements in the dealer network. In response you repeated your previous arguments for the 80 per cent figure – as he did for the 70 per cent.

A haggle now ensued, the outcome of which was that you both agreed to move. The deal finally emerged at 75 per cent of your original asking price together with some improvements in the services of the dealer network. You were happy. Although he did not know it, you had settled well within your negotiating parameters. You went out that night for a meal together. Relationships were excellent. You paid the bill.

Some not altogether untypical negotiations which nearly failed. If they had broken down it would have been in the interests of neither party, and their failure would have been directly attributable to a lack of understanding of the inner game. For example, the importance of developing empathy, of identifying needs and of establishing common ground before making a proposal, was ignored as was the need to create a credible platform for the proposal. Again, there was no real understanding shown of how to use time and pressure in negotiation. And there was no sense that the supplier was in control of the period when his initial proposal was predictably rejected. When it came to getting movement after the near breakdown, luck and the emergence of better technique began to pay off for him, but again his touch lacked the certainty of a negotiator who was in full control of the processes of movement.

It is on such points as these that agreement hangs, and to negotiate well requires a level of insight and understanding that enhances them. It is therefore to this 'inner game' that we first of all turn.

2

Enhancing personal credibility

Of paramount importance to the negotiator is the image he presents. It is not just a desire to be respected or liked as a matter of ego satisfaction, pleasant as these might be. It is more because of a deep certainty that critically important moments occur in negotiation when an assessment is being made of him as an individual – his personal credibility is on the line. Is he to be believed? To be trusted? Will he back off or will he stand firm? Has he got authority?

The view he gains of your personal credibility often starts as a number of straws in the wind. Did you match up to his expectations of what a negotiator of substance should look like? Did the tone of voice sound confident and was the position put with authority? Did the rest of your team clearly respect you? From these and others his opinion begins to take shape. Then he finds that you can support your position, that you have done your homework, that you can deal with his queries or objections and that, more subtly, by countering some of his points while responding more positively to others, you are beginning to shape the discussion. And so on.

His opinion of you as an individual and as a negotiator now starts to become firmly fixed, and consciously or not he now uses it to filter all that follows. Ultimately it has an effect on the outcome. It may even make or break the deal. But it started in the first moment of your first meeting. Indeed, it might have been earlier. If you have a reputation, it probably preceded you.

So personal credibility and the image you present are important. Hence creating, nurturing and defending them are key elements of the inner game. But on what are they based?

Attributes of personal credibility

It is known as 'the negotiator's dilemma'. Should your style and approach be tough or tender? Should you appear firm or flexible?

17

On the one hand both research and experience point to the fact that toughness can pay, and that to start high or low as the case may be, and to move slowly and with an irregular concession pattern can yield handsome returns. But on the other hand, the risks are equally well known. Such an approach prompts the other party to do the same, with stalemate or loss of face the outcome. On the other hand to be seen as the 'great concessionary' and flexible beyond belief is even worse! So the image which it is prudent for the negotiator to create and sustain requires some thought. It has various attributes.

Capability and strength

Both experience and research[1] point to the fact that it is desirable for a negotiator to be seen as both capable and strong. Once the point has been stated, it seems self-evident. But I can testify to the fact that there are occasions when it would appear unknown. Capability amounts to being seen to be in control of the negotiating position and its detail, and being generally perceived as a competent negotiator. Strength lies in the way the position is put across and is supported and maintained thereafter.

The value of being seen as capable and strong is apparent whichever way the negotiator looks. If it is across the table at his opponent, he must be impressive. If it is to those who gave him his mandate and who look to him for results and for information and guidance as the negotiation progresses, he must inspire confidence. If it is to his peers or subordinates, he must demonstrate that he is in control.

But alone these are not enough. Is he an outright bluffer of whom you can never be sure of anything? Hardly the reputation that a negotiator of substance would want – which is where the elements of trust and integrity come in.

Trust and integrity

There is a popular image of negotiators as crooked men conniving at crooked deals in smoke-filled rooms at 2 a.m. Of course it happens, but normally as a result of a desperate effort to find a deal that they can live with rather than none at all. And it happens less frequently than is often supposed.

The truth is that negotiators know that if there is to be anything like a productive long-term relationship between them, trust and integrity are vital. The experienced negotiators were unambiguous on this. There are four reasons why. First, since negotiation puts a tremendous strain on reserves, there has to be *trust in intent* between the parties that each is serious in its intention to attempt to find an agreement – that it is indeed negotiating 'in good faith'. Second, there has to be some *trust in process* that they will act 'fairly' towards each other in that they will observe at least the minimum conventions of negotiation. We discuss conventions in Chapter 10: suffice to say that although they are probably only intuitively known and applied, if they are broken, negotiation starts to founder with total collapse as a very real possibility. Third, there must be *trust in implementation* so that if an agreement is reached, each has the intention and resource to implement it.

There is also a fourth reason why the reality of trust and integrity is so important. It relates to *productive negotiating behaviour*. Dealing with the negative first, it is well known that when trust is replaced by suspicion, negotiators will make slow progress. They will be less likely to get down to negotiation proper. They will tend to fence and to prevaricate. In addition they will be more likely to lie and to resort to threats, and they will give little information on which the other side can build. [2] However, moving to the positive, there are five reasons why a climate of trust is beneficial for negotiation. There are less likely to be incidents of the sort of nonproductive behaviour we have just mentioned; trust by one party will tend to beget trust by the other; communication by each party is more likely to relate accurately to things as they really are; it is also less likely to be misconstrued by the other; and finally there is more likely to be the sort of flexibility of thinking that finally leads to settlement.[3]

The value of having a relationship based on trust has been well put. 'The fact is that trust appears to be an unmixed asset in negotiations. There is little to commend a policy of fostering distrust.'[4] The only exception to this would be the back-street trader or his cultural equivalent who does not even think of repeat business, and is out to exploit each transaction to the full regardless of the consequences. He is not concerned about relationships beyond the immediate encounter. He is not worried about reputation. But these are the mavericks of negotiation. They are avoided by others – even their own type – wherever possible. Deal with them, and the game is wild, with power the only currency that counts.

Four attributes therefore that give a negotiator personal credibility: capability, strength, trust and integrity. But there is a fifth which in my view is vital. It is empathy. Without it a negotiator might be respected, but he will also be seen as the sort of man with whom it is difficult, if not impossible, to deal, with all that that implies.

Empathy

Negotiators need each other. They will therefore probably deal with each other much more productively if there is personal respect and empathy between them. But there is another reason why empathy in style is important. It harks back to the negotiator's dilemma of whether to be firm or flexible. Both will almost certainly be required according to the situation; but both have their penalties. Firmness can generate frustration and anger. And flexibility will have to be restrained by opposition so that concessions can be gained as well as given. So on both counts, negotiation can all too easily degenerate into a hostile ego battle. But where empathy exists between the parties, personal antagonism between them is far less likely. As with the other four attributes, empathy is a great facilitator.

Personal credibility is very much a matter of the inner game. It is under the surface, yet it pervades all. I have suggested that it possesses a positive image in which capability and strength, trust and integrity, and empathy figure strongly. How this positive image can be created and sustained we will see as we now turn to what we call 'managing the inner game'.

Managing the inner game

Developing a positive image

Few people can act out a lie. For most, when the heat goes on they revert to type, and for me at any rate the image we present springs inevitably out of the values and beliefs that we have. But given that the attributes of personal credibility that I have suggested are broadly consistent with these, there are some ways in which we can better project our credibility – even add to it. Since the attributes of trust and integrity are the tenderest of the five, we will make some suggestions in this area first.

Trust and integrity
   Find out about your opponent's track record
If you can, actively seek information about your opponent before
you meet for the first time. First, can there be trust in intent? Does
he embark on negotiation from well-researched positions? When
he speaks, does he have the authority of his organisation behind
him? Has he a record of mature negotiation which produces
agreement? Second, can there be trust in process? Does he
negotiate fairly? Does he observe the conventions? Does he set out
to resolve issues, or to destroy people? Third, can there be trust in
implementation? When he makes an agreement, does it turn out
like that in practice? Is the spirit of the agreement also observed?

   All these questions are very relevant. If in fact the answer to
each one were to be in the affirmative, your opponent would be
too good to be true! But they will certainly show a pattern that will
tell you whether trust-building measures on your part will
enhance or destroy your personal credibility with that particular
negotiator.

   Project your own trustworthiness
Clearly this is influenced by what you find out about your
opponent's track record, and also by whether your trust-building
attempts are being reciprocated. But unless there is clear reason to
the contrary, initiation of trust-building measures can be of real
benefit. Initially these are the small body language signals such as
good eye contact, an open and business-like manner with no
defensive gestures such as arm folding and mouth covering, good
use of open palms and an empathetic body position. Then, as
negotiation unfolds, there are more substantial indications. Can
you support positions? Are 'the facts' demonstrably so? If a
genuine weakness or admission is identified by your opponent, is it
acknowledged by you? Are you clearly operating the conventions
of negotiation yourself? If you are consciously and genuinely
doing these, you will find that your personal credibility really does
start to rise.

   Look for reciprocation
This, however, is always the test. Because trust is such a tender
quality, because it can so easily be abused, particularly in negotia-

tion, it is always prudent to look for reciprocation. So what are the responses to your body language – similar or opposite? What is the line taken on your 'facts'? Are they taken at face value, or are they immediately twisted or attacked as an invention? Does a genuine error on your part beget a 'Brownie point' on his? And the conventions – what are the signs from him? Does he appear to be observing them also?

In my experience, it is well to trust your own feelings on all of these. If you are in real doubt, *slow down*. Start to protect yourself. Ask further questions to get reactions on any point on which you are doubtful. If, however, you feel that your trust is being reciprocated, press on.

Test in the low-risk areas first

The first area is almost certain to be body language. So look out for non-reciprocation. After that, testing is a progressive affair and the acid test is always *common ground*. If you summarise common ground as you understand it as it develops, and consistently there is disagreement, watch out. Your understanding may be at fault once or twice, but unless you are consistently using the tactic of the 'false summary' (which is unwise), it is unlikely to be all the time. Again, look out for his sidetracking; beware when he indulges in recrimination. Both are the forerunners of prevarication. Both put a question mark over trust.

Guard your integrity

There are times when a negotiator should bristle. One is when his integrity is directly attacked. Clearly, since negotiation may include selectivity with the facts, differences of interpretation, different assessment of priorities and so on, there are bound to be times when his own judgement, experience or truthfulness is being questioned. But these are the times when reputation should be jealously guarded. If there has been an error, admit it and, in my view, apologise. But if the question related to such matters as opinion, interpretation or judgement, repeat your rationale, and take it from there. More will be said of this later.

In these ways, trust can be generated and integrity shown without the risk that it will be turned to disadvantage.

Capability, strength and empathy

We have already seen that a positive image in negotiation has much to do with assessments which are made as to the capability and strength of the negotiator, with strength being tempered by empathy. But the creation of image is a subtle affair. For the most part it rests on inferences which you hope will be drawn by the other party. So what are the areas in which to concentrate so that the right inferences are indeed drawn? Here are some points which should help.

Demonstrate access to authority and power

In their essay on 'Communication in bargaining and negotiation', Tedeschi and Rosenfeld[5] make the point:

Control over material resources in bargaining situations provides the negotiator with the ability to back up his threats, keep his promises, and acquire knowledge and skills. The other negotiator is unlikely to believe his opponent's communications if the latter does not appear to possess or have access to the kinds of resources his threats and/or promises require, no matter how high his personal credibility.

So to demonstrate his access to authority and power the negotiator has certain devices available to him. For example, if he feels that his authority to negotiate is being questioned, he will indicate his close contact with the sources of power in his organisation. So the commercial negotiator will quote his director, the acquisitions negotiator will demonstrate his intimate knowledge of the forces and thinking of the personalities who influence the stock market in that business sector, and the trade union negotiator will hint darkly about 'the mood of the membership' or will quote one of the resolutions of Delegate Conference. Or he may surround himself with 'experts' in his team such as lawyers, merchant bankers, accountants and so on. Clearly, in their own specialist areas, their contribution is going to be important in any case. But the status they give to the position being taken by him can be considerable.

Demonstrate expertise

Closely connected to the previous point is that of demonstrated expertise. Indeed when we look at the next dimension of persuasion, we will see just how important it is to have a rationale backed up with supporting detail. But here we are concerned with the requirement, if personal credibility is to be achieved, for the negotiator to demonstrate expertise in the detail of his own and, if possible, his opponent's position. To do this, he will welcome the opportunity to back up his statements with examples, calculations, illustrations, quotable quotes, etc. Also he will accept that if he is going to make assertions, he has the responsibility to support them. Indeed it is this ability and willingness to explain a position with the relevant detail that makes a negotiator and his position look impressive. Equally, it is a failure to do so that causes personal resentment and disdain.

Develop empathy early

Unless the negotiator wishes to give a very strong signal of formality or of difficult negotiations ahead, before he gets down to business he will spend time in small talk. If the parties do not know each other this can be anything ranging from the weather to sport to the journey the other negotiator has just had, and so on. However once they know each other, the conversation is more specific. But it is non-threatening in content and is really saying 'We might be heading for disagreement. But we won't take it personally. As individuals we do have quite a lot in common, and in fact as a person I both respect and (perhaps) like you.'

Small talk is valuable. It enables you both to give and to look for signals. It sets the tone and hopefully develops the empathy that can be very useful later – particularly if the going gets rough.

There is, however, one important point. Unless it is controlled, small talk hardly gives the impression of capability and strength. So the general rule is to embark on small talk with a genuine interest. But then to control the time that is spent on it and to be the first to get down to business.

Acknowledge the points he has made

This does not mean that you agree with them, but it does mean that you let him know that they have been received and understood. Without this acknowledgement his tendency will be to believe that you are belittling what he says or ignoring it, and empathy will ebb away.

Be hard on the argument but soft on the man

It is an old maxim, but it has played its part in preventing heated discussion from turning into bitter personal hostility time and again. It is wholly consistent with the development of the 'tough but tender image' that we are discussing. Clearly, it should be sustained throughout negotiation, and it is one of the characteristics shown by skilled negotiators. They hammer away at the argument put forward by the other party and then say that they cannot accept his position. But they do not attack the man. Average negotiators on the other hand are prone to say that they disagree with the other party as an individual, thereby making the chance of personal antagonism greater. However if this line of 'hard on the argument, soft on the man' is consistently followed in negotiation, the reconciliation of power with empathy is by no means as difficult as it might at first appear.

Depersonalise the conflict

Allied to the previous device is this one. Instead of saying, for example, 'I disagree with you', the negotiator trying to maintain empathy will tend to say 'The arguments being adopted don't really seem to me to justify your position on this.'

Avoid 'Brownie points'

Avoid the little one-up points, such as 'What, haven't you done your homework yet?' or 'You're looking a little bit peaky this morning'. They might make their initiator feel a bit better. They might even raise half a smile by the other party. But in my experience they almost invariably produce a counter Brownie point a couple of minutes later — just to restore the psychological balance. This in turn will lead to a yet more speedy response to regain what is now beginning to be seen as an important psychological edge. So it goes on, and before you know where you are, resolution of the issue has been replaced by a deep ego battle.

Demonstrate confidence

We mentioned body language earlier. Perhaps some of the assertions made by its protagonists seem a bit excessive. For example Allan Pease writes:[6] 'Research shows that non-verbal signals carry about five times as much impact as the verbal channel and that, when the two are incongruent, people rely on the non-verbal message; the verbal content may be disregarded.' Again he quotes research[7] 'that the total impact of a message is about 7% verbal (words only), and 38% vocal (including tone of voice, inflection

Indications you can give

Of trust and empathy	Of capability and strength
A non-defensive body position	Firm handshake
A relaxed style and manner	No fidgeting and little body movement
Friendly eye contact	Use of firm gestures to emphasise selective points
Appropriate smiling	
Acknowledgement gestures, e.g. nodding	Leaning forward – dominating 'no man's land'
Mirroring of gestures as appropriate without copying them	Control of material and team
Use of open palms	Purposeful style
	Direct eye contact but without 'eyeballing'

Indications to look for

Interest and evaluation	Rejection or doubt
Sustained eye contact	Sustained arm folding
Head inclination	Reduced eye contact
Chin stroking	Hand covering mouth
Forming a steeple with the fingers	Fidgeting
Leaning forward	Fingering of collar/rubbing of eye
	Palms out of sight

Figure 2.1 Some indicators from body language

and other sounds) and 55% non-verbal.' To me, this hugely underrates the value of content. You cannot propose or support a position by body language alone. But I think it does rightly point out that tone of voice, posture and appearance do have their effect on the assessment that is being made, and anyone who is involved in negotiation would do well to look at the book by Allan Pease already mentioned or at that by Nierenberg and Calero.[8] They both raise awareness in this important field. Figure 2.1 shows some indications that can be given and looked for from body language.

So the presence of trust and integrity and an image of capability, strength and empathy go to create personal credibility. But a catalyst is required: one other attribute that must be present. That catalyst is self-confidence, and to this we finally turn.

Self-confidence

Clearly, self-confidence affects believability. If it is lacking, the words will have a hollow ring and both style and negotiating

behaviour will lack panache. Virtually all the experienced negotiators commented on this. As one of them said, 'If you don't sound
as though you believe it, why should they?'

But there are two other, perhaps deeper, reasons why it is so
important. First, possession of self-confidence normally means that
pressure will be handled more positively. Taking the other side of
the coin for a moment, there is good evidence to suggest that those
with low self-confidence – or, as the researchers tend to call it, 'low
in self-esteem' – are more likely to make unproductive responses
when under pressure. For example it seems that they handle
threat by bringing even more threat into the situation.[9] While
there are occasions when to answer threat with threat may be the
best reaction, those with greater self-confidence are more likely to
stand off for a moment and actually consider their next productive move rather than merely react by matching hostility with
hostility. So self-confidence affects the handling of overt pressure.
The same applies to the handling of covert pressure. Take, for
example, the situation in which there is an imbalance in status
between the negotiators. All the studies on this indicate that on the
one hand the negotiator of higher status will tend to exploit his
advantage, while the negotiator of lower status will tend to show
considerable deference to the other, with the strong inclination, if
he is left to his own devices, to adopt a submissive pattern and to
yield on a selective basis.[10] In short, then, if one negotiator pulls
rank, the other will need a reserve of self-confidence to see him
through the crisis.

The second reason is that when self-confidence is present,
necessary risks are more likely to be taken. It is apparent that risks
must be taken throughout the negotiation process. For example, if
the probing and conditioning stage is to be effective, questions
must be asked – many of them. But insecure negotiators do not
ask questions; they fear losing control. Again if agreement is to be
reached, almost certainly movement will have to be given. But
insecure negotiators find movement uncomfortable. In general
they dislike the ambiguity which is so much a part of negotiation.
And if dogmatism is seen as the intolerance of ambiguity, it is well
worth mentioning the effect which dogmatism has on negotiation.
The research is conclusive: 'Subjects high in dogmatism tended to
make fewer concessions (with less yielding), resolved fewer issues,
and viewed compromise as defeat more often than those who were
low on dogmatism.'[11] If it is a lack of self-confidence as opposed to

a strong rational base that is leading to a fixed and unyielding position, the effect that this one point alone has on the likelihood of success is considerable.

Before we see self-confidence as wholly good, there is the obvious note of caution which sounds from its excess – the twin evils of arrogance and complacency. Arrogance destroys empathy and in so doing adds to the problems of conflict resolution. Complacency undermines preparation and results in under-researched positions and half-baked strategy. So self-confidence there must be. But it must be the sort that results in eager anticipation rather than in personal or intellectual disdain.

Generating self-confidence

It was the above-mentioned eager anticipation that was a common denominator among the experienced negotiators. With one exception, they all admitted to feeling nervous before major negotiations. But they were not the nerves that kill performance; quite the contrary. They were the nerves that sharpened the mind ready for the battle that was to come, because underneath the tension was the deep reserve of self-confidence on which they could draw. They *knew* they would perform well.

So what is their secret? What is it that enables experienced negotiators to have this inner confidence? Here are some of the points they made, and others that I have found for myself that enable them, you and me to generate the self-confidence that wins.

View negotiation dispassionately

This is really a polite way of saying 'view negotiation as a game' – they do. In the Introduction I also called it a game since it has strategies, tactics, ploys and so on. But here the experienced negotiators are really saying something different, something which might make some readers feel more comfortable. They are saying that as they negotiate, it is not necessarily the real them they are showing. They do not spend their life negotiating on every-thing. But there are occasions when they meet with others to negotiate. They then act a role according to a script – a script of their own making. The script is really only a sequence of cues with a lot of supporting notes, but it keeps them going until the final curtain. I might say most of them appear to enjoy their own performance! But the point is, they are performing. They are actors in a role, players in a game.

The consequences of this are considerable. Because it is a game and their opponent is another player, they are far less likely to make personal attacks or to respond to them. They do not 'rise to the bait'. They view negotiation as a series of moves to be made. They are involved, yet they can remain aloof. This is the sort of detachment that works wonders for self-confidence.

Develop your game plan

This is closely allied to the previous point, but the emphasis here is to analyse, along the line of the systematic approach we have already given in the outline in the previous chapter and will develop in detail later, so that you know that when you embark on negotiation you have a plan that gives you the best possible chance of success. Then to sleep peacefully the night before in the sure knowledge of that might be asking a lot! But *knowing* that you are as well prepared as you ever will be and that you have developed the optimum strategy, gives you an inner certainty that is worth a lot.

Allow time for assimilation

There is never enough time! Preparation is almost always a last minute affair – that is the way of things. But I must say that from my own experience, performance in negotiation is never as good if it follows immediately after preparation as if there is a pause between the two, a time for reflection, even if it is only twenty-four hours. If the negotiation is important, the preparation should have been detailed. But it takes time for the detail to sink in, for the strategy to become part of you; and, I might say, to forget enough of it and be sufficiently on edge so that you have the much-needed resilience to handle what you have not anticipated. This opportunity for assimilation, which is probably as much a subconscious as a conscious activity, is one that should be actively fought for in the schedule of work leading up to negotiation.

Use your team

Again, it is a matter of time, but as we will suggest, there is great value in the negotiating team working together to develop strategy. The danger is obvious: as they say of economists, put five of them in a room to come up with an answer, and they give you six to the question you did not ask! But as we saw earlier, the benefits of using the team in preparation are immense, and using the techniques given in Part II of the book, I can vouch for the fact that greater insight is achieved, greater unity is developed and greater confidence is generated. As one of the experienced negotiators commented, 'The extra energy, the extra courage that comes from working as a team – *that is important*.'

Practise the first five minutes

The opening moments can be critical. That is why some negotiators deliberately try to unsettle their opponents by bringing in something which is unexpected. It may happen. Nevertheless there is great value in practising in detail the first five minutes of your game plan. Then, if possible, in finding one of your team who can act as devil's advocate to practise on. If it does not work out as planned, you have still 'tuned' yourself in. But more likely than not you will find that in general terms it will work, and you are then into your stride.

Stay positive

'Expect the negative reaction – that's what he is there for.' 'Don't react unfavourably to your own mistakes – everyone makes them.' This is some of the advice I give when I am involved in training. If you can accept that there will be difficulties, that you will make mistakes, that you will have to think on your feet, I find the mind is quietened considerably. The fact of the matter is that there is not a lot that can come up, other than you making a totally counter-productive direct commitment, that perceptive preparation, good team support or an adjournment cannot handle. So be assured.

Review negotiation

The value of consciously reviewing negotiation can be considerable, and as we will see when we look at the role of the team, your colleagues can help a lot. But try to find the critical moments. When did negotiation start to move in the direction it took? When did it change course or pace? What happened immediately before? Why? If you can answer such questions as those and take whatever action is necessary, you will improve your understanding and style, and your self-confidence will grow.

Personal credibility and how to enhance it have been the starting point of our insight into the inner game. It is worth reminding ourselves that not only is it a major component of negotiation, but all the available evidence from experience and from research suggests that, the greater the adversarial nature of the negotiation, the greater is the importance attached by the parties to personal credibility.[12] So it matters.

But personal credibility is without purpose if it stands alone. If the persuader is to persuade, like the singer, he must have a song. There must be a negotiating position, and that position must have credibility. So it is to this that we now turn.

Summary

1. Personal credibility in negotiation results from developing a positive image which possesses:
   (a) capability and strength;
   (b) trust and integrity;
   (c) empathy.
2. Self-confidence is the catalyst that is required for them all.

Nineteen means of developing personal credibility were given.

Key question: Since it matters considerably, how do you set about enhancing your own personal negotiating credibility?

References

1. See for example the work in this field of D. G. Pavitt and D. F. Johnson; M. Deutsch; B. R. Schlenker.
2. See for example the research of H. W. Kee or R. K. White in this field.
3. Walton, R. E. and McKersie, R. B. (1965) *A Behavioural Theory of Labor Negotiations*, McGraw-Hill, New York, pp. 141–3.
4. Ibid., p. 358.
5. Tedeschi, J. T. and Rosenfeld, P. (1980) 'Communication in bargaining and negotiation', in M. E. Roloff and G. R. Miller (eds.), *Persuasion*, Sage Publications, Beverly Hills, CA, p. 242.
6. Pease, A. (1984) *Body Language*, Sheldon Press, London, p. 14.
7. Mehrabian, A. (1971) *Silent Messages*, Wadsworth, Belmont, CA.

8. Nierenberg, G. I. and Calero, H. H. (1973) *How to Read People Like a Book*, Thorson, Wellingborough.
9. Walton and McKersie, op.cit., p. 194.
10. See for example the findings of Faley, T. and Tedeschi, J. T. (1971) 'Status and reactions to threats', *Journal of Personality and Social Psychology*, vol. 17, pp. 192–9.
11. Rubin, J. Z. and Brown, B. R. (1975) *The Social Psychology of Bargaining and Negotiation*, Academic Press, San Diego, CA, p. 178.
12. Perloff, R. M. and Brock, T. C. (1980) 'And thinking makes it so', in Roloff and Miller, *Persuasion*, pp. 70–2; Tedeschi, J. T. and Rosenfeld, P. (1980) 'Communication in bargaining and negotiation', in Roloff and Miller, *Persuasion*, pp. 234–5.

3
Developing positional credibility

As we discuss the inner game of developing positional credibility and how to set about managing it, we are concerned mainly with what is said. I am the first to accept that on occasion action speaks louder than words, and that good strategy embraces what you do as well as what you say. But in the final analysis, actions foreshadow or reinforce what is said – they can never be a substitute for it. So on to what is said. Since we are talking about negotiation, we will be talking about creating *arguments* for our positions. After all, negotiation is about arguing, is it not?

There are three reasons why I think this view is mistaken. The first is to do with the overtones that surround the word. While it has a number of meanings, apply 'argument' to negotiation and you get associations such as 'altercation' and 'aggression', and being 'contentious' or 'quarrelsome'. And above all, that arguments should be won. Now that may be true on occasions. But not always. And it certainly can take your eye off the ball. Negotiation in the final analysis is about finding successful deals rather than winning arguments.

Second, arguments, when they are produced as reasons for a position, are the end results of your own thought process. They tend not to take the other party through the factors that have influenced you, such as the pressures that were present, the context in which negotiations are taking place, the underlying values which are considered important and so on. Such points as these are in fact highly relevant to the negotiation if a rational, credible position is to be established, and my experience is that if arguments are the prime consideration, such factors as these tend to get lost.

The third reason has to do with time. As we will see, it takes time for people to adjust to new positions. The trouble with arguments is that they can have a short life-span. They are used, and they are spent. But if you are to persuade, you will need something that lasts.

So it is for these reasons that to talk of arguments is not all that helpful in our understanding of negotiation. I would suggest that it is far better to think and work in terms of *themes*. Dictionary definition has it that a theme is 'an idea or topic expanded in discussion; a unifying idea repeated throughout a work.' Now that is just what is required. A continuing theme or, as we will see, a series of themes that is progressively developed as the context for the proposal which is to be made. Indeed, it was remarkable how often, without any prompting from me, the experienced negotiators used the same word. 'Developing the themes', 'working the themes', 'playing the themes' were phrases I often heard.

So as we discuss the development of positional credibility we talk of themes, not arguments; themes which are the forerunners of proposals. At best their purpose is to move the other party from his position of indifference, scepticism or hostility to an eager anticipation of your proposal. At worst they should serve to develop an awareness that he cannot stay with his own thinking and that the proposal that you have in mind is at least a viable one.

With themes now firmly established as a key ingredient we look first at the inner game of positional credibility and see that what is sometimes regarded as the ritual of negotiation – the part when each side has 'its say' in support of its first position and the other appears to pay little attention to it or to treat it as an Aunt Sally to be knocked down – is in fact a very important part of the negotiating process. Success here is of lasting benefit throughout the negotiation that follows. We will then look at some of the principles and techniques which can be of value as you set out to develop and sustain a platform which is firm and strong enough to see you through.

The inner game

It is very rare that you have the luxury of dealing with someone who comes new to a subject. At the least they have a set of hopes, fears and expectations. Perhaps they are only vaguely defined or intuitively felt; but they are there. At the other extreme you can be faced with an opponent whose mind is made up: 'I know what you're going to say and I don't believe it/don't accept it; so you can save your breath.' Yet as I suggested before, creating a context in

which a first offer is at the very least seen as credible is tremen-
dously important. Just look at what happened in the case study 'A
close run thing' when it was ignored. Almost a breakdown. And
why? Because precious little real effort had been spent in putting
forward and sustaining a rational base on which the first proposal
could be made; hardly any attempt at structuring expectations had
been undertaken; very little common ground had been achieved.
Small wonder then that a total breakdown was only narrowly
averted.

So what does it take to develop positional credibility? I suggest
there are three requirements that have to be met. First, and most
obvious we must build *the platform* which is strong enough to carry
our proposal. The more extreme the proposal, the stronger the
platform must be – and dogma, prerogative and dictum will not
do. To give it strength it must have within it reasons that will hold
good for the other side.

Second, if we are to get movement from the other party, we
must first create a sense of unease in his mind in the position he is
currently adopting. It is like moving a heavy object with light
tackle – the first movement is the crucial one. In the same way in
negotiation, before positions change, thought processes relating to
them have to alter. The respectable term for this is the development of *cognitive dissonance*. Though we will use it, for me
'psychological wobble' will do!

Third, as much as possible of the previous two (your platform
and his cognitive dissonance) should be converted into *common
ground*. Now common ground by itself does not necessarily make a
proposal any more acceptable. But it does make the risk of a
breakdown following it far less, and the difficulty for the other
side of rejecting it outright that much greater. So its creation is
very important and is in fact the *raison d'être* of much of platform
building and of the development of cognitive dissonance.

Let us therefore look more closely at each of these three.

The platform

One of the oldest debates in the matter of persuasion is whether it
is better to develop themes that appeal to the emotions, or to stand
square on the assumption that man is a rational being and
therefore to aim at his intellect. Regrettably the results of research
are ambiguous. The only clear conclusion is that it is normally best

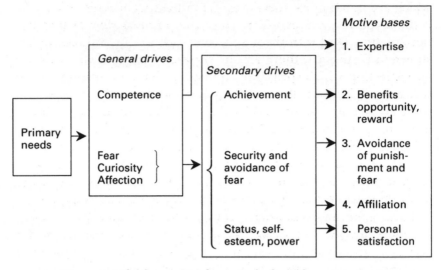

Figure 3.1 The five motive bases and where they come from

to hedge your bets by doing both. But to leave it at that is not really very helpful: thankfully we can do better.

The psychologist will tell us that most, if not all, of our behaviour is 'motive led'. By this he means that we have needs that drive us and that our life is spent in trying to satisfy them. Clearly how we act to satisfy these drives is very much affected by the culture and environment in which we operate. If we take negotiation, the way we conduct business in Tokyo is very different from the way we do a deal in Texas. And in addition, our own personality and past experience or learning will also have their effect. But the point is that we behave in a manner which we believe will satisfy our needs, and that in negotiation if we are to achieve our preferred settlement, we must deal with, though not necessarily satisfy in full, the needs of the other party as part of the process.

However, before applying this directly to negotiation, we must go a little deeper. Satisfaction of the basic or so-called primary needs of hunger, thirst, sleep and sex is crucial, with the last being of least importance. While their relevance to negotiation is apparent – exploiting jet lag, extending negotiation into the small hours, ignoring lunch breaks as a means of asserting pressure to clinch a deal and so on – we are more concerned here with the drives that are most likely to result from them. These are the so-called 'primary drives' which are general, and the secondary drives which are much more specific to the individual and his culture. It is the secondary drives which, from the point of view of negotiation, matter. Deal with them and you really are in business. So, as shown in Figure 3.1, there are the general drives of fear, curiosity and affection which speak for themselves. The interesting one to which most, but not all, psychologists subscribe, is the competence drive. It was first suggested by R. W. White who thought that it must be present since all animals have a capacity to interact effectively with their environment.[1] Hence he believed that since people attempt to exercise control or competence over their environment, they need to know what they are doing and why. They then order their activities so that they make things happen.

These general drives work through into secondary drives. They are more specific and are the focal point of our behaviour. So we aim to be secure and to avoid fear, to achieve in our chosen field, to affiliate to and to be accepted by our chosen group, to have a higher status than those with whom we compete, to be happy with ourselves and our performance in our chosen fields, and to exercise power over others.

Finally these drives are directly translated into what we call the *motive bases*, and these we can apply directly to negotiation. We can say that if these are the drives that are important to the man sitting opposite you and to those he represents, and in some or part they will be, then for each there is a motive base that we must address if we are to develop credibility in his eyes for our proposal.

Let us now look a little more closely at what this means for the inner game.

The five motive bases

Expertise

Expertise is given priority for three reasons. First, of them all, it is the only one over which you have total control. The themes that constitute the rational base, the 'why' which demonstrates that your proposal represents the superior course of action, are yours to determine.

Second, our culture attaches much importance to the imperative to 'be logical' or to 'be rational' – so much so that if a rational base is not forthcoming the proposer can be made to look foolish.

Third, the requirement to demonstrate expertise – to 'prove it' – is such that it extends to each of the other motive bases. So for every theme it should be remembered that there must be evidence, supporting detail, projections, chapter and verse – whatever is appropriate to back it up. No theme stands alone: all require support. To all this we give the generic name of *staff work*. It is a crucial ingredient of any negotiation. It is often *the* deciding factor.

The importance of using and satisfying the motive base of expertise is nicely summarised in the 'law of certainty' put forward many years ago by R. H. Thouless. It runs as follows:

> When, in a group of persons, there are influences acting both in the direction of acceptance and of rejection of a belief, the result is not to make the majority adopt a lower degree of conviction, but to make some hold the belief with a high degree of conviction while others reject it also with a high degree of conviction.[2]

In other words, when nobody knows with any certainty what the truth is, people adopt extreme positions either for or against. Hence, given the nature of negotiation, if there is a lack of expertise pointing in favour of the proposal, it is almost certain that there will be a considerable reaction against it.

Dealing with the need base of expertise is as important as that.

Benefits, opportunity and reward

Each of these might be called a 'positive inducement', but in fact their emphasis in negotiation is very different. It is therefore useful to comment on each. *Benefits* are those factors of value to the other party that are intrinsic in the proposal or the position. So, for example, in 'A close run thing', the supplier used the benefits of the dealer network and the modifications which his company had given. *Opportunities* are clearly different. They are the favourable possibilities or prospects which can occur for one or both parties out of a positive approach to negotiation in general or to the proposal in particular. An example of this from the case study would be the opportunities for the purchaser that would arise from alterations to the service given by the dealer network. *Rewards* carry along the same continuum, but introduce more specifically the requirement of having to be earned. Again in the case study they would have been proposed by the supplier along the lines of 'If you agree to our price structure of X we might be able to look at the alterations to the service which our dealer network currently provides.'

I would suggest that this distinction is important. Benefits are useful to have, and are fine for the salesman, but for the negotiator their value is limited. For example in the case study the supplier gave three in his opening statement, and it got him nowhere. Why? Because for the purchaser they were already in his possession – he did not have to do any more to get them. But when you look at opportunities and rewards they become increasingly useful. They are more specific in that they relate to certain possibilities, and they form the basis of the negotiator's three best friends – linkage, trading and joint abandonment – since they can be prefaced by the magic word 'if': 'If you were to do this, we might be able to look at that.' Movement by both sides is proposed and the foundations of a deal are laid.

So if there is a message here from the inner game, it is that the value to the negotiator of these three elements is considerable, with the greatest benefit coming from reward.

The avoidance of punishment and fear

Just as we referred to elements of the previous motive base as 'positive', so we might call these 'negative inducements'. But they are powerful motivators, arguably more so than the previous group, at least over the short term. For obvious reasons they are dangerous. However, there are a number of well-researched conclusions which are worth bearing in mind if we are to use them.

First, fear seems to follow an inverted U-shaped curve. In other words, there will be a point in time when fear loses its impact.[3]

Second, fear has different effects on different individuals. It depends on such factors as personality type, the level of importance of the topic and the credibility of the source. In fact it can be said that the more important the topic and the greater the credibility of the source, the greater is the impact of fear.[4]

Third, when parties are engaged in serious conflict, the introduction of threats (which is likely to occur anyway), introduces a downward spiral in which they are more likely to be seen by the proposer as justified and are more likely to be believed.[5]

Fourth, when parties start to use fear and punishment as the basis of their persuasion, the amount of their communication is likely to decline. T. M. Newcomb has called this 'autistic hostility'[6] in which the amount of communication declines and the level of distortion of the smaller amount of information that is exchanged increases.

Fifth, because the presence of threats increases the competitive aspects of negotiating behaviour, their introduction also increases each party's concern for their own reputation and self-esteem. They are therefore more likely to lose sight of the task of resolution and to concentrate on an ego defensive game – or just be intent on revenge![7]

These add up to some fairly powerful reasons for avoiding the use of punishment, threat and fear in negotiation. But fear is also a powerful motivator – too powerful to ignore. Despite the adverse effects given above, the conclusion is clear: threats work. True, they have to be seen as both credible and as unpleasant, but as Rubin and Brown[8] point out in their survey of research on the matter 'In general it appears that threats and to a lesser extent promises, tend to increase the likelihood of immediate compliance and concession making by the other.'

So the conclusion for the inner game is clear. Punishment and fear have their disadvantages but equally they constitute a pressure point which is too valuable to ignore.

Affiliation

This need arises, as we have seen, from the desire to be 'one of the group'. Clearly it is particularly high when a negotiator has been mandated by his peers – a director negotiating on behalf of his board, or a trade union negotiator on behalf of his members. Indeed in one elegant piece of research by Blake and Mouton[9] in which groups prepared their solutions to a problem and then delegates met to negotiate which solution would apply, loyalty to the group won hands down over the logic of the best solution. Only two out of sixty-two negotiators went outside the parameters given them by the group. The rest stuck to their mandate. Rubin and Brown take this point further and suggest that as the pressures from the group they represent increase, so this affects the negotiator's ability 'to perceive alternatives posed by an opposing party and to act affirmatively on them if necessary.'[10] In short, if a negotiator feels he is going into territory which is out of touch with the expectations of those he represents, he will almost certainly draw in his horns. How to deal with this we will discuss later.

Personal satisfaction

We have already seen that for most negotiators this means dealing with an image that the other party has of himself of capability and strength. He will want to show that he has fought his corner, has gained movement from you, his opponent, and has achieved an acceptable level of settlement. We look at this in considerable detail in the next chapter when we deal with handling personal needs. But it is worth making the point here that if the other motive bases have been addressed, they will have given him at least some level of satisfaction in this last. So, for example, themes developing the rational base for your position will have made their appeal to his motive base of expertise, themes revolving round opportunity, benefit and reward will also relate to his need for achievement, and so on.

In sum, therefore, use of these five motive bases offers a rich source for themes which give credibility to your position. But more than that they are introduced from the point of view that is most likely to succeed: that of his own needs.

Cognitive dissonance

People, it would seem, have a desire for order in life. They seek explanation, they look for reason. They dislike uncertainty and inconsistency; these make them feel uncomfortable.

It was in 1957 that a psychologist, Leon Festinger, developed a term which described this unease. He called it 'cognitive dissonance' and he described it as an 'imbalance between one's thoughts, beliefs, or attitudes, and one's behaviour. It is a tension state people are motivated to reduce.'[11]

Peter Warr in his book *Psychology and Collective Bargaining* calls it 'psychological inconsistency', and writes of it: 'We often experience discomfort if our mental world contains inconsistencies (suppose someone you dislike does something likeable) and as a result we adjust our behaviour and perceptions to bring our ideas back in line with each other.'[12]

Most people set a high value on consistency and go to great pains to demonstrate that what they do is consistent with what they think. So if we want to change what they do, we first have to generate cognitive dissonance by making them uneasy with what they think. To illustrate the point, a general strategy for this is suggested by George Miller who states that:

This high value people set on being consistent in their opinions gives us excellent leverage for persuading them to change their opinions. The recipe runs something like this: if you want someone to revise his considered opinion *a*, first find another opinion of his, *b*, and convince him that *a* and *b* are inconsistent. Since you now have the tendency to eliminate inconsistencies working in your favour, offer him a simple resolution of the problem which involves changing *a*. [13]

So relating this to negotiation, if we want the other party to change his stance on *a*, we first have to set about developing an inconsistency in his mind between it and the various reasons, *b*, he has for holding it. And if we are successful in this, if in fact we can move him to accept that *b* has changed in that, for example, the 'facts' relating to *a* really do not apply any more, or the benefits of keeping to the *a* position are nowhere near as great to him as he thought, there is then mental discomfort, there is inconsistency, there is a lack of logic. In short, cognitive dissonance has been created and with it a gap is opening up which is there to be filled.

Now the consequences of all this for the inner game are considerable. The first relates to *time*. If it takes time for cognitive dissonance to occur – as it does – it will take time for positions to change. So as Francis Bacon wrote in his essay 'Of negotiation' in 1621, 'In all negotiations of difficulty, a man may not look to sow and reap at once; but must prepare business and so ripen it by degrees.'

The second consequence relates to *sequence*. Cognitive dissonance is an evolutionary affair. It develops gradually rather than in one move. The effect which this has on negotiation is that there is a requirement for a number of themes rather than just a few; and that there is a need to phase in their introduction rather than to show them just once in a glittering show case.

The third relates to *proposition*. Quite simply, when do you make your first proposal? Before you have attempted to create cognitive dissonance? That will make his back teeth rattle! But it will also put a negotiated outcome very much at risk. Or alternatively as negotiation develops as a means of either filling the gap or of reinforcing the dissonance? Now that is using the inner game to real advantage.

The fourth relates to *reaction*. Clearly he will resist proposals or conditioning with which he disagrees, and how this disagreement is handled will have a significant effect on the outcome. Do you back off hoping you have made the point? Or reinforce and sustain it? If cognitive dissonance is to occur, there is only one answer. It is for this reason that negotiation is not for the faint-hearted.

Cognitive dissonance therefore is more than just jargon. If you are to build a platform for your position there must also be some weakening in the way he sees the credibility of his own. Cognitive dissonance must occur.

Common ground

Quite a good case could be made for defining negotiation as 'the progressive development of common ground between two or more parties'. It has the right overtones of initial difference, of movement from fixed positions and of settlement. It also highlights the fact that negotiation is a progressive process which starts with insufficient common ground to achieve settlement and ends when there is enough to satisfy at least the minimum requirements of the two parties as they see them at the time.

Clearly therefore the development of common ground continues throughout the negotiating progress. But we take it at this point as part of the inner game because it is here that it first assumes importance. Going back to the case study 'A close run thing' there has been, in the opening moves, the normal interplay of scene-setting and conditioning by each side. Using the parlance of the two requirements we have already discussed, each party has started to build its platform using themes from selected motive bases, and in so doing has been trying to develop cognitive dissonance. Two of the requirements for positional credibility are being met at least to some degree. But neither party has made the effort to develop them into either overt common ground or, at the very least, a tacit understanding. So there is nothing that will bind them into the negotiating process when first positions are put.

The term 'common ground' has a wonderful ring to it. It smacks of firmness, of mutual agreement. Reality, however, is that until the final agreement, common ground is often more tenuous. This is particularly so in the opening stages. So while first prize is always that common ground is overtly stated and has the full agreement or acceptance of both parties, you normally find you have to settle for the second, third or even consolation prize. But make no mistake, any prize is better than none. Second prize falls short of 'full acceptance' of, say, themes *a* and *b*, and goes into the category of 'acknowledgement' that they have considerable relevance to the matter under discussion. Third prize is merely that they are 'understood'. Consolation prize is not overt at all but amounts to a tacit understanding that they do have a bearing on the subject.

In fact, at any point in time, common ground is all you have to hold on to in negotiation. It is as critical as that.

The inner game of developing positional credibility suggests that the opening moves of negotiation are far from ritual. Rather you create a platform with determination and purpose. With some vigour you set about developing cognitive dissonance in the other party. And you progressively develop elements of both into common ground. Let us now turn to some of the practicalities of each of these as we look at how to set about managing the inner game.

Managing the inner game

Building the platform

A useful way to generate positional credibility in your opponent's eyes is to check off the themes that you consider using against the five motive bases which will exist for him. In this way themes and strategies can be created which develop this first element of positional credibility. We will look at each of the motive bases in turn, and then we will suggest ways in which the variety of themes that you now have can be managed to good purpose.

Expertise

As we saw from the inner game, concentration on the themes and detail that give your position a rational base is going to be crucial. Whether success here will carry the day on its own is probably doubtful – the other four motive bases will also be important. But failure on expertise will almost certainly mean that you lose. So here are some points which are worth bearing in mind.

Themes

Have at least two or three themes which initiate the rational base for your position and play them early – they will give you the initiative and will enhance personal as well as positional credibility. They may well be disputed by the other party, but if you can sustain them you will have set the tone of negotiation as objective and rational and have established a sound platform for your proposal.

Develop your staff work

As mentioned earlier this is the detail which supports your rational base. In fact *no* theme, be it expertise or any of the others, speaks for itself. All require supporting information ranging from that based on reason such as projections, data, market share, analysis and so on to the emotion of the homely illustration or the dramatic scenario. Staff work is crucial to the achievement of themes.

Make the expertise relevant

In other words ensure that wherever possible the themes that you use fall within your opponent's own expertise. If they do not, you have an educational problem to resolve which, should you fail, will probably generate substantial hostility.

Defend your expertise at all costs

One of the experienced negotiators put it to me like this: 'I develop a strong intellectual argument, and I hold on to it tight.' And so you must, because of all the themes, those based on expertise are yours. They are at the very heart of your position. And if he does not accept them, unlike the others, the burden of proof to the contrary rests with him.

Benefit, opportunity and reward

Although expertise is the motive base over which you have greatest control, as we have seen, inducement is probably going to be the one that will matter most to him. Your position might be as rational as Pythagoras but if there is nothing in it for him, why should he change? And I have already suggested that rewards in the form of linked proposals are of greater value in negotiation than benefits. Here are some suggestions about managing the themes for this particular motive base.

Needs must be identified before benefits can be given

This is one of the reasons why so much importance is given to questioning by the experienced negotiators – as one of them said, 'good negotiators ask lots of questions'. And in the selling field, Neil Rackham for example, has developed a system for making major sales which is based almost exclusively on the use of questioning.[14] Now this is not to say that since the introduction of themes which relate to benefits, opportunities or rewards rests on responses to questions, they should not or cannot be planned. Reasonable assumptions have to be made. But it does mean that where appropriate and before they are initiated, questions should be asked and signals received so that benefits can be launched on the basis of the information gained.

Needs emerge and change as negotiation continues

Following from the previous point, it is only as negotiation develops that a real feeling for what is going to be seen as a benefit or what is an appropriate level of reward is gained. So rather than wading straight in with 'benefits' or 'opportunities' there is much to be said, particularly if it is you who wants the change, for developing the rational base of your position first. Then as negotiation proceeds and by judicious use of questions, you will more clearly determine his needs so that benefits, opportunities and rewards can be played to better effect. If we look back at 'A close run thing', it was only when the supplier mentioned the lower running temperatures that he got the feedback that told him that this might well be a benefit. And it was only after a fair amount of conditioning that expectations on price had changed sufficiently to enable minor improvements in the dealer network to constitute sufficient reward to narrow the difference.

Talking about benefits and opportunities

Talking of benefits and opportunities can have a significant effect on how negotiations develop. Notwithstanding the previous point about how themes highlighting benefits can be developed as needs emerge, it is worth bearing in mind that there is a wealth of research that confirms what is called the 'lock-in effect'.[15] In short, the lock-in effect is the tendency for negotiators to get into a certain mode, for example in pressure bargaining the mode of belittling, threatening or of ego point scoring, and then find it very difficult to get out of it. One of them has to take the lead and he increases his risk of losing the psychological battle if he does so. Now the point here is that it is known that cooperation, as marked by themes revolving round benefit, opportunity and reward, begets cooperation. And that high incentives, embodying themes relating to opportunity, generate a significantly greater amount of cooperation than anything which smacks of low incentive or threat. So the consequences are clear. Themes relating to benefits or opportunities should not be delayed too long. And when they are introduced, much should be made of them in both position and style.

Reward is crucial and should be planned

As we have seen, reward in negotiation is introduced most frequently in the form of what we can call a 'linked concession': for example, 'If you give us X, we might be able to look at Y'. Kennedy, Benson and McMillan in their book *Managing Negotiations*[16] call it packaging, and make much of it, rightly so. Now for the rewards to be used to their best advantage, movement should be planned in advance. It is for this reason that it is normal for negotiators to develop what are called *'parameters of negotiation'*. As we can see from Figure 3.2 each side establishes for as many items as are on the table a series of positions from which they can move and still get what they want. This we call their *initial position*. Then, moving further towards the other party, is their *realistic position*. In fact this is the package that each is hoping to achieve: it is their negotiating objective. Finally each establishes its at worst position

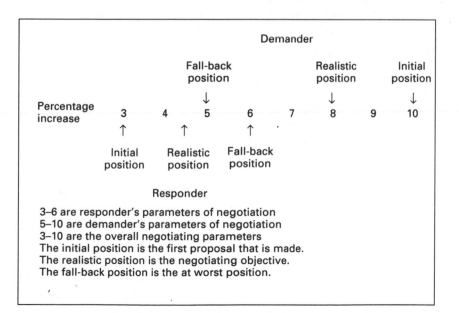

Figure 3.2 The parameters of negotiation

which is normally the minimum demands it requires and the maximum concessions it is prepared to give. These we call its *fall-back position*. These three positions constitute the parameters of negotiation.

Clearly there is more to it than that. Positions cannot just be plucked out of the air merely for the sake of ensuring that movement can be given. They must be seen as credible at the time they are put. Nor is it always possible to move on every item. Sometimes the initial, realistic and fall-back positions on an item are all the same. And again, final agreements often fall between parameters. But the notion of negotiating parameters is a key concept. It means that reward is planned and that the movement on which agreement almost certainly depends is managed and directed to good effect. We will return to this point again later.

Benefits, opportunities and rewards are fundamental to both the strategies and tactics of negotiation. Clear thought on how they are used will yield substantial returns.

Punishment and fear

If the inner game of benefits, opportunity and reward is interesting, that of using punishment and fear is more so. The difficult moments of negotiation are almost invariably stressful when frequently the desire is to inflict punishment in one form or another on the other party. Handling it is a matter of control which again takes us back to personal credibility, and the level of the negotiator's self-confidence. As far as consciously using punishment and fear is concerned, the principles of the inner game hold good. To these we can add some practical points.

Make punishment and fear the last rather than the first resort

Probably the most important point that can be made is that because of their adverse side-effects, themes which deliberately evoke punishment and fear should be delayed and only used if all else fails. They might sound grand, they might intimidate the other party, they may well establish a position of psychological superiority, but they generate reactions which are counter-productive to positive negotiation. Hence in most circumstances they are the last rather than the first resort.

Develop a legitimate reason

The secret in reducing or avoiding counter-productive reactions seems to lie in legitimacy. As Tedeschi and Rosenfeld write:

> Research has shown that doing harm of any kind provokes anger and retaliation when it is perceived as unjustified, but that these volatile responses do not occur when the source can justify the use of coercion . . . History, science and common sense all agree that negotiators often take great pains to justify their use of coercion as legitimate, defensive, and necessary.[17]

So to extend this line of thinking, if themes or positions incorporating punishment or fear can be seen as *legitimate*, i.e. deemed as necessary because of the actions or position being taken by the other side, as *defensive*, i.e. they would not be initiated except for the actions or position of the other side, and as *appropriate*, i.e. there is a rational base for them and they are not an over-reaction, then both their effectiveness will be greater and their negative effect on resulting negotiation less.

Depersonalise punishment and fear

From the previous point, it follows that the use of fear and punishment should be depersonalised. It should be played on the basis that it is not the case of one individual taking action against another, but rather that an individual finds himself as having no alternative. It is an inevitable consequence of the position of the other side – and the attitude is one of sorrow and not anger.

Affiliation

As we saw from the inner game the affiliation motive is a strong one. It is a brave man who goes against the values of his group. It is an even braver one who negotiates outside his mandate without first clearing it with the person or group to whom he is answerable! The essence of managing the inner game lies in anticipating the affiliation need so that themes are introduced and positions adopted with this requirement very much in mind. Some of the factors which assist in this have already been mentioned, particularly the development of themes of expertise and of positions which allow movement. They both enable him to rationalise his own movement to himself and provide him with a means of selling it to his colleagues. There are other points which can be of value.

A 'new angle'

Develop a theme which represents a 'new angle' and use it when he is quite clearly looking for a means of rationalising the need for his own movement. Such a theme may be a 'bombshell' which amounts to a compelling reason kept in reserve and which puts further pressure on his position. Or it may be a different perspective such as 'the way the business will look to an outsider', or as in 'A close run thing', the fact that recent price increases of a major competitor did not make the proposal look that extreme. But whatever it is, the theme should represent something new so that the other party can use it as the new factor which legitimises movement on his part, and he can put this to his colleagues as the basis of movement by him.

Make the change required as undramatic as possible

When it is clear that he is operating under a strict mandate, set out to reassure whenever possible that the change you are looking for is not threatening. It might 'be the norm for the industry', 'be what any professional business would look for', 'constitute a basic requirement of fair practice' and so on. Where the change is substantial, set out to alter the frame of reference in which he operates by setting it in the context of the long term or by introducing the theme of 'statesmanship'.

In one sense handling his need for affiliation is not your problem. But in another, if you do not take it into account and fail to develop both themes and strategies to handle it you are ignoring what might be the difference between him wanting to say yes but having to say no.

Personal satisfaction

As mentioned in our discussion of the inner game, the motive base of personal satisfaction is bound to be affected by what you do in the other four. So should you consider doing anything which explicitly deals with his desire for status, self-esteem or the exercising of power? Should you go beyond the development of empathy which I have already suggested is so important?

Of all the motive bases, this clearly is the one that most closely relates to the personality of the man sitting opposite – a wider subject which is dealt with in the next chapter. But there are three points which are worth making here.

Think carefully before you risk enhancing his power base
Meeting any of the needs of this motive base by ingratiation is bound to be risky. Ingratiation is a chancy affair with bribery, its logical extension, a possible outcome at the end of the line. So as a deliberate ongoing strategy, ingratiation is dangerous. Cultural differences obviously affect things, but since the process of ingratiation first of all enhances his power base before (you hope) he voluntarily decides not to use it because 'you seem a decent fellow', its conscious use has very clear implications.

Ingratiation can help in a weak position
Despite the previous point, if your ability to use the other motive bases is severely limited and your power base is small, your only real hope may lie in making the sort of appeal which you trust will dissuade him from using the strength of his own position. So ingratiation – the only real option open to you – may well have to be the order of the day, unsatisfactory as it is.

Compliments
Complimenting and thanks are low-risk strategies but can yield high returns. Perhaps the best option in this field lies in giving compliments or thanks where there is good reason, for example, on a well-researched case, on his willingness to meet you at short notice, on the business-like way he is conducting negotiation and so on. This does serve to increase his self-esteem but in a way that rebounds to your interest, and it acknowledges any special effort he has made. As commented by Tedeschi and Rosenfeld 'Complimenting others tends to produce the intended effect because of the general and perhaps universal norm of reciprocity which stipulates that one ought to return the positive acts of others.'[18] So where there is genuine reason, complimenting or thanking can yield good returns.

The five motive bases we have discussed form a very useful starting point for strategy and particularly for theme identification and development. So before we leave them we will look at some ways in which they can be managed to good effect.

Managing the themes

I have already declared my preference for thinking in terms of themes rather than arguments, the principal reason being that they reflect much more the continuing nature of the persuasion process. It really is a matter of having a series of themes that you will use, of using them and getting the reaction, then of using this reaction to develop either cognitive dissonance or common ground. Here, therefore, are some points about managing the themes so that they can be used to good effect.

> *Persuasion is a function of a number of themes that can be brought into play*

Quite clearly there has got to be an upper limit to numbers and any attempt to use them all at once would be utterly counter-productive. For all the obvious reasons it would be the worst of all strategies. But there are three good reasons why a number and variety of themes are of value.

First, there is such a thing as weight of argument. We have already seen that the aim is to build up a state of tension – cognitive dissonance – in the mind of the other party. Introduced on a progressive basis, both a number and variety of themes will accomplish this more successfully than just one or two.

Second is the point of their potential for developing common ground. The importance of the progressive creation of common ground is immense. If there are few themes, the opportunity for common ground development is correspondingly less. But once a theme is at best accepted or at worst understood, it can become the first ray of light in what until then has been a dark sky.

The third reason for a number of themes rather than a few is the straight point about handling disagreement. It takes time for parties to become aware of psychological inconsistency, and it takes time for them to rationalise new positions. Again in normal circumstances, the greater the level of opposition, the longer this takes. During this period it is more than useful to have something new to say. This will maintain the pressure, provide an added rationale for change and, perhaps most usefully of all, reduce the chances of a dog fight developing out of sheer boredom when your opponent cannot bring himself to say yes and equally you have nothing new to say. In this instance new arguments and different angles are like a breath of fresh air.

Wherever possible, prepare the ground

In many ways initiating and developing themes is similar to learning. You are attempting to put something new into the thinking of the other party. So what is important in this process? Bernard Lovell has no doubt and puts the point succinctly: 'What is certain, however, is that the most important single factor influencing new adult learning is what the learner has learned already and has organised in his conceptual structure.'[19] So if we are to introduce themes which are either alien to the thinking or outside the experience of the other party, it is well to prepare the ground first. We will discuss this as a matter of strategy in Chapter 9.

Plan the sequence of your themes

We have seen that themes have their greatest value if they are introduced progressively into negotiation. But in what order? And what time-scale? There are two principles to guide us here:

1. *Primacy and recency.* From our own experience we can probably confirm that when we are faced with having to recall something that is new to us, we are most likely to remember our first and last impressions. These are in fact examples of what are known as the laws of primacy and recency. The first impression we get of a person or topic is likely to remain prominent. And the last impression we have is the most recent in our memory, so again it has a specially important place. Clearly this does not always happen, but the tendency is there; and the information in the middle of our recall tends to become blurred. So themes should be initiated with this point in mind.

2. *The attention span.* This is the time that is available to you to make an impact. While it is extended if there is interest or involvement, it is surprisingly short – say ten to fifteen minutes. So again this argues against conducting negotiation by means of making long presentations; rather the series of short bursts as each theme is introduced, supported, discussed and at best converted into common ground, is the more effective method.

Introduce the least contentious themes early

We have already mentioned the lock-in effect in which once a general pattern of behaviour is initiated it tends to be reciprocated. We also know that it is often quite hard to get out of that particular mode. It therefore follows that while there might be high drama in starting with the most contentious themes, and while there might be a feeling that to do so will mean that your opponent's defences are rapidly trampled down, the strategy should be resisted. If you do start with a blast, drama there will be, but you are locked into adversarial conflict which pervades nego-tiation from then on. And because he will recognise that they really are the contentious areas, he will man the barricades. So unless you actually want drama or a confrontation, the general rule is to introduce the least contentious themes first and develop them into common ground so that when the going gets tough later, you can refer back to them to relieve the tension.

Do you really have to give a downside?

One of the problems for the negotiator is whether or not to pre-empt counter-arguments by pointing them up and dealing with them at the same time as developing his themes. Certainly to do so demonstrates an openness of mind and an even-handed approach. But it might also mean that the attack is blunted. So which is the best option?

The research on this is interesting. In some very comprehensive analyses, it was found that:

The two sided presentation was more effective with better educated men; the one sided presentation was more effective with less educated men. Habits of thought acquired in high school and college tended to make the educated listeners resist a one sided presentation, whereas their less critical, less educated friends were impressed by the one sided programme and would not challenge or think of possible objections to it.[20]

So, on balance it might appear that for educated negotiators, you should at the very least indicate that you have considered and already taken account of likely counter-arguments. But watch out! The same piece of research found that when the even-handed approach was used but one major counter-argument had been left out, once this admission had been identified by the hearers, there was a huge boomerang effect and the communication was resisted even more than if no counter-argument had been mentioned at all.

So for us the message is clear. If for whatever reason you are going to counter-argue your own themes, you must guess at the areas which will be important to the other side and deal with them.

And if you miss an important one, your even-handed approach will rebound.

In the light of this, the lower-risk and arguably higher pay-off strategy is to make it quite clear that your themes support your position and that you expect him to think of his reactions for himself. Hence you do not need to counter-argue.

Develop your cover positions

The final point in this section follows from the last. The other party will have his own themes. True, they can only be guessed at, but it is more than prudent to anticipate as many as you can and to develop for each what we call a *cover position*. This is a theme, argument or device you will use to avoid the awkward silence or the dropping jaw which will otherwise occur when you cannot think of what to say next. Obviously your cover positions represent the defensive aspect of theme development, but they are no less important for that.

In sum therefore I would suggest that the inner game of platform building and its management is an important one. Succeed here and you are on the way to developing positional credibility.

Let us now turn to management of the second element of positional credibility, to cognitive dissonance.

Managing cognitive dissonance

From my own involvement in negotiations, and in training others, one of the biggest failings I have found in negotiating behaviour stems from the assumption that if you have said something, then it has been received, understood and unless there has been fairly rapid feedback to the contrary, accepted. Questioning to test acceptance of a theme or just to find out how it is going down are the exceptions to the rule. Development and reinforcement are embarked on with reticence. Yet the hard truth is that if a theme is worth getting, it will almost certainly have to be fought for. 'The wobble' will only come if there is a push or, perhaps more to the point, a series of pushes. So what do we do? Keep hammering on the door in anticipation that it will finally open? Perhaps, and tenacity certainly pays. If nothing else it reinforces determination and commitment, and against a weak opponent that can count for a lot. But the danger is apparent. Too much repetition is a turn-off. Perloff and Brock commenting on mainstream research in this field put it well when they write of research in this:

> Repetition of message arguments provides subjects with increased opportunities to cognitively process the communication and to recognise the cogency of the arguments. Thus, when the communication was repeated a moderate number of times, counter-argumentation decreased and agreement increased. *However*, when the message was repeated many times, boredom and reaction ensued, thereby motivating subjects to criticise the communication. Consequently, counter-argumentation increased and agreement declined.[21]

So the underlying point about the reinforcement which is bound to be necessary if cognitive dissonance is to be achieved is that it should be undertaken with empathy. Apologising for 'having to reinforce the point', accepting that it is your fault if 'the point hasn't got across' and like comments are ways of reinforcing with empathy. With this in mind, here are some other points about managing cognitive dissonance.

Do not shy away from repetition

Despite all that we have said, the evidence does show that without repetition, learning does not take place. So themes should be repeated. But in full? With all the supporting detail? This smacks of lack of empathy. And what a bore! This is where the device of the *key commitment* comes in. A key commitment is a phrase or short sentence not very different in form from an advertising slogan. It encapsulates the theme that you are developing. It has impact; it is memorable. In fact it is the pressure point for the whole theme. So in 'A close run thing' you, as the supplier, had themes which related to the value of your dealer network and the benefits to him of you being sole supplier. Key commitments for these could therefore be, 'Our dealer network has served you well' and 'We meet your needs uniquely'.

Good key commitments have great value. They can summarise the outcome of a complex theme. They can be repeated frequently to emphasise it. They are the trigger point to the thought process that lies behind it. And they are very useful for rapid, relevant summary. As we will see they figure prominently in both preparation and negotiation.

Have something new to say

Clearly the danger here is that if new themes are introduced too quickly, they can dilute the impact of the existing ones. Yet the benefit of having something new to say by way of reinforcement is considerable. The best way of doing this is gradually to introduce staff work which supports the theme. So in this way the theme remains constant but it is reinforced as new perspectives are put.

Question to develop involvement

Questioning is the key to getting involvement. Philip Lund in his book *Compelling Selling*[22] gives six reasons why we should ask questions. Questions, he says, allow you to retain the initiative in discussion, give you control of the conversation, make you appear a pleasant and interesting person, allow you to adapt your conversation and modes of expression to the characteristics of the man you are talking to, clarify and elucidate your points, and finally they can be used to establish commitment. Again, Neil Rackham in some interesting research found that skilled negotiators spent more than twice as much time asking questions as did their average counterparts.[23]

I would suggest that questioning – be it open or closed – falls into three categories. These are the questions for *information*, designed to find out more about his position, how he supports it and what lies behind it. Questions for *clarification* relate to his responses to your themes, proposals and comments; they include the very important questions designed to find out priorities in his position or reactions. Finally, there are questions for *commitment* which are asked to identify common ground, agreement or potential agreement. In combination they should get involvement from the lowest of the low responders. It is only by questioning that negotiation can progress.

Use the pressure of silence

Most of us in the Western culture find silence embarrassing. We tend to feel that it smacks of weakness, of not knowing what to say, rather than of measured reflection. It is therefore a gap to be filled, and the great danger is that we fill it even though it is 'our silence' and the onus of response rests on him. So silence, particularly after the question is asked, is indeed golden. One of the experienced negotiators put it like this: 'Never underestimate the value of deliberate silence and eyeballing. Many negotiators find it difficult to handle. There is a compulsion to contribute after opening doors.'

Be careful of language intensity

It may seem that use of intense language such as the very positive or forceful affirmation, the overstatement, the swear-word, or the intense phrase would, like a bright colour, have the greatest impact. Reality is that because of the reaction it generates, it is more likely to generate a boomerang effect. There is good evidence to say that using a relatively low intensity of language – for example, suggesting rather than demanding – is more persuasive than arguing very intensely. Indeed if you have a weak power base, there is probably little useful alternative.

An interesting development of this is the finding that people in a stressful situation such as negotiation are more likely to respond positively to lower levels of language intensity and to reject persuasion which incorporates language of high intensity. The same is true of language which is opinionated, particularly if it comes from a person who has a low level of credibility.[24] In this, as in all assessments of whether or not language is intense, much depends on what is regarded as 'appropriate for the context'.

When approaching an impasse in platform building, move on

I would suggest that this last point is probably the most important of all. As cognitive dissonance develops, it is almost certain to be accompanied by some hostile and negative reactions. It then becomes a fine decision about whether to extend discussion and involvement to reinforce the theme and your commitment to it, or to back off and move on. Continuation may not just be bad for you in that you are banging your head against a brick wall, but also bad in the effect that it is having on him. So when the really negative reactions start to show (these are the so-called defence mechanisms that we will discuss in Chapter 5 as part of the rejection pattern), perhaps now is the time to move on to another theme or topic. Unless you want to make it almost a 'breakdown issue', moving on is almost invariably best. As the fisherman would say, there is little point in working an empty pool; you can always come back to it later when conditions might have changed. But now is the time to move on. Try another pool and see how that goes. By progression from one theme to another, at the end of the day you will have a number of them 'in the bag'.

Being aware of the need to create cognitive dissonance and then using sound technique to manage it are important. But as with platform building, they are a means to an end. Both are aimed at developing sufficient common ground on which the first position can be put. So it is to this third element of positional credibility that we now turn.

Developing common ground

Besides mentioning the key importance of the progressive development of common ground, our discussion of the inner game made the point that although the term has a definitive ring to it, in negotiation it is rarely so precise. There are varying levels of common ground. At best the other party accepts the point as common ground and there is full agreement on it between you. More likely, he acknowledges it as representing the basis on which your proposals are made. At worst he understands it. Hence even though he may reject your proposals, he will have at least acknowledged that to you at any rate they have a rational base. So summarising whichever of these aspects of common ground applies is very important. Here are some points to bear in mind.

Summarise progressively
Keep the momentum of negotiation going by summarising themes and positions, priorities and indications as they are given, and agreement as it develops.

Summarise accurately
There may well be a temptation to go for the loaded summary or to use the tactic known as the 'false summary'. Well, it is a tactic which, if it works, enables you to shift negotiation to the position you summarised in your favour rather than the state of negotiations as it actually was. But against a good negotiator it will probably fail, and played too often will destroy your credibility. So the general rule is to summarise accurately.

Use summaries to signal
The previous point may have implied that all that a summary does

is to recap. Not so. In the hands of a good negotiator it will do much more. By highlighting certain points and lowlighting others, by commenting on certain aspects, by using it as a platform to question or to propose, he will use it to signal requirements that he wants met, areas he might abandon, and possible lines of negotiation that might prove fruitful. In short, he will use it to give and to test reaction.

Use summaries as a platform

Finally, summaries make a platform from which to launch the next move. Before a negotiator goes to his next position, he will try to secure his base. Before he launches a proposal he will try to develop enough common ground and he will summarise it. Then, if he gets a negative reaction, he will either go back to platform building and the task of generating cognitive dissonance, or he will let the point hang as he moves on. But if he gets enough of a positive reaction, he will make it the platform for his next move. In this way negotiation develops' with a natural rhythm that demonstrates order and purpose.

In conclusion then, establishing positional credibility is crucial. If we fail here, proposals which are put forward to resolve areas of difference are seen as arbitrary and unreasonable. But if we are successful, we create a solid platform on which successful negotiations can prosper.

With two of the dimensions of persuasion in negotiation now discussed, it is to the third, which we call opponent management, that we turn in Chapter 4.

Summary

1. There are three elements that make for the development of positional credibility:
   (a) *the platform* on which you launch your first proposal;
   (b) *cognitive dissonance* which makes him less certain of his own position;
   (c) *common ground* which as it is progressively developed consolidates both the platform and the development of cognitive dissonance in your favour.
2. The platform should consist of themes, developed on a progressive basis with the appropriate staff work, which cover

in particular the motive bases of expertise, benefit, opportunity and reward, and the avoidance of punishment and fear:

(a) *Expertise* which gives the rational base for your proposal is essential.

(b) *Benefit, opportunity and reward*, particularly reward, are the positive inducements to get movement. Reward is used on the basis of movement gained for movement offered. It is likely to lead to reciprocation and so to positive negotiation.

(c) *The avoidance of punishment and fear* is a powerful persuader, but must be seen as both a defensive measure and a legitimate one.

3. Themes, of which you need a number, should be progressively introduced so that cognitive dissonance, which is an evolutionary process, can more easily occur.

4. There are three levels of common ground. At best it is agreed; at second best it is acknowledged; at third best, it is understood.

5. The first negotiating position – called the initial position – should only be launched from a credible base. This means that as much of the platform and as many as possible of the elements that make for cognitive dissonance, should be converted into common ground before it is.

Thirty-two means of developing positional credibility were given.

Key question: Which aspects of the inner and outer game of positional credibility are most relevant in the negotiations you normally face?

References

1. White, R. W. (1959) 'Motivation reconsidered: the concept of competence', *Psychological Review*, September, p. 329.
2. Eysenck, H. J. and Wilson, G. (1975) *Know Your Own Personality*, Penguin, Harmondsworth, p.36.
3. McGuire, W. J. (1969) 'The nature of attitudes and change', in G. Lindzey and E. Aronson (eds.), *The Handbook of Social Psychology*, Addison-Wesley, Reading, MA.
4. Burgoon, M. and Bettinghaus, E. P. (1980) 'Persuasive message strategies', in M. E. Roloff and G. R. Miller (eds.), *Persuasion*, Sage Publications, Beverly Hills, CA, pp. 141–69.

5. Tedeschi, J. T. and Rosenfeld, R. (1980) 'Communication in bargaining and negotiation', in Roloff and Miller, *Persuasion*, pp. 225–48.
6. Newcomb, T. M. (1947) 'Autistic hostility and social reality', *Human Relations*, vol. 1, pp. 69–86.
7. Deutsch, M. and Krauss, R. M. (1960) 'The effect of threat on interpersonal bargaining', *Journal of Abnormal and Social Psychology*, vol. 61, pp. 181–9.
8. Rubin, J. Z. and Brown B. R. (1975) *The Social Psychology of Bargaining and Negotiation*, Academic Press, London, p. 283.
9. Blake, R. R. and Mouton, J. S. (1961) 'Loyalty of representatives to ingroup positions during inter-group competition', *Sociometry*, vol. 24, pp. 177–83.
10. Rubin and Brown, op. cit., p. 54.
11. Coon, D. (1983) *Psychology: Exploration and application*, West Publishing, St Paul, MN, p. 614.
12. Warr, P. (1973) *Psychology and Collective Bargaining*, Hutchinson, London, p. 27.
13. Miller, G. A. (1962) *Psychology: The science of mental life*, Penguin, London, pp. 366–7.
14. Rackham, N. (1987) *Making Major Sales*, Gower, Aldershot.
15. Rubin and Brown, op. cit., pp. 265–71.
16. Kennedy, G., Benson, J. and McMillan, J. (1980) *Managing Negotiations*, Hutchinson, London.
17. Tedeschi and Rosenfeld, op. cit., p. 237.
18. Ibid., p. 243.
19. Lovell, R. B. (1982) *Adult Learning*, Croom Helm, London, p. 63.
20. Miller, op. cit., p. 354.
21. Perloff, R. M. and Brock, T. C. (1980) 'And thinking makes it so', in Roloff and Miller, *Persuasion*, p. 74.
22. Lund, P. R. (1974) *Compelling Selling*, Macmillan Press, London, pp. 6–7.
23. Rackham, N. (1971) *The Behaviour of Successful Negotiators*, Huthwaite Research Group, Sheffield.
24. Burgoon and Bettinghaus, op. cit., p. 152.

4

Effective opponent management

So far we have looked at persuasion very much from your own point of view; you have an objective to achieve and your aim is to persuade the other party to accept it. Hence we have concentrated on how to develop your own personal and positional credibility. But, obviously, this is only one side of the coin. In most negotiation the other party has objectives and needs of his own. Just as you are out to develop an image of capability and strength which is softened to a degree by empathy, so is he. Just as you have a position you wish to achieve, so almost certainly will he. Hence as far as he is concerned, both his personal and positional needs must be addressed if there is to be any real chance of a successful outcome as, for example, in the case study 'A close run thing'. First, the positional needs of the purchaser were met by the opportunity that he could see arising from the lower engine running temperatures and from the possibility of achieving a more competitive price. Second, his personal needs for achievement and power were met as price began to be adjusted and his own proposals relating to the improvement of the service given by the dealer network were incorporated into the discussion. Then the negotiation really started to make progress. In short in these, as in virtually all other successful negotiations, when the means are found of incorporating some at least of the needs of the other party into the discussion, negotiations begin to hum.

At this stage therefore, I suggest that there are three what I would regard as basic 'truths' which can be stated about negotiation. Like many of their type they may appear to be almost self-evident, but are none the worse for that, and they take us rapidly forward.

First, while it is essential – absolutely essential – to develop personal and positional credibility of your own so that the conditioning which supports your proposal is effective, it is only when the same needs of the other side are addressed that the basis of settlement begins to emerge.

Second, like your own, the positional and personal needs of your opponent are interlinked. Satisfaction of one inevitably has an effect on feelings of satisfaction relating to the other. Clearly an acceptable outcome requires that an adequate level of satisfaction is given.

Third, since negotiations start with conflicting interests or positions, satisfaction is normally only possible after expectations have been revised. Even the best of win–win options usually requires that at least some adjustment of the first preferences of both parties is made. It is therefore at this point that what we call 'opponent management' enters.

To some, opponent management might be an emotive phrase which gives them difficulty, so let me start by saying what I do *not* mean. I do not mean full control so that your opponent is virtually your prisoner. When he has choice, as he has in most negotiating situations, that is impossible anyway. And, more fundamentally, I have enough faith in my opponent and experience of the process to believe that where there is conflict, better results come from free negotiation anyway. But what I do mean is that almost invariably the aspirations of the other party must be lowered and his arguments dealt with if we are to have any chance of finding resolution. So to this extent I must set about managing both his positional needs and the arguments he uses to support them, and his personal needs and the personal style that he uses to express them.

In this chapter therefore we discuss the management of our opponent's positional needs and his negotiating style. Our starting point is the inner game when we consider how to set about understanding his needs. Then, as we look at the practicalities of opponent management, we discuss how to set about managing them.

The inner game

Understanding positional needs

Opponent management starts with insight, and the experienced negotiators were very clear on what this meant. For them it was not just a matter of considering their opponent's stated positions.

They wanted to feel the pulse. 'Getting tuned in to his position', 'identifying his needs', 'understanding where he is coming from', 'looking for his concerns – and happinesses' were just some of the many phrases used. So, yet again, insight is the key, and this insight is at two levels. The first is that which relates to the needs of the organisation he represents over the longer term and in a wider context, and to which these negotiations may only partly be relevant. These we can call the *strategic needs* of the other party and rest either formally in the organisation's corporate plan, or informally in the hopes and fears of its senior executives. The second level is much more specific and relates to the *immediate negotiating* needs of the other party as he attempts to get specific arguments established and positions accepted.

Let us take an example, familiar to us all: negotiating with our bank manager. When we meet, we know very well what our own needs are. But insight into opponent management only comes when we consider his. So what are they? Does the bank in all its might, or its manager as its representative, have any positional needs at all? They are likely to include the manager's need to satisfy himself and to show to his superiors that there is a sound business base for the loan, and that it is not being made to support an imprudent or implausible request. The extension of this is that there is security on the repayment of the loan. These are needs which will have to be satisfied if we are to exercise any positional control at all, and their effect on our negotiating style and stance as we determine how to handle them is obvious. But it is his third need – to increase his future business with us – which is the one which, if we can satisfy it even in part, will bring a gleam to his eye. Hence if we are to develop any positional control, it is the one that is of greatest interest to us. If he actively wants something that only we and our business can give, it puts a different aspect on the discussion.

I am the first to accept that making or attempting to make a distinction between strategic and immediate negotiating needs is fraught with difficulty and danger. And yet if you stop insight into positional needs short of the wider context that surrounds them, you may well be missing a trick. Equally, if you deal with context to the exclusion of specifics you will be hopelessly ill-prepared. So insight must relate to both strategic and immediate needs. The technique we will use to gain this insight is the expectation test which is discussed and illustrated in Chapter 7. But the point here is that if the positional needs of the other party are consciously considered, the sort of opponent management we mean can become a very real possibility.

Let us now turn to the other aspect of the inner game of opponent management. As well as having positional needs which must be understood before they can be managed, your opponent will have personal needs which very much affect his negotiating style. A brief discussion will show how.

Understanding personal needs

I have already suggested that personal and positional needs are almost invariably closely linked so that personal satisfaction with the process has an effect on the acceptability of the terms. That is true even for the most tightly mandated and junior of negotiators. And when you are dealing with the top man, understanding of this can make all the difference.

One of the areas in which I asked for the views of the experienced negotiators was in the factors which for them made for successful negotiation. 'We got on well together', 'the chemistry was right', 'I felt I could do business with that man' were typical of the many comments made about the interrelationship of personalities. But, of all people, they realised that you could not pick and choose the people with whom you negotiated. Hence they also spoke of 'understanding your opponent', 'reacting to your man' and 'adjusting your style to deal with his personality'.

So how to handle personal needs? How to get the chemistry right? How to deal with your opponent? These are questions of never-ending interest and speculation. If we could only box our opponent into a certain personality type, we could then set about predicting how he would behave and adjust our line of negotiation accordingly. It is an approach which the purists would condemn. But the practitioner is in fact having to make decisions, at times very rapidly indeed, as he negotiates. He has to take a view, which is almost certainly an over-simplified one, on his opponent's personality and negotiating style. So although making general assessments of personality and style and then generating a line of negotiation to handle them falls short of any rigorous analysis, we have to do it. So let us look at the inner game of understanding our opponent's personal needs by taking what in my view is the best workable theory that is available.

Rubin and Brown have brought together the wide and varied research which has been done on personality type as it affects negotiation.[1] They suggest that there are three crucial variables that influence negotiating behaviour. The first is the level of what they call 'interpersonal orientation' that the negotiator has. By this they mean both his social ability and his social awareness. Someone high in interpersonal orientation is 'responsive to the interpersonal aspects of his relationship with the other. He is both interested in, and reactive to, variations in the other's behaviour.' Conversely, someone low in interpersonal orientation is characterised by a 'non-responsiveness to interpersonal aspects of his relationship with the other. His interest is neither in cooperating nor competing with the other but rather in maximising his own gain – pretty much regardless of how the other fares.' We will call these high or low sociability.

The second variable is what they call 'motivational orientation', which is simply whether the negotiator is by nature and inclination a cooperator or a competitor. The third variable is power which Rubin and Brown define as the 'ability of one individual to move another through a range of outcomes.' It is different from the other two variables in that while they describe what by nature we are – a tendency to sociability or unsociability, to cooperate or to compete – the variable of power is laid upon us by the situation surrounding our negotiating position. While we can influence it, it is basically not of our making. But the way we respond to it will depend very much on our existing predisposition.

From this a matrix can be created which first comprises the two variables of sociability and negotiating disposition; second, describes the behaviour of four main types of negotiator; and third, allows the overlay of the other variable, power, to demonstrate how this further shapes the negotiating behaviour caused by the interaction of the other two. The basic matrix is given in Figure 4.1. Here is a pen picture of each of the negotiating types.

Positive Peter

Peter is well known and much sought-after in negotiation – particularly by his opponents – for several good reasons. He is pleasant to deal with. He is responsive to the other party as an individual and will go to considerable lengths, including exceeding his mandate, to maintain a positive relationship. He is interested in

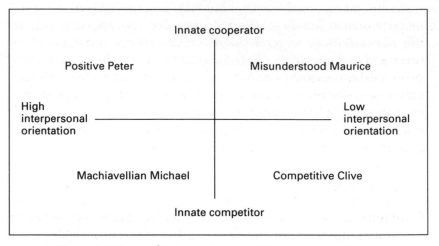

Figure 4.1 Personality types in negotiation

and reactive to changes in behaviour, and is tolerant of ambiguity and positions. He will respond to mission statements and has a concern for those who share his ideals. He tends to be straightforward about threats and promises and generally acknowledges that he will have to give if he is going to get. This means that he will go to some lengths to create win–win options. He will probably be prepared to take risks with his own side in order to find an agreement. He is ideally suited to the joint problem solving mode of negotiation. All this makes opponents such as Competitive Clive and most of all Machiavellian Mike long to meet him. But even they should beware because he tends to take adverse comments as a personal attack and reacts emotionally and with considerable hostility to them. And if he feels that his positive style is being exploited – by which we mean *really* exploited – he will go to the other extreme and become suspicious, resentful and, above all, hostile.

Recognise him? Let us try another.

Misunderstood Maurice

Maurice is full of positive intent and really wants to find a good agreement. He can often see one. But regrettably he does not make a good negotiator for the simple reason that because of his low sociability he tends to ignore the requirement to persuade. In short, influencing and persuading are not really part of his make-up. So he tends to spend too little time developing personal or positional credibility in negotiation, does not much believe in the persuasion or negotiation processes either, and makes one offer and one offer only. Then he gets resentful when his 'sensible proposals' are thrown back at him, and runs the twofold danger either of giving in to pressure or of terminating the discussion – even though all the signals are that movement from the other side is available. In theory he should not be called on to negotiate. In practice because it is 'part of his job' he all too frequently is.

Competitive Clive

Clive is the archetypal mainstream negotiator. He is not interested in cooperating or competing, in being sociable or unsociable – only in doing well. He is cool under pressure, and well able to cobble together a deal if he has to. But to get it, he will tend to give as little away in either information or position as possible, he will try to dominate his opponent and he will be happy to talk of threats rather than opportunities. If things start to turn against him, he will resort to personal attack and positional subterfuge. He is tough, but for the most part is fairly transparent in motive and method. However if you do not play his game you will probably lose. You have been warned!

Machiavellian Mike

He is Michael to some, who say it with respect. He is Mike to others who admire his manipulative style. To others he is Mac the Knife – never to be trusted, always to be avoided. In fact Mike has a tendency to be the 'tricky negotiator' *par excellence*. The only thing that perhaps might restrain him is if he has a personal code of ethics or an acceptance of negotiating conventions. But his tendency is to the Machiavellian. His high sociability gives him all the advantages of reading people, but his high competitive streak means that he has little compunction in manipulating them whenever he sees it to be to his advantage. He will spend time getting to know his opponent, but not from the point of view of establishing a positive relationship; rather he seeks to identify strengths so that he can nullify them, and weaknesses so that he can exploit them. He will play his power base to the ultimate. In many respects these characteristics should make him the most effective of all four types, and indeed for genuine 'one off' negotiations where he need never be heard of again, this may be so. But the big disadvantage for him is that his notoriety rapidly spreads and that, if it is at all possible, his opponents, unless they are of the same type, refuse to do business with him. Or if they have to, they will plan to beat him by force. When he loses, he tends to lose both heavily and messily!

Certainly, these four types are at the extreme. But the attributes and characteristics they show are well researched and ring true. I would acknowledge that by no means are all negotiators at these extremes. But negotiation is a high-profile activity that tends to attract fairly emphatic personality types, and I would think that those who negotiate freely with a wide range of opponents will have little difficulty in fitting faces to these descriptions.

Let us now look at the effects of power on these four negotiating types. There are some general points which are worth bearing in mind. The first, and most depressing, is that if there is a significant imbalance in power between the parties, it will tend to be exploited. Certainly Machiavellies will do this more than co-operators, but the tendency is shown by all. 'Bargainers with high power relative to that of their adversary tend to behave manipulatively and exploitatively, while those with low relative power tend to behave submissively.'[2]

There are other known effects of power. I have given them various names. There is what we can call the 'warring tribe effect' as seen for example in the Lebanon and Afghanistan – the more people with coercive power, the more likely it is that all will use it. There is the 'wild cat effect' as in the lightning, crippling strike – the more precise and usable the power, the more likely it is that coercion will occur. More positively, however, is the well-researched[3] 'MAD effect' (MAD as in Mutually Assured Destruction) which occurs when there is a high but roughly equal power distribution. The parties will tend not to use their power and would rather prefer to engage in meaningful negotiation. Regrettably, only the last has any real degree of comfort for us.

Given that there are these general effects relating to coercive power which seem to apply regardless of personality types, there are marked differences, given in Figure 4.2, in the way cooperators respond to coercive pressure compared with competitors. Cooperators will initially at any rate tend to pay less attention to power imbalance and will be less likely to set about exploiting it or

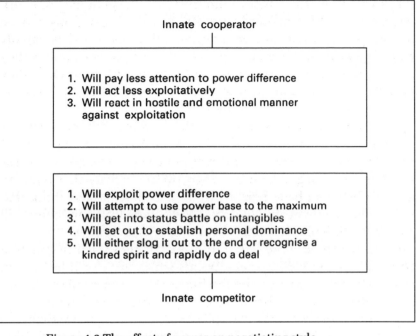

Figure 4.2 The effect of power on negotiating style

succumbing to it. But, as with the tendency shown when personal relationships are broken, once they feel that power is being used to exploit them, they will either react heavily against it or leave the field. Competitors, however, take a look at power and ask themselves how they can use it to gain maximum advantage. This ability will compound the advantage that they already have in most negotiation in relation to cooperators. However, if they are dealing with one of their own kind (and this applies particularly if Machiavelli meets Machiavelli) one of two effects can occur. Either they will recognise a kindred spirit and they will rapidly do a deal, or they will slog it out to the bitter end.

So for the inner game of opponent management, I have suggested that insight is the key. First, insight into your opponent's longer-term strategic needs, and then into the more immediate negotiating needs relating to the positions he will take and the rationale he will put forward. Second, insight into his personality type so that the general pattern of his negotiating behaviour can be identified and understood.

This insight can be put to good use. So we will now deal with the management of each of these starting with his positional needs as we look at some ways in which positional control can be developed.

Managing the inner game

Developing positional control

In the last chapter we discussed ways in which themes could be created, developed and sustained. The purpose of doing so was twofold: first to build a platform on which you could launch proposals and second to set about generating what we called cognitive dissonance – psychological wobble – in the mind of the other party in relation to his own position. In fact it was all rather straightforward in that because you knew what you wanted to achieve you could develop the themes that you hoped would give your position a credible base. But now that we are going into the other party's camp, and need not only to understand his needs but also to manage them, a very legitimate question to ask is just how far is this possible? Can you seriously embark on the strategic assignment of controlling your opponent's position and arguments and, more fundamentally, the needs that give rise to them?

Quite clearly the answer directly relates to how important his position is to him, and what sort of alternatives you are going to be able to put forward. But even within these two constraints, success in developing positional control depends on how you perform in three areas. First on how successful you are at anticipating his needs and in developing strategies to handle them. Second, on how much you are able to clarify his position and get some idea of the priorities that relate to it. And third on how well you are able to shape his position so that his expectations are structured in your favour. We will deal with each of these.

Anticipating needs

Some negotiators appear to have an intuitive sense which guides them. When you talk with them about their experiences, it often seems that at one stage in their career they have been in the other camp. This helps to explain the sixth sense they show about the negotiating positions and ploys of the other party. Almost subconsciously they put themselves in his shoes. This helps them enormously. It gives them some sort of empathy and it helps them to read behaviour and to decode signals and needs. Yet it almost always appears to be an intuitive activity. However in the expectation test (Chapter 7) we make it a more overt activity. Meanwhile, here are three suggestions which will help the process further.

Understand the pressures he is under

Perhaps more realistically, *try* to understand the pressures he is under, since to get the full truth is going to be impossible. This should take account not just of the normal pressures of business activity, but should extend wherever possible to any pressures he is under away from work. I would defend the value for making this extension for two reasons. First, I have found that to show empathy to an opponent who is suffering personally in some way is not only good in itself, but can also have lasting beneficial effects on relationships. And second, the man who is under great personal stress outside negotiation will tend to behave differently – and make different decisions – from the man who is at ease in his personal life.

Use pre-negotiation meetings

The virtues and values of the informal pre-negotiation contact, be it a telephone call, informal meeting or lunch or dinner date, are immense. They are covered in greater detail when we look at strategy. But if ever there were a way of taking the guesswork out of anticipating needs, this is it.

Identify possible concessions

To the average negotiator or his less-gifted colleague, to think in terms of concessions implies weakness. To the effective negotiator concessions are a source of strength for several reasons.

First, very few negotiating positions are so strong that they can be all take and no give. Even if they are, the other party will rapidly latch on to what is happening and will become disenchanted with a process that offers him so little. So since concessions are normally inevitable, there is a great value in identifying them in advance and using them to maximum effect. This will normally be on a linked basis so that concession by him is demanded in return for concession by you.

Second, the possibility of concessions introduces what has been called 'the tension of movement'. Positive inducements to move are given to both parties.

Third, instead of slamming all doors in the face of your opponent, they represent the basis of a discussion which can interest him.

Fourth, if negotiation is sterile or is approaching an impasse, they can provide the momentum which can lead to breakthrough.

Concessions therefore are too valuable a commodity to leave to chance or pressure. Where possible, they should be identified in advance and then incorporated into the negotiating parameters at the level of settlement that is thought to be appropriate.

These are some of the means of anticipating needs and are the first step in developing positional control. Clarifying positions and priorities is the next, and it is to this that we now turn.

Clarifying positions and priorities

Perhaps one of the greatest dangers that arises from any sort of need analysis is that having thought through his likely positions and arguments, you tend to take them for granted. This can have a number of adverse consequences, the worst of which is that negotiations develop without you having fully determined what he is looking for or tested him on the reasoning that lies behind it. In short you are trying to hit a target which is a moving one, largely because you assumed that you knew what it was, and you therefore have not pinned it down. You can then find that too many of the shots you have available have fallen short or wide of the mark.

So clarification of positions and their supporting rationale, and then, usually later in negotiation, of priorities is important. Here, then, are five suggestions that can help in managing this particular aspect of the inner game.

Questions

Questions clarify positions and arguments – particularly if they are vague! As we have seen, good negotiators ask many questions – for information, clarification and commitment. But arguably the questions aimed at clarification are the most fruitful. They are open-ended, they lead on, they reveal. So such questions as 'What exactly are you looking for?' 'What are you saying to us in all this?' ''What is it that is making you take this line of argument?' 'Where is the evidence for that?' and so on have the potential to get you somewhere.

Test him in his reasoning

Testing serves a number of purposes. The first, and most obvious one, is that it stops him from coming to the conclusion that because you have not done so, you agree with him. Again as you take him up on his own themes you can get some idea from how well he supports them, of where his priorities lie. And again as you test his rationale, you start to find the basis for your counter-attack.

If you do not understand him, say so

For reasons of ego preservation, there is always a temptation to back off if for any reason you are not understanding him. But it is worth remembering that the onus of proof always lies with the proposer. If you have difficulty in understanding the rationale for his position, he usually has more to gain from allowing your confusion to continue than from enlightening you. The irony is that it is often the questions that come from ignorance or misunderstanding that open up the major flaw in his position.

Get your timing right

As mentioned earlier, questioning for positions and arguments tends to take place earlier in negotiation. However, as far as questioning aimed at finding priorities is concerned, it is unlikely that he will give you any real idea until he has come to the conclusion that he cannot achieve his first position. Normally, therefore, questions such as 'Which particular aspect of this proposal gives you the greatest difficulty?' or 'Where do you suggest that we put our major effort to find agreement?' are best delayed until he is aware that he cannot stay where he is and that movement there must be.

Be alert to signals

Signalling is one of the major arts of negotiation, and we cover it extensively in the next chapter when we see it as the means of transition from positional conflict to adjustment and accommodation. It is sufficient here to say that if you believe that you are being given a signal, ask a question aimed at clarifying it. Such questions as 'What do you want us to understand by that?' or just plain 'Tell us more' can be the means of taking negotiation rapidly forward.

These five points are useful to bear in mind for what some less-experienced negotiators find to be one of the more embarrassing aspects of the negotiating process. But the requirement for clarifying is important for it leads to the final and most important step in developing control of the other party's position – to shaping the discussion so that when the stage involving adjustment and accommodation is reached, it is away from his position and towards yours. It is therefore to shaping that we now turn.

Shaping his position

In the last chapter we looked at how to develop a platform on which to launch your proposals, and we noted that this would have its effect on developing cognitive dissonance in the mind of the other party. Since the purpose of shaping is to lower his expectations in relation to his own position, creating cognitive dissonance is once again important. Here, then, is a brief summary of the main points made about it so far:

1. Cognitive dissonance is created as your own themes are developed and either agreed, acknowledged or understood.
2. Themes will be more effective if they take account of the five motive bases, are supported by good staff work and introduced and reinforced on a progressive basis.
3. The creation of cognitive dissonance takes time.
4. Hence the second wave of themes, or the 'second push', is normally the most effective.
5. If possible, your initial position should be delayed until a strong platform to make it credible has been built and cognitive dissonance has been created.

With these points in mind let us now look at how cognitive dissonance can be created in relation to the other party's position and then controlled so that negotiation moves in your favour.

Develop empathy by acknowledging positions and needs

As far as he is concerned it is only when you have acknowledged what he has said, usually by summarising it back to him, that you have any base from which to start. The added benefit of doing this is that under most circumstances it will develop empathy between you and him in a way that appearing to ignore his position or arguments certainly will not. Clearly the one thing not to do at this stage is to agree with his position or any elements of it unless it is clearly within your strategy to do so. But you can always acknowledge that you have heard him.

Identify and use cover positions

One of the benefits of the analytic technique known as the expectation test (which we will discuss in detail in Chapter 7) is that it encourages you to develop cover positions. These are the arguments you will use or the themes or positions you will adopt in response to positions or arguments of his. In short they avoid you being caught 'with the dropping jaw'. How they are developed is explained in Chapter 7. It is sufficient here to say that as far as is possible, just as you develop themes and staff work to build your own platform, so you develop cover positions and, where necessary, staff work to deal with his.

Do not be afraid of an argument

Some readers might be surprised that this point has been so long in coming! Well here it is. There are occasions – quite frequent in the conditioning stage – when in order to demonstrate firmness and commitment, you have an argument. Hopefully you handle it more as an aspect of negotiation than as a verbal brawl – though there are occasions when that is necessary too. But more normally, you stick to your guns by developing your themes, introducing different elements of staff work and hammering away at your key commitments. You set out to win your argument.

In fact in my experience, most people are well able to have the argument; the difficulty is what to do after it. The general rule is that if you are going to argue, do it during the conditioning stage when the markers are still being set.

You do not have to win

Following on from the previous point, the good thing about arguments on your opponent's themes is that you do not have to win them. In fact if you try to win them all, it will be too much for him and the odds are he will get annoyed and, perhaps, will walk away. In fact, your aim in arguing is to block and blunt rather than to conquer; to create cognitive dissonance rather than mayhem.

Match tenacity with temperance

There is no doubt that tenacity is an important attribute of the negotiator – the experienced negotiators told me that often enough for me to be left in no doubt! But with tenacity should go temperance, because without it pressure can become a destructive force. So just as developing and sustaining your themes and mobilising your cover positions are important, so is either moving on or backing off. As we will see, too much pressure is counter-productive – a point which lies at the heart of the psychology of negotiation.

Where you can build

What a difference there is between on the one hand rejecting an argument because you cannot accept 90 per cent of it, and on the other building a response on the 10 per cent you can consider. The former gives little alternative but counter-argument; the latter gives you the floor and then takes you forward. It is the hallmark of a good negotiator that where possible, instead of outright disagreement, he will be far more likely to take what he is able to use in a position and then to build his own themes, positions or proposals on to it.

So far we have looked at managing the inner game of positional control. But opponent management is just as much to do with handling the personal style that the other negotiator has. We suggested that his negotiating behaviour could be identified as falling into one of four types and that although you have little, if any, control over which negotiating type you deal with, understanding can give influence. It is to this that we now turn in the second part of managing the inner game.

Handling negotiating style

Considering how to handle your opponent's negotiating style is important. While it is impossible to have such flexibility yourself that you can deal equally well with all men, you can be sensitive to the direction of the wind and trim your sails accordingly. Here are some suggestions that may help.

Where you can, match like with like

We know the minefield. High-sociability cooperators and low-sociability competitors have views and approaches to negotiation which are so different from each other that to put these types together is to risk one outcome: that negotiations will degenerate with the cooperator becoming more suspicious and the competitor more frustrated so that either they break down or the cooperator capitulates and the competitor wins all.

Now take the other two types. One is a born loser in negotiation, the other a born winner. The loser is the low-sociability cooperator. He should never be asked to negotiate.

The born winner is the high-sociability competitor – the Machiavelli. If he is low on business and negotiation ethics, he is an extremely efficient killer – the shark of the negotiating sea. There is only one who can match him, and that is another of his own type.

In the light of this, if a choice is available, should you select negotiators on the basis of the context of negotiation, or on the innate style of the negotiator with whom they will be dealing? It is a difficult question to answer. Certainly cooperators are better if the context is one of joint problem solving; competitors are better if it is trading that will be required. But on the basis that the context of negotiation is only the context as it is seen by the other party – in other words perception is all-important – I would suggest that, if it is possible, to match negotiators with similar styles constitutes the safest approach.

If there is a mismatch, exercise strong self-control
This applies particularly if you have the tendency towards high sociability and cooperation. In fact there is a lot going for you. Odds are you will be more likely to see alternatives and options in negotiation and use them; you will be better able to read the other man and hence to react quicker; and you will be altogether more fluent in your style and the way you handle your position. But for the reasons already given you are very vulnerable. To a lesser degree this applies to the low-sociability competitor who may well lose out by failing to use opportunities in negotiation simply because they are not within his mandate.

When you know there is a mismatch, there are two golden rules. The first is to be aware of your tendencies and short-comings and to be very much on your guard against them. The second rule follows from it. It is to slow negotiation down. For example, have more shorter meetings rather than few longer ones. Give yourself more thinking time in negotiation. Very definitely think once before responding and twice before moving.

And if you have a team, use it to monitor negotiation. Then be prepared to take its advice.

Try to develop power parity before you negotiate

This is covered in detail in Chapter 8, but we have already seen enough of power to know that the tendency is always for the powerful to exploit their position and for the weak to succumb. The first conclusion that follows from this is to be aware of this effect of power. The second is that if you are the weaker party, to do all you can to enhance your power base.

Give him one chance

Since for most negotiation there is always another round ahead, optimum negotiation behaviour can normally be seen to lie in both cooperation and competition. One of the effects of this is to make innate cooperators a bit more competitive and innate competitors a bit more cooperative. And we have already seen how cooperation in the form of movement, at the right time, begets reciprocal movement. So there is much to be said for setting the tone of cooperation. Hence when appropriate, make the cooperative proposal. Give him a chance to respond positively. If it is reciprocated, continue. But if it is not, become overtly less cooperative yourself. In short, give him one chance.

Be aware of specific consequences

From the research[4] into negotiation it is possible to draw some conclusions of a more general nature about personal style and how to deal with it. They are given, briefly, as follows.

It would appear that negotiating ability has little to do with *intelligence* and that possessors of high IQs do not necessarily make the best negotiators. But it does seem that those with *numerical ability* might behave less competitively than those without.

As *age* increases there is a progressive reversion to type. So a young tough nut is a hard nut to crack, but an old tough nut is harder still.

It would appear that the effect of *social class* lives on. It is the same as for power. Negotiators of a higher social status than their opponent will tend to exploit it, and those of inferior social status will tend to defer to it.

Sex counts! Females tend to have the preferences and insight into negotiation associated with high sociability. Males on the other hand tend to negotiate in the pattern relating to low sociability. This means that for example unless they have good reason to act to the contrary, females tend to be more trusting and trustworthy than males in the early stages of negotiation. But faced with what they regard as a lie, a breaking of a commitment or a breach of agreement, they respond defensively, even vindictively, and stay in that mode longer than males.

People high on the *authoritarian* scale tend towards competitive behaviour. They also tend to be less trusting of their opposite number and to have an expectation that they will be exploited by him.

Innate competitors tend to believe the world is full of other innate competitors. They therefore find it very difficult to change their style.

Finally there is the effect of *self-image*. To a degree we have already looked at this from the standpoint of the importance of self-confidence. But the part played by self-esteem is obviously considerable. Will the other party see a statement as a threat or as an opportunity? Will he trust his own ability to handle a proposal so that he changes it to his own advantage? Or will he reject it because he feels that anything that does not fall exactly within his game plan is an insult to his ego ('I didn't think of it so there can't be any merit in it') or a threat to his psychological security? This is well put by Tedeschi and Rosenfeld:

A person's self esteem represents a bias in his or her expectations of receiving benefits and punishments from others. Low self esteem persons may generally believe they will be disliked and punished by others, while high self esteem persons may expect others will approve of and reward them. Although low self esteem persons are apt to be more self destructive in their responses to threats, high self esteem persons may be more compliant when it is in their best practical interests to be so.[5]

In short we are back to self-confidence and how well the personal needs of the other party are being met as he negotiates.

All very interesting!

In this chapter we have looked at the third dimension of persuasion, at the positional and personal needs as they affect the style of the other party in negotiation, and at some of the ways in which they can be handled. We have been bold enough to call it opponent management. But because success in it and in the other two dimensions of persuasion is so elusive, because it is rare indeed to be able to meet the needs of the other side at least until aspirations have been moderated, there is normally a period of disenchantment, disillusion, even despair in the process which may cause a partial or even total breakdown. One or probably both parties dislike what they are hearing and, whether they realise it or not, they enter into what we call 'the rejection pattern'. So it is to this that we now turn as in the inner game we identify what it is and the influence it has on negotiating behaviour, and then as we consider ways in which it can be more successfully managed.

Summary

1. The inner game of opponent management is based on identifying your opponent's positional needs and understanding
   the effect which his personality will have on his negotiating
   style. For the former, strategic need analysis and the expectation test are useful. For the latter a matrix taking the variables
   of high to low sociability and cooperative to competitive
   disposition can give good insight.
2. The positional control you achieve is to a degree influenced by
   success in developing your own positional credibility. It then
   rests on anticipating his positional needs and handling them by
   clarifying, shaping and then dealing with them by concession
   or opposition.
3. Handling his negotiating style is very much a matter of being
   sensitive to the likely patterns of behaviour and of negotiating
   with them in mind.

Nineteen suggestions for managing the inner game have been given.

Key question: How do you set about handling the task of opponent management to better effect?

References

1. Rubin, J. Z. and Brown, B. R. (1975) *The Social Psychology of Bargaining and Negotiation*, Academic Press, London, pp. 158–9.
2. Ibid., p. 221.
3. See, for example, the findings of Murdoch, P., Thibaut, J. and

Gruder, O. L. in this area in the *Journal of Personality and Social Psychology*, vols. 9 and 11 (1967 and 1969).

4. The sources of this research are given as appropriate in Rubin and Brown, op. cit., pp. 179–91.

5. Tedeschi, J. T. and Rosenfeld, P. (1980) 'Communication in bargaining and negotiation', in M. E. Roloff and G. R. Miller (eds.), *Persuasion*, Sage Publications, Beverly Hills, CA, p. 240.

5

The rejection pattern

Rejection is taking place throughout negotiation, but it is normally at its most intense in the first two stages as themes seen as hostile are introduced, and indications which conflict with expectations are given. This process comes to a head when the initial positions of one side or both are formally put. It is a dangerous time. Indeed when I asked the experienced negotiators about the stages of the process when they felt a negotiated outcome to be at greatest risk, most of them said it was when first proposals were put on the table. Here, they said, was where the peak of rejection was reached. Let us look more closely at it.

The inner game

Over my years of involvement in negotiation, I became more and more aware that disagreement and, in its extreme form rejection were more than just events which occurred when your powers of persuasion were exhausted! But it was only when, completely outside the context of negotiation, I came across the 'crisis model' which gave the general pattern of behaviour that any of us is likely to exhibit when faced with information that comes as a shock, that I saw a sequence that described what I had seen time and again in negotiation.

The original version of the crisis model[1] is given in Figure 5.1. To illustrate it we will take the example of an unexpected

Figure 5.1 The personal crisis model

bereavement. First there is a period of *shock* as we find it difficult to believe that the bereavement has happened. The senses are numbed and life continues almost normally. But it is the calm before the storm. Second is the stage of *defensive retreat* when our reactions will tend to one of two extremes. Either we will show anger, bitterness, resentment and hostility as we look for someone or something to blame. Or we will turn these emotions in on ourselves with a sense of recrimination, depression or a desire to avoid coming to terms with reality. It is important to note that we might not progress beyond this stage and will remain bitter about what happened for the rest of our lives. But if we do progress, we move to the *acknowledgement* stage in which although the legacy of emotion from the previous stage lingers on, there is progressively an understanding that the old order has changed and that the new situation has to be dealt with. Finally, as acknowledgement deepens, we are able to think more positively about what must be done to adjust to the new situation and the period of *adaptation and change* begins. As I say, it is a well-established sequence or pattern that is likely in any situation in which major stress is experienced.

Let us take this a step further. I would suggest that the parallel between the personal crisis model and crisis in negotiation is a close one. Perhaps it could be argued that in negotiation, since both parties are expecting disagreement, the duration of the crisis pattern will be shorter, and that since we are negotiating, some of the emotion at least will be feigned. But from my experience, the crisis model is as real in negotiation as it is in a personal crisis of everyday living. Applying it to the case study 'A close run thing' will show what I mean.

While present at different stages, crisis was most marked when the first proposal on price was made. The shock stage was accompanied by incredulity which soon gave way to a long and unpleasant period of defensive retreat. It was characterised by anger, hostility, repetition of old arguments and the very real possibility of breakdown which was only narrowly averted by adjournment. After a cooling-off period the stage of acknowledgement was reached as the benefits of a continued relationship were reaffirmed. This was followed finally by the long discussion of the basis of an agreement as adaptation and change took place.

So the 'shape' was there. But, looking at it a little closer in the negotiating context, the crisis model as it stands does not formally take account of the point that the other party can walk away.

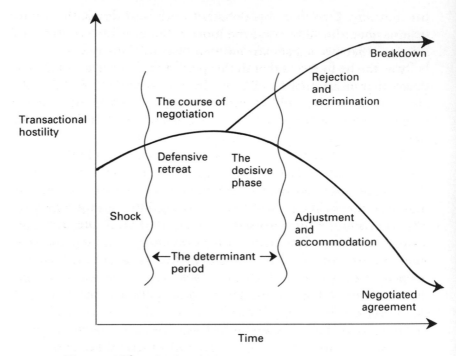

Figure 5.2 The rejection pattern

Negotiation can move towards breakdown as well as towards settlement. So a modification is required, and this is shown in Figure 5.2.

As can be seen, the pattern starts in the same way with a period of shock which may be characterised by spontaneous behaviour such as lack of comprehension, failure to grasp the point, incredulity and the like, which can then lead to 'treading water' devices such as backtracking, blocking or the introduction of the red herring. But since the proposal that gave rise to the sequence was probably anticipated, there is usually a fairly rapid transition to defensive retreat during which, predictably, old themes and cover positions are rerun. They are, however, the relative calm before the storm, because once the parties get into defensive retreat proper, the level of what we call 'transactional hostility' rises sharply. Transactional hostility is no more than the mutual distaste that parties demonstrate for each other. A high level of transactional hostility is marked by such behaviour as anger, bitter personal attack, a slanging match and the like. A low level has all the hostility of an amicable debate. In practical terms, the higher transactional hostility rises, the more difficult it is to control and the more likely it is that extreme responses will be given.

Now the bad news is that in this period of defensive retreat, the level of transactional hostility is virtually bound to rise. But the good news is that within broad bands, we know the sort of behaviour we can expect and how to control it. But first, a little more about what happens as this period develops.

One or both parties will now be feeling frustrated and anxious. Frustrated at 'the lack of progress', and anxious because they begin to see that they may not achieve their preferred solutions. In this state they will set about defending not just their positions but themselves – and this means their ego. So they will subconsciously implement one or more of what are called the 'ego defence mechanisms'. These are defined as 'unconscious psychological devices used to reduce or avoid anxiety'.[2] And loss of temper with its associated hostility, personal attack and slanging match that we have just mentioned, is just one of them.

So there will be this period of defensive retreat which will almost certainly be marked by an increased level of transactional hostility. During it, one or more of the defensive mechanisms will occur. How long the period continues, and what happens after it, is very much dependent on how it is handled. But as we can see from Figure 5.2, soon after it, the course of negotiation divides and leads either through rejection and recrimination to breakdown, or through adjustment and accommodation to negotiated agreement. Just before it does divide, however, there is this phase that we have called the decisive phase. It is during it that feelings about negotiation in general and the other party in particular, about the prospects of resolution and the sort of deal it might turn out to be, are likely to become firmly fixed. And from then on, it will be very difficult to change perceptions. They will have become so established that whatever is said or done will be interpreted in the light of them.

So when we look at the rejection pattern, we can see that what happens finally is very much influenced by what happens in the defensive retreat period which then leads into the decisive phase. Because they influence the outcome to such a degree, they constitute what we have called the 'determinant period'. It is worth seeing what can happen during it.

The determinant period

The determinant period is one of those times when people with a real flair for negotiation tend to show it. Perceptive use of pressure is at a premium. Too much pressure and the determinant period leads on to rejection and recrimination. Too little and adjustment and accommodation yield insufficient movement by the other party. Almost intuitively, it seems, good negotiators know when to put the pressure on and when to back off; when to assert a position and when to leave it; when to show real empathy, and when to distance themselves. In fact much of this feeling for negotiation comes from an awareness of the danger signals that demonstrate that the pressure is now becoming counter-productive, and then from the negotiator's good judgement on what to do about it. So as we take the inner game a stage further, we look in more detail at some of the signs that can indicate that all is not well, and at what is likely to happen if they are ignored.

Things can go very wrong in the determinant period. The statement or proposal that initiated the rejection pattern is seen as an attack; the level of transactional hostility therefore rises. As it does, there are outbursts of resentment and perhaps a heated moralising denunciation of the other's behaviour. Or there is the seemingly inexplicable refusal to consider a proposal even though it meets many of the other party's needs; or a refusal to negotiate even when there is everything to gain at this stage and little to lose; or a bitter personal attack or an outburst of temper. These and other reactions happen particularly at the difficult moments of negotiation. Normally they are not planned: they are involuntary gut responses. But almost invariably, they hinder productive negotiation. So why does the other party, why do we if it comes to that, give the reaction, even make the very moves that are likely to benefit no one?

The answer to this lies in the fact that people under attack defend themselves. If it is physical, they fight back or they run away. But if the attack frustrates them, and particularly if it deprives them of the motive base of status, self-esteem and power, they enter the period of defensive retreat as they protect their egos by adopting one or more of the so-called 'defence mechanisms'. These mechanisms for the most part are subconscious and involuntary, but they are well known.[3] Those that apply to negotiation are worth mentioning here.

Anger, hostility and aggression

These are probably the most obvious trio. Put them together and they constitute one of the biggest hindrances to productive negotiation of them all.

Rigidity of response

Perhaps better known as 'tunnel vision'. Under pressure we tend to abandon complex thinking and revert to simple. To add to this there is a tendency to think of one possible solution only, and to refuse even to consider alternatives even though they might serve as the basis for a negotiated outcome.

Reaction formation

This is, quite literally, 'going to the other extreme'. Faced with the prospect of not achieving our initial position, we quickly go to the other extreme which is that we refuse to move at all. Thus the middle ground of possible compromise is never even explored, let alone agreed.

Regression

Regression to a form of behaviour which used to work in childhood, as, for example, the violent outburst of temper which used to work when we were 3, 4 or 5 but which is totally out of place now that we are 30, 40 or 50!

Evasion

Evasion, if contrived, could well contribute a useful cover position. But here it is an instinctive reaction which first leads the other party to query our motive and then to despise our intellect.

Projection

Our own fears or perceptions may be projected onto the other side. For example, we feel uneasy about the validity of some of our staff work, but then we project this doubt of our own position onto our opponent by calling him a liar!

Fantasy

This can account for the proposal made which is so wildly optimistic in terms of the possible movement of the other side that it is seen either as an insult or as just plain ridiculous. It can also account for much superfluous discussion within a team during an adjournment as one of the members promotes a strategy which is based on the premise 'if only'. Such discussion is usually best nipped in the bud.

Vacillation

Vacillation or wavering between two courses of action results in a seeming impossibility for the other party to make up his mind. However, it is one of the few reactions to frustration which at times can be helpful to negotiation since it has the effect of keeping positions fluid and of reducing the likelihood of rapid polarisation. But its presence in the latter stages of negotiation can be most frustrating.

Rationalisation

Like the previous mechanism, rationalisation can be helpful in that it enables a party to rationalise or explain away the abandonment of previous positions: 'Oh well, we never really thought we would get that anyway.'

Apathy and boredom

Rather than appear to become involved in what is likely to be a difficult situation for him to handle, the other party just opts out and unconsciously adopts an approach similar to that of the low responder. In other words he makes little response and gives little involvement. In its extreme form it is the far more dramatic mechanism of *leaving the field* – otherwise known as the 'walk out'.

Brownie point scoring

Finally there is this half-serious, half-humorous, potentially lethal mechanism. Realising that they are in a situation in which psychological edge is important, one or both parties cannot resist the temptation to try to score over the other with comments such as 'I see you're not quite prepared on this item', 'My word, it must have been a heavy night last night' and so on. The irony is that Brownie points often start in half-humour. But of all the reactions to frustration, they are the most insidious since they almost invariably beget a counter Brownie point, which in turn begets another and so on until negotiation spirals down into an ego battle.

For the negotiator, most of these defence mechanisms are

danger signals. They hinder negotiation. Angry men will not listen
to alternatives; negotiators who have gone to the 'fight or flight'
extreme will reject moderation; those suffering from tunnel vision
will be incapable of responding to possibilities outside their script.
So the dangers of the determinant period multiply and the
likelihood of the decisive phase leading to rejection and recrimination increase.

The inner game shows us just how important an understanding
of the rejection pattern is. In particular, seeing what can go wrong
in the determinant period and how this in turn affects the decisive
phase prompts the question 'How then do we deal with it?'

Managing the inner game

Handling the determinant period

In fact, handling rejection and dealing with disagreement is an
ongoing activity in negotiation as each side attempts to establish
positional credibility which the other denies him. But handling of
the determinant period is usually at its most important when the
initial position is put. It is a balancing act which is all about the
handling of pressure: too much and the defence mechanisms
obstruct progress; too little and the momentum to get movement
is lost. So let us look at some of the ways in which the determinant
period can be managed so that negotiation progresses more
securely to a successful outcome. Having made the unspectacular
but nevertheless important comment that simply an awareness of
the rejection pattern and the importance of the determinant
period can help enormously, the suggestions that follow fall into
three main groups.

First, since transactional hostility, if left to itself, can well become
a very real barrier to progress, we talk of some of the ways of
handling it. Second, since pressure is so important, we look at how
it is used in negotiation and particularly at its control during the
determinant period. Third, again because of the considerable part
it plays in determining the outcome, we look at the decisive phase
and at how it can best be managed.

Controlling transactional hostility

Anger, emotion and the other defence mechanisms associated

with the determinant period are very much a part of negotiation. It may be tempting to dismiss them as over-reactions which on occasion border on the absurd. But this is to miss the point. To the other party who is so enraged that he is about to break off negotiation, they represent a legitimate reaction which is promoted only by the provocation of the other; and to attempt to handle them by some sort of blame apportionment is almost certainly only to add to the problem. There are, however, a series of more positive points which it is useful to bear in mind.

Successful conditioning affects the level of transactional hostility and the length of the determinant period

We have already discussed at some length the need both to develop a platform and to create cognitive dissonance. So important are they that all the top negotiators with whom I spoke reckoned to spend 60 per cent or more of the total face-to-face negotiating time on it. But related as it is, there is, I believe, another reason since, if handled correctly, conditioning constitutes a considerable forewarning exercise.

As we know from our experience of life, if we have forewarning of bad news we come to terms with it more readily and with less emotional overspill. In terms of the crisis pattern, we move more rapidly from shock and defensive retreat to acknowledgement and then to adaptation and change. So it is in negotiation. Once cognitive dissonance has been created, the likelihood of any of the defence mechanisms taking place and *becoming firmly fixed* so that negotiation never recovers is far less. Hence success in the conditioning stage of negotiation is also a good insurance cover against emotion taking over later on.

The existence of empathy and common ground shortens the determinant period

Like the previous suggestion, this point builds on what we have already seen – that personal credibility which is based not just on capability and strength but also on empathy is the blend which is most likely to succeed. Also with common ground progressively established, the likelihood of rejection is bound to be less. So if empathy is present, it means that personal antagonism is likely to be less; and if proposals which would otherwise trigger a defence mechanism are launched on common ground, the determinant period will be easier to handle.

Acknowledge the other party's emotions and the reasons for them
All the techniques for dealing with anger and emotion have this as their starting point. In negotiation, acknowledgement that a proposal has caused surprise, disappointment or anger is particularly appropriate for two reasons, First, and most obvious, once an emotion is acknowledged as received and understood, particularly if this is done with empathy, the force of the emotion is part way to being spent. This is one of the principles on which all forms of psychotherapy are based. Second, if emotion is being used as a deliberate tactic, acknowledgement serves the same purpose, but for a different reason. Like any other tactic, it loses its force once it has been identified as just that. It may take a while to disappear from the scene – the other party cannot afford to be seen to be playing games especially when emotions are involved. Nor can he be seen to be immediately doing your will. But if it is a tactic, once the emotional outburst has been acknowledged and its effect neutralised, it ceases to have any real value. So either way, to play back his emotions to the other party is sound practice. It is good human relations and it is good negotiating strategy.

Live through the period positively
Even with good forewarning and empathetic handling, it can be a miserable time. The negative reactions are in full flow, and it is all too easy to counter emotion with emotion. So evasion is countered with rigidity of response, recrimination with reaction formation, aggression with aggression and so on. Yet these are normally the least productive ways of handling the situation. Here, then, are some suggestions that might help you to stay positive during what can be a difficult time.

Expect a period of hostility
As we have seen this will be initially because there is frustration on the other side as his own aspirations come under attack, and then later in the defensive retreat period as he is subconsciously coming to terms with the possibility that he might have to change. But he is continuing to state old positions. As we have already suggested, the low key and, wherever possible, supportive response which keeps empathy is the one that is most likely to encourage change. So forewarned of the likelihood of a period of hostility is forearmed.

Try to reduce your own tension

The defensive retreat phase of the determinant period is a time when you are vulnerable. Odds are that you will be sustaining his heaviest attack, perhaps on a personal basis. He will certainly be trying to weaken your position. So the pressure is very much on you. In these sorts of instance it helps to make yourself both physically and psychologically comfortable. Physically by such simple devices as sitting back rather than forward; by consciously relaxing; and by giving yourself thinking time before responding. And psychologically by viewing his response as a natural one and hence by not reacting emotionally yourself unless you decide, for example, that you must match anger with anger since without it you will be unable to recover psychological parity.

Have something in reserve

Have something new to say that will help him rationalise his position. There is much to be said for keeping a pressure point in reserve to use at this stage. Hawks and doves in negotiation will play this device differently. The hawk will keep a sizeable and aggressive point which he will throw in knowing that it will raise the emotional response. He is gambling that once this additional pressure has worked its way through the system, it will generate a more yielding response. The dove on the other hand may well back off by playing a new pressure point. But it will be a softer one aimed at helping the other party to rationalise movement. He might even start to take the pressure off by giving reassurances or by signalling a possibility of movement. The latter has real benefit in that it gives a signal for the decisive phase that his intention is adjustment and accommodation. But the danger for the dove of indicating this too soon is obvious.

These are some of the ways of handling transactional hostility. If there is one message that is central to them all, it is to view the adverse reaction as normal and to handle it accordingly.

Let us now look at pressure and how to use it in the determinant period and indeed at any point in negotiation.

Using pressure perceptively

As the reader will know, one of the purposes of this book is to take the mystique out of negotiation by relating practice to what we can gain from research. However, to my considerable surprise, when it came to the use of pressure in negotiation, although I felt I knew about how it worked in practice, I found remarkably little research on which to draw. Yet if there is one thing that characterises negotiation, it is pressure, and when I asked the experienced negotiators about applied psychology in negotiation, all of them referred to it. But I would suggest that understanding pressure and using it perceptively are very important indeed.

Let me start by giving some general points about pressure as it applies to negotiation:

1. Pressure will be necessary for positions to change.
2. Pressure can be on positions or on those holding them, or both.
3. Pressure on the position or the person will almost certainly cause stress on the individual.
4. Stress on the individual is not necessarily bad. Following the research of the late Hans Selye there is *eustress* which is the 'stress of achievement, triumph and exhilaration', and this is good. But there is *distress* which is the 'stress of losing when we feel insecure, inadequate, helpless, despairing and disappointed.'[4]
5. Stress has a physiological concomitant. That is one of the reasons why negotiation is such an exhausting activity.
6. While we wish to feel eustress ourselves, it is hardly in our interests to create it in the other party. Our aim therefore is to cause him a measure of distress. The means of doing this relate to the use of pressure.
7. The psychological effects of distress, however, are characterised by the defence mechanisms already mentioned. As we have seen, most of them are counter-productive in achieving movement and compromise.

All this serves to make a general but very important point: while pressure is necessary to change perceptions and positions, because of the distress it generates, too much pressure is counter-productive.

So how should pressure be used in negotiation? The basis of the answer has been around for a very long time as William Sargant in his book *Battle for the Mind*[5] demonstrated. More recently, since the work of Pavlov, the theory and practice of brainwashing and hostage negotiation have been carefully studied. Clearly negotiation is not in the same league of persuasion as these! But an understanding of how pressure is used in interrogation can give us a very good understanding of how it can be applied to negotiation. So distasteful as this may be, it must be mentioned.

Once more according to Sargant, there are two requirements that must be met if interrogation using the psychology of pressure is to be successful. The first is the requirement to get the subject's 'undivided and anxious attention'. The second is the need to generate mental confusion. As Sargant writes:

The interrogator must try to prolong a state of artificially induced tension to the point where the brain starts to become fatigued, disorganised and what Pavlov would call 'transmarginally inhibited'. Then normal behaviour and judgement become disturbed. If the arousal and maintenance of anxiety is not sufficient to achieve this by itself, then it is necessary to bombard the brain with a variety of changing stimuli and a random switching of conditioning signals. Thus the hungry anxious prisoner is given a series of confusing or alternating signals by the interrogator; and the more he tries to sort out and make sense of these quite senseless signals, the more confused and disturbed he becomes; and the more successfully he is being softened up and hastened towards the final stage of breakdown and the desired state of brain 'transmarginal inhibition'. In this condition the prisoner is now susceptible to new proposals.[6]

Now negotiation is not interrogation if only because in negotiation the other party can walk away. He may be bound by his mandate, but he is not in chains. So if the reactions of fight or flight are to be avoided, the application of pressure must be diluted. However, as a brief look at Figure 5.3, comparing some of the tactics of interrogation and negotiation, shows, they are on the same continuum.

With all this in mind therefore what do we do if we are to use pressure perceptively? I suggest there are three points to bear in mind.

Pressure must be present, but must be controlled

As Sargant writes there must be sufficient pressure to obtain 'undivided and anxious attention'. Without this, its subsequent use will fail and any movement by the other party will only be on the basis of benefits and inducements, the costs of which course of action alone will almost certainly be prohibitive. But, equally, too much pressure causes the extreme reactions of fight or flight, let alone the more moderate defence mechanisms. So the good negotiator will be aware of how and when to put the pressure on.

Interrogation	Negotiation
1. Switch conditioning signals: friendly becomes hostile; helpful becomes obstructive.	Alternate between heavy and light conditioning. Have a 'hard' and a 'soft' negotiator in the same team. Alternate 'carrot' and 'stick' themes.
2. Outline the unpleasant effects of continued resistance.	Outline the unpleasant effects of rejection of your proposals.
3. Have a series of interrogators.	Change key personnel in your team.
4. Put the prisoner in a cell/solitary confinement.	Have the key meetings on your territory.
5. Repeat anxiety-laden questions *and wait* (for as long as is necessary) for a reply.	Repeat the 'stick' themes. Use the pressure of silence.
6. Quote unpleasant past behaviour and habits.	Hint at his previous 'shortcomings' or 'failures'.
7. Generate physical debilitation.	Extend negotiating sessions and reduce the level of amenities.
8. 'Come clean'.	'Come clean'.

Figure 5.3 A comparison of some of the tactics of interrogation and negotiation

It was no coincidence that a majority of the experienced negotiators put 'too much pressure' high on their list of the negotiation pitfalls to be avoided, and that 'a belief in the requirement to dominate' featured in the weaknesses which they believed were shown by the inexperienced. So while pressure must be present, it must be actively controlled.

The secret lies in alternating pressure with relaxation
To achieve success in interrogation much rests on the development of unease and then of confusion. Relating this to negotiation, we have seen that the unease of cognitive dissonance is a state that it is desirable to generate. But the state which can follow, of extreme confusion, is probably not. So the art of using pressure lies in relaxing it; and from what we have already seen, it should not be surprising that it is often as you relax pressure that you get movement. For example, you have had a major and heated disagreement. An acknowledgement that you may have over-reacted – most of all the giving of an apology – will almost invariably generate an equivalent reaction from the other side. Again, it is for this very reason that the linked concession which in fact constitutes mutual relaxation is so successful a tactic.

So the art of using pressure in negotiation is very much the art of withdrawing it. As we shall see later, much strategy hangs on this fact.

Be alert to the danger signals

It is therefore crucial to be alert to the danger signals which are the defence mechanisms that will indicate that there is too much pressure on the other party, particularly during the determinant period. Since this leads to the decisive phase which you trust will in turn progress to adjustment and accommodation, it is most likely that your response to the danger signal should be in line with what I have already suggested. But the point here is that whether they realise it or not, it is on the basis of these signs that negotiators adjust their pressure. And it is as pressure is adjusted and readjusted that positions change, and movement and settlement emerge.

I would suggest that pressure is an integral part of negotiation, and that perceptive use of pressure is a key skill of the negotiator. The art of using pressure lies not just in putting it on: that really is quite easy. Anyone can have a fight. But true skill lies in taking it off in such a way that reciprocal movement, which is waiting to be tapped, is achieved.

This leads us naturally to the pivotal point of negotiation, the decisive phase. It is here that personal credibility, platform building, cognitive dissonance, opponent management and pressure all come to fruition. It is here that negotiation starts to wither or to prosper. And it is to its management that we now turn.

Managing the decisive phase

One of our continuing themes has been that although your aim is to manage, direct and control negotiation, you can only do so much; and that since it is the other party who will finally agree or not, the most you can hope for is to generate sufficient pressure on the one hand and offer the possibility of sufficient movement on the other that you induce him to change his position in your favour. It is now in the decisive phase that this is put to the test. So what can be said of managing it? There are, I think, three points that it is useful to keep in mind.

Look for signals and give them

We have already mentioned in the previous chapter the need to be alert both to signals from the other party and, if the time is right or a signal is necessary to keep negotiation moving positively, to the requirement to give them. But it is here in the decisive phase that signals really do come into their own. The trading, if that is how negotiation is going to develop, has yet to come. But it is here that signals have to be given that this is so. A signal, by definition, is 'any sign, gesture or token that serves to communicate information; anything that acts as an incitement to action.' In negotiation the most normal incitement is to movement. Hence anything which amounts to a change in argument or position is a signal that is worth following up. As such signals are explored, they can indicate that a change in position is possible, but that usually a similar change, a trade-off, a quid pro quo is sought in return. So the basis of linkage is established. Hence mutual signalling in the decisive phase is the key to movement after it.

Summaries in the decisive phase are crucial

We have already mentioned how important summaries are in negotiation and how they lead from one step to the next. Summarising in the decisive phase is in fact the most important, since it now brings together all that has gone before, and as each party summarises, he points in the direction he thinks negotiation should go. So summaries here should make particular reference to the following:

1. The positions of the parties, the themes that supported them and how they have changed in emphasis or in substance.
2. The positive indications that have been given, and the possibilities that have been identified.
3. Areas which may still constitute 'a major problem'.

Only with summaries which are accurate and even handed can negotiation now move clearly forward.

If you have to, settle for second best

There is no doubt that the ideal situation is one in which full clarity is given by both sides about the basis for negotiation which now exists. But this might not be possible, for three reasons. First, as we have already noted it takes time for positions to change; and with that, it takes time for new positions to be thought of as even worthy of consideration. Second, the basis of a new position might not yet be sufficiently clear. Certainly the need to abandon the old one is now acknowledged, but what to go for in its place may well depend on other factors which are also under discussion. Third, overt acknowledgement of the changed position might be more than the party can bring himself to give. Although he might think it, at this stage 'yes' is more than he can actually say.

In this situation, therefore, it is a matter of settling for second best. This means achieving the clarity for the positions that you can, and accepting ambiguity for those that you cannot since any positive indication is better than none at all. The only caveat is to hear the warning bell that excessive ambiguity should ring.

So with the decisive phase, the determinant period is at an end. Tenacity, personal and positional credibility, opponent management and pressure have paid off and the shape of a negotiated agreement is beginning to emerge. There is now a change of pace as the linkage and trading of adjustment and accommodation are attempted. It is to this that we now turn.

Summary

1. The inner game of handling rejection amounts to an understanding of the sequence of the rejection pattern and of transactional hostility and the defence mechanisms that are part of it.
2. The determinant period with its decisive phase is a critical time in negotiation.
3. The duration and outcome of the determinant period are very much influenced by:
    (a) what has happened in the build up to it;
    (b) how transactional hostility is dealt with;
    (c) how pressure is used;
    (d) what signals are given.

Thirteen suggestions for handling the determinant period were given.

Key question: How should the rejection pattern be managed in the next set of negotiations?

References

1. Beak, K., Fink, J. and Taddeo, S. J. (1971) 'Stages of reaction to crisis and change', *Journal of Applied Behavioural Science*, vol. 7, pp. 15–37.
2. Coon, D. (1983) *Psychology: Exploration and application*, West Publishing, St Paul, MN, p. 615.
3. See 'defence mechanisms' in any good textbook of general psychology.
4. Stanton, H. E. (1983) *The Stress Factor*, Optima, London, pp. 25–6.
5. Sargant, W. (1959) *Battle for the Mind*, Pan, London.
6. Sargant, W. (1980) 'The vital interrogation question: Just how voluntary is a voluntary question?' *The Times*, 26 May.

6
Adjustment and accommodation

The effort of negotiation is, for the most part, behind you. Specific positions have been put and, perhaps, signals have been given of possible ways of moving from them. You have lived through the dramas of the major determinant period and have paused in negotiation to assess the position and to consider the next stage. This has indicated that a negotiated agreement is seen as the most likely outcome and hence that adjustment and accommodation are now required.

For the inner game, there are three forces that are now at work. Two are familiar to us. The first is the change in original perceptions and expectations that has occurred as you have developed your own personal and positional credibility, and as you have dealt with his. The second, following from it, is the cognitive dissonance that has been created and with it the tension for change that is now present. Both of these are forces which are working in your favour. They are the context in which progress is now possible.

But a third force must be created if adjustment and accommodation are to occur. It is the powerful force of movement. And behind it lies the equally powerful principle of *mutuality*. In its widest sense, all negotiation is based on barter and exchange, and the best way of getting movement from a reluctant party is to be able to offer movement in return. This expedient is so well established that it leads to the principle of mutuality – that movement by one party gives it an entitlement to expect movement by the other. There is nothing to say that such movement has to be equal, greater or less: that is a product of what the parties perceive as necessary at the time. But movement by one begets movement by the other. Movement and mutuality therefore are the stuff of which negotiated agreements are made.

In this chapter therefore we will look in the inner game at the three forces already mentioned. We will briefly summarise the first two since they have already been discussed at length. But on the third we will spend more time: just what is required if parties are to move? Then we will suggest a series of features which are likely to encourage the movement that is necessary if adjustment and accommodation are to occur.

The inner game

Perception change and cognitive dissonance

The three dimensions of persuasion that we have already discussed have dealt with perception and the development of cognitive dissonance. We have seen how important trust, the creation of a positive image and the possession of self-confidence are in developing a relationship in which you will be believed. We have emphasised the point that only by developing a platform of your own, and by managing the positional needs of your opponent, can you influence perceptions and shape expectations so as to create the sort of cognitive dissonance that will benefit you when it comes to negotiating specifics. All this is now well established. But just how compelling these two forces alone can be is well illustrated by a strategy which, although it is widely known and much practised, does not as far as I know have a name. So for the reasons that will become obvious, we will call it QED.

QED goes like this. Your new car has broken down three times in the last four weeks. On each occasion you have had to be towed in. Each time the repair has been undertaken by an accredited service agent. When you see the general manager of the garage that supplied the car, you are annoyed, but you stay cool and decide to use the two principles of perception change and cognitive dissonance.

The perception change is easy. You have three incident reports that demonstrate mechanical failure. True, the general manager argues the toss, but he never manages to establish positional credibility and you do, largely because your staff work is too good for him. Now you summarise his perception change: 'So we agree that through no fault of mine, I have suffered a degree of inconvenience which is intolerable.' He mumbles a bit, but you press him until he gives you the reaction that demonstrates that his perception change is acknowledged as common ground: 'It would appear so, Sir.' You then use cognitive dissonance: 'What are you going to do about it?' And you await the reaction.

You have not won the game yet but you have developed a series of winning options. An understanding of the inner game has paid off. The sequence has followed a predictable path. *Quod erat demonstrandum!*

Regrettably for most negotiation, there is more to it than that. It is indeed unusual for perception change to be wholly by one side or the other. Negotiation at the probing and conditioning stage usually indicates that there is credibility which is highly defensible on both sides. And even if this is not so, needs are often present which if they are not met, at least in part, will mean that there is no deal. So negotiation normally needs the third force of mutual movement if adjustment and accommodation are to progress. But if this force is to be used, what conditions must be present? It is to this aspect of the inner game that we now turn.

The five conditions for movement

Viewed in general terms, there are five conditions which if present will mean that movement and hence rapid progress in negotiation should take place. I would stress that it is *not* necessary for them all to be present but undoubtedly the more there are, and the greater their emphasis, the better.

The requirement to change positions has been acknowledged

We have already made the point that although the means for achieving movement is by offering reciprocal movement, there is nothing which determines what the level of that movement should be. Certainly, at the end of negotiation when both parties have already moved but there is still a narrow gulf dividing them – 'I'm at 10 and you're at 12' – fairness indicates that we both move to find agreement and that we therefore settle in the middle. But before that, whether you have moved five points to my two or vice versa is really a matter of how we have reacted to conditioning, and what we believe we have had to concede to stay in the game. So the first condition that must be present if movement is to occur on any sort of reciprocal or mutual basis is that parties must genuinely feel that they cannot stay where they are, and that to do so would no longer be defensible.

The consequences of negotiating power are understood

Following from the previous point is this more specific one which really relates to an understanding by each party of roughly how much movement it will have to give if settlement is to be reached.

This brings us straight up against the feature of negotiation which, with the exception of a brief discussion in Chapter 1, we have so far avoided, namely negotiating power. What it is, how it affects negotiating objective and how it is used, are covered in detail in Part II. All I would say here is that if negotiation is to be realistic, if 'Micky Mouse movement' is to be avoided and meaningful movement is to occur, the conditioning that has taken place and, better still, the common ground that has been achieved, should by now overtly reflect the relative distribution of negotiating power. The harsh reality is that by now parties should be pretty clear of the movement they will have to give if they are going to get an agreement.

At least minimal benefit from movement is apparent

The third condition that must be present if movement is to occur is that both parties must have some fairly good grounds to believe that there is a willingness on the part of each to meet at least the minimal needs of the other. This comes partly from the trust between the parties that we noted earlier, and partly from the general impression that is created by signalling. It lends further weight to the point that some signalling – and perhaps quite a lot – should take place before the decisive phase of the determinant period after initial positions have been put.

Movement should be possible

This point has been made a number of times already. It is obvious; it lies at the very heart of negotiation. Yet it is all too often forgotten when, as parties come to negotiate they allow themselves little or no room for manoeuvre between their initial, realistic and fall-back positions. Clearly movement on all items is often impossible. An item may be quite literally non-negotiable, or credibility might determine that there is little or no difference between initial and fall-back positions. In such instances either the conditioning undertaken should be strong enough to make the lack of move-ment credible, or every attempt should be made to identify an option which can be put into the negotiation at a later stage which does generate room for manoeuvre – the alterations to the dealer network in the case study 'A close run thing' would be a good example. But without flexibility in position or the means of introducing a productive variable into the negotiation, the best means of creating the basis for mutual movement is lost.

Negotiators should be willing and able to negotiate

The phrase 'willing and able to negotiate' is a well-established one. I have used it before. But it says much, particularly at this stage of the negotiation.

The word 'able' implies that each negotiator will come with a mandate that allows him to move, and with an ability, dependent on the terms, to both trade and settle. Clearly this means that he has the full backing of his organisation generally and of the director, the board or whoever to whom he is responsible in particular. It also implies that he has both the self-confidence and the skill to negotiate to reach settlement.

But it is the word 'willing' that is the interesting one. Clearly, to a considerable degree it is dependent on being 'able'. But in my experience, willingness is also affected by the relationship that now exists between the parties. At the lowest level this should be sufficient to ensure that negotiations have not degenerated into acrimonious ego point scoring. But it really needs to be better than that. The experienced negotiators, you will remember, placed considerable emphasis on respect of each other so that the parties negotiated in a businesslike and professional way. To this I added trust, so that at least the minimum conventions would be observed, and empathy, which would mean that hard talk and hard positions were more likely to be resolved. So yet again the value of a positive relationship is underlined. The feeling that 'I can do business with this man' really matters.

These five conditions are in fact dependent on each other for effectiveness. One alone will be insufficient; the presence of two or three might enable negotiation to limp along. But all five together provide the right combination to enable adjustment and accom-modation to occur. Indeed, I have found that the value of using them as a check-list prior to the beginning of decisive movement to assess the likelihood of a successful outcome is considerable.

With the importance of all that has gone before established – of the three dimensions of persuasion, of getting the psychology of pressure right, of handling rejection and the determinant period, and now of the conditions which are necessary for movement to occur – we will turn our attention as we manage the inner game to some factors which, if taken into account, will serve to encourage the process that is so important: the process of movement.

Managing the inner game

The ten facilitators of movement

Informal pre-negotiation discussion

The emphasis laid by the experienced negotiators on the pre-meeting discussion over the telephone, over a meal, in the corridor, in the club (anywhere so long as it was in private and informal) was immense. Indeed when asked to look at negotiations which had gone particularly well, most mentioned pre-negotiation discussion as a factor of major importance. And reviewing the research on this, Druckman, for example quotes various sources which give a clear indication that the value of informal meetings lies in the following areas.

1. It enables the clarification of issues that will be formally discussed.
2. It makes possible the development of a positive relationship informally which will enhance the possibilities of cooperation later.
3. It allows a time lapse between informal and formal discussion thus enabling the information given and received in an informal setting to be acted on in advance of the stating of formal positions. It therefore reduces the likelihood of parties digging themselves into positions only to have to dig themselves out of them.[1]

So the potential of informal meetings is considerable. Indeed other research goes as far as to indicate that communication which takes place prior to bargaining may be more important than that which takes place during it, especially if the opposing parties attempt to explore a range of 'fair' proposals.[2]

But before we leave such meetings, it should be noted that there are both conventions and dangers surrounding them. The dangers are for the most part obvious and arise from not viewing informal discussion as part of the negotiation process. However, the conventions that apply do provide a useful safety net. They are discussed at some length in Chapter 10.

A favourable negotiating environment

One of the experienced negotiators who was involved in much acquisition negotiation made the point that he preferred a series of short meetings rather than fewer longer ones. And he went on to say that he always made a point of trying to ensure that the crucial ones were held on his territory.

Of course he was right. The matter of location can be important. We know there is considerable psychological value in being the home player, particularly in the opening stages of negotiation. Generally, home players tend to be more relaxed, more dominant and more successful in the settlement they achieve.[3]

Yet there are two problems. The first is that for the same reasons, although they may only intuitively feel them rather than know them to be true, visitors will be naturally more defensive and less willing to give positional movement on their opponent's territory. And second, like all psychological ploys, if they are seen to be overt attempts at manipulation, they will be resented. So the point that comes out of this is that while there is value in being the home player – and this applies whether it relates to international negotiation or to negotiating in your own country, never mind on your own premises – if it becomes a matter of ill feeling or even dispute, it is far better to agree on a neutral venue. It is for this reason that much profitable negotiation is done in hotels, country clubs and the like. Neutrality is enhanced by the more relaxed atmosphere in which parties can break from each other and from negotiation, yet still stay together.

The same point about psychological ploys applies to such points in the negotiating environment as differences in the height of seats between the parties, whether both parties are being treated in the same way as regards ashtrays, water and glasses, whether the visitors have space for writing, have light in their eyes and so on. To me these are the ploys of the novice. All they will serve to do is to irritate the other party, and if they are seen to be deliberately manipulative, they will antagonise him. They are hardly the means of enhancing mature discussion between intelligent men, let alone of facilitating movement. On the other hand, if the environment is conducive to empathetic, orderly negotiation, it is more likely that movement will occur.

Developing movement

While we have said much about creating the basis for movement, there are two specific points which apply to developing momentum. The first has been described as the 'foot in the door'. It is a form of progressive inducement:

> The major assumption underlying the foot in the door technique is that a powerful predictor of future compliance is past compliance; that is, a person who has been induced to comply with a small request is more likely to comply with subsequent, larger demands. This knowledge is certainly intuitive to those in the advertising world. Many campaigns attempt gradually to induce people to become regular buyers by initially asking them to respond to requests even if the response is simply evaluating a product.[4]

The effect of this for the conditioning stage of negotiation is clear. You try to get agreement on your least contentious themes before progressing to the more contentious ones so that, as we have said, you develop common ground incrementally. And for achieving adjustment or accommodation, it is equally apparent: progress in negotiation is best achieved if agreement on the less contentious areas is attempted before going on to the areas of greater difficulty. It is this which is at the heart of Roger Fisher's proposals in *Basic Negotiating Strategy* when he suggests, 'Give them a Yessable Proposal'. Now this may seem obvious, yet there is often a desire to 'speed negotiation along' by tackling items the other way round. It should be resisted.

The second force is that of reciprocation. We have already seen that movement by yourself which is offered in return for movement by him – the stuff of which linkage and trading are made – uses the desire of the other party for reward, and that this force alone can be strong indeed. But there is the second force of reciprocation which is at work at the same time. It comes from human experience in the requirements of everyday living and is so strong that at its worst it gives rise to blood feuds and wars while at its best it ennobles the human race. Apply it to negotiation, in which it is well researched[5] and is known as the 'reciprocal concession pattern', and the very fact that one party is offering movement, say from its initial to its realistic position, puts pressure on the other to do the same.

These two additional forces of progressive inducement and reciprocation when added to those that we know are already at work make a powerful combination to maintain the momentum of movement.

The 'fair' proposal

Much of our discussion of conditioning in negotiation has been to do with developing a platform for the initial position which can be defended at the very least as 'credible' in the light of the themes that have underpinned it. So for launching the position from which we can move, credibility is the key note. But if we look for the rationale for making a proposal that is aimed at providing the basis for resolution, it is in 'fairness' that our best hope of acceptance lies. Again both experience and research confirm this point. 'The more parties communicate statements which suggest "fair" resolutions or other shared values, the easier it is to reach an agreement and the less likely will the bargaining relationship break down.'[6]

So what constitutes 'fairness'? First, it is to do with reciprocal movement: 'It is fair for me to ask for movement by you from your position, if I offer movement to you from mine.' Second, it is to do with the fact that movement also involves you in cost or loss: 'It is fair that I should propose this to you because it means sacrifice for me as well as for you.' Third, it is to do with needs: 'It is fair that you should consider this proposal because it is meeting at least some of your needs as well as mine.' And fourth, it is to do with achieving resolution: 'It is fair that I should put the proposal to you because it takes us further towards a negotiated agreement which is our joint objective.'

If a proposal can therefore satisfy any of these four aspects, it is well on the way to being defensible as 'fair'. But one aspect is still lacking. It is the aspect of valuation. Even if other aspects can be met, if I am proposing major movement by you and offering only minor in return and this is seen as inconsistent with the way negotiations have proceeded so far, you will throw it back in my face. So, fifth, fairness is to do with fair gain or loss: 'It is fair that I should put this proposal to you because the movement it suggests is consistent with the way negotiations have progressed to date.'

If a 'fair' proposal really does commend itself as being fair in these ways, its impact on the speed and direction of negotiation will be considerable.

Additional incentives

The power of the fair proposal can be enhanced in a number of ways. The first of these, which is much used, is to view all items under negotiation as a package so that, by mutual agreement, no single item is considered settled until all have been finalised. Clearly this allows great scope for linkage and trading of items, and gives the negotiators far greater opportunity for finalising acceptable compromise than the so-called 'seriatim' or 'one-by-one' approach in which no progress is made to the next item until the current one has been settled.

Within this approach major issues are broken down into smaller parts, again so that progress can be more easily made, yet the final outcome on the whole is preserved. And as we have seen, once the momentum of agreement on sub-items is built up, the most complex of issues becomes manageable.

The second device on the surface is an obstructive one, and if played to the extreme it can certainly impede progress. It consists of deliberately generating disagreement, leaving it in abeyance and then offering agreement in return for movement by him in another area. So into this category would go, first, the *phoney demand* – the demand which is only made so that it can be abandoned later in order to get final movement from the other party or to break what would otherwise be a locked situation. And, second, the *phoney disagreement* which is the refusal to agree on an item or in an area, even though in fact it is not unacceptable to you, again so that agreement can be offered to achieve the final last movement out of the other party. But both of these 'phonies' should not mask the very real value they have of injecting the means of movement into what might otherwise be a locked situation.

An irregular movement pattern

We have already seen that the amount of movement achieved is a function of how the parties perceive what they have to concede in order to stay in the game or to settle it. Movement does not have to be equal, only sufficient. But there are a number of interesting conclusions coming out of research and experience that relate to the patterning of movement. They are worth mentioning here.

First, consciously or not, parties take a view of how far and how quickly each other will move on the basis both of the strength of the conditioning that supports the initial position and on the tenacity with which it is maintained.[7]

Second, negotiators 'are more responsive to an opponent who employs a changing concession rate strategy than to one who concedes at a constant rate.'[8] The most likely version of this is a substantial move from initial position to realistic followed by smaller 'topping up' moves to get final agreement.

Third, relating to the previous point, is what we can call the 'roundness of position'. By this I mean whether we start for example with an offer of 6.18, 6.25 or 6.5 per cent. Clearly the second and third versions give the feeling that there is more whole movement available in a way that the first does not, particularly if it is supported by meticulous and credible staff work. And again a move of another 0.25 or 0.5 per cent gives the feeling that there is more available in a way that a move of 0.17 per cent does not.

Fourth, notwithstanding the previous point, there is a time for rounding numbers up or down or for 'splitting the difference'. It is during the end game that the final inducement is offered to close the negotiation. Splitting the difference is the final 'fair' sacrifice for both to make.

Developing tangibles

The clarification of positions that takes place in the opening stages is aimed, among other things, at getting away from general hopes – 'a substantial improvement'; general fears – 'not a job will be safe'; and general emotion. These are the intangibles which can be all things to all men and around which it is impossible to negotiate. It is only when they are translated into specific positions that they can be dealt with. The same applies to the general comments such as 'now you're being unreasonable'. And unless nipped in the bud this can degenerate into what Rackham[9] calls a 'defend/attack spiral' in which negotiation degenerates into an emotional slinging match. So if adjustment and accommodation are to blossom, intangibles should, by questioning, be converted into tangible positions. They can then be dealt with accordingly.

Graduated reduction in tension

Graduated reduction in tension, GRIT for short, is the name given by C. D. Osgood to an overall strategy of particular value in major negotiations such as arms control. It is of particular value in breaking an impasse because, without conceding everything or indeed very much, the veil is lifted from a negotiating position and the basis of a final deal is outlined. The strategy

consists of a set of preannounced unilateral and noncontingent rewards which are given to the adversary together with a request for some form of reciprocation. These unilateral initiatives may start with very small rewards and gradually increase in magnitude. However, parties adopting a GRIT strategy must be firm and not allow the opponent to take advantage of them or to give the appearance of appeasement. Thus, the initiatives are limited to those voluntary ones chosen by the active strategist, and demands or attempts by the opponent to take competitive advantage must be rebuffed. Of course, this strategy cannot be carried on indefinitely without reciprocation from the opponent. Fortunately, evidence reviewed by Lindskold (1978) indicates that GRIT strategies are effective in defusing hostilities and that it does facilitate compromise solutions to conflict situations.[10]

In short therefore, following the points made earlier relating to the 'door in the face' approach, if parties are faced with an impasse there is considerable value in making a small concession and then standing firm. The onus is then passed to the other side to reciprocate.

The third alternative

It is here that in my view the 'principled negotiation' approach of R. Fisher and W. Ury that we mentioned in Chapter 1 comes into its own. If the gap between the fall-back position of the two sides is at this stage clearly too wide for them to find settlement, yet both parties are genuinely seeking agreement, now is the time for a radical rethink. Existing positions and approaches are seen by all concerned to be no longer relevant, so there is a real will to start again. There must be if it is to work. So it is here that their four-element approach[11] comes into its own:

1. First, separate people from the problem. To do this, each side puts itself wholly in the position of the other.
2. Second, focus on interests not positions and bring them clearly into the open.

3. Third, develop options on a genuinely creative basis which concentrate on mutual gain.
4. Fourth, insist on objective criteria as you try to identify the best solution.

As a technique and discipline, this offers excellent new opportunities. It does require either that new personnel are introduced into the negotiation or that the negotiators on both sides are big enough to swallow their present failure. It also requires both faith in each other and a willingness of their respective organisations to embark on a radical rethink. Given that all these are so, an attempt at developing a third alternative can be well worth making.

The expiry of time

The part played by the passing of time has been put as follows:

An approaching deadline puts pressure on the parties to state their true positions and thus does much to squeeze elements of bluff out of the later steps of negotiation. However, an approaching deadline does much more . . . It brings pressures to bear which actually change the least favorable terms upon which each party is willing to settle. Thus, it operates as a force tending to bring about conditions necessary for agreement.[12]

Both research and practical experience point to the fact that the approach of a time limit or the expiry of a deadline concentrates the minds of the negotiators and tends to soften both positions and strategies. But there are two important provisos. The first is that the existence of a time limit must not be seen as an arbitrary constraint imposed by just one of them. At best it is mutually agreed by the two parties. Failing that, it is imposed by external circumstance such as the expiry date of an old agreement, or by forces such as the exchange rate, market forces or government edict. At its worst there must be some benefit to the other party even if it is only that 'we can finish now and get a good night's sleep'.

This brings us to the end of the inner game of adjustment and accommodation, indeed to the end of our discussion of the inner game generally. We have spent a considerable amount of time and effort in an attempt to understand the processes that are at work as we negotiate so that insight and understanding can replace intuition and opinion. Judgement there must be at all stages in negotiation and on many issues. That is one of the reasons why negotiation is such a fascinating activity. Nevertheless I have tried to take as much of the blind guesswork out of it as possible and to give the rational base on which any negotiator can build. The insight it gives we will now use as we move to the first assignment of negotiation proper, to the task of incisive preparation.

Summary

1. All movement starts with the development of personal and positional credibility and the creation of cognitive dissonance.
2. Achieving adjustment and accommodation is then a matter of attempting to create the right environment in which it can take place. It is here that the existence of the five conditions of movement is of benefit – the more the better.
3. Specific movement will be more likely to occur if the ten facilitators of movement are taken into account.

Key question: How much account is taken of creating a climate of movement and of using it?

References

1. Druckman, D. (1973) *Human Factors in Interactional Negotiations*, Sage Publications, Beverly Hills, CA, p. 23.
2. Krauss, R. M. and Deutsch, M. (1966) 'Communication in interpersonal bargaining', *Journal of Personality and Social Psychology*, vol. 4, pp. 572–7.
3. See for example the research of Martindale, D. A., on the effects of territorial dominance presented to the 79th Annual Convention of the American Psychological Association, 1971.
4. Burgoon, M. and Bettinghaus, E. P. (1980) 'Persuasive message strategies', in M. E. Roloff and G. R. Miller (eds.), *Persuasion*, Sage Publications, Beverly Hills, CA, p. 155.
5. Cialdini, R. B., Vincent, E. J., Lewis, K. S., Catalan, J. and Wheeler, D. (1975) 'Reciprocal concessions procedure for inducing compliance: The door in the face technique', *Journal of Personality and Social Psychology*, vol. 31, pp. 206–15.
6. Druckman, op. cit., p. 28.
7. See for example Druckman, D., Zechmeister, K. and Solomon, D. (1972) 'Determinants of bargaining behaviour in a bilateral monopoly situation: Opponent's concession rate and

relative defensibility', *Behavioural Science*, vol. 17, pp. 514–31.
8. Druckman, op. cit., p. 29.
9. Rackham, N. (1987) *Making Major Sales*, Gower, Aldershot.
10. Tedeschi, J. T. and Rosenfeld, P. (1980) 'Communication in bargaining and negotiation', in M. E. Roloff and G. R. Miller (eds.), *Persuasion*, Sage Publications, Beverly Hills, CA, p. 239.
11. Fisher, R. and Ury, W. (1982) *Getting to Yes*, Hutchinson, London.
12. Stevens, C. M. (1963) *Strategy and Collective Bargaining Negotiation*, McGraw-Hill, New York, p. 100.

Part II
Incisive preparation

Introduction

Sound preparation is the key to success. All negotiators agree on this. For negotiations of importance, I have already suggested that the best method of comprehensive preparation lies in the four-stage approach.

Stage 1: Identify the negotiating issues and use them.
Stage 2: Assess negotiating power and enhance it.
Stage 3: Create the overall game plan.
Stage 4: Check the detail.

In Part II we will concentrate on the first three stages. In Chapter 7 we show how to set about identifying the issues, generating negotiating positions and parameters, creating themes and key commitments, and laying the base for a coherent strategy. In Chapter 8 we take the next stage and show how that illusive but crucial variable, negotiating power, can be identified and used. In Chapter 9 we look at the standard strategies of negotiation and at how to set about creating the game plan.

We illustrate the techniques with short examples as we progress. But since they are related in developing an overall strategy, we use a central case study throughout Part II which demonstrates how they are brought together and how strategy is progressively developed and built. The case itself is fictional but is close to reality. It is given next. It relates specifically to major contract negotiation. The techniques themselves, however, can be applied singly or in combination to negotiation on anything.

Case study: The space defence contract

It is 1998. Barataria is a Western-style democracy. Its government is concerned about the country's space

117

defence system. With potentially hostile orbiting weapons systems able to strike from space, it is vulner- able to attack. What is now desperately needed is a new satellite-launched seek and destroy anti-missile system to replace its obsolete earth-based interceptor missiles.

The Baratarian Space Defence Department (BSDD) foresaw this need seven years ago. But rather than enter into a collaborative venture with Communication Technology Ltd – the leading company of Grandia (Barataria's major ally) whose research even then in this field was far advanced – it was decided at the highest level that Barataria would develop its own system. It seemed to provide a unique opportunity to use existing satellite design, suitably modified, and to develop Baratarian technology for tracking, launching and controlling missiles in space. It was recognised then that this was leading-edge technology that would test the resources of Barataria to the utmost. But equally it was an opportunity to develop the technological capability with some very valuable commercial spin-offs. After two years during which the various contracts were put out to tender, the contract for the major electronics research and production work was awarded, after intense competition with its major rival Tirac Ltd, to the Advanced Electronics Corporation (AEC) with a lead time of six years. Although cost estimates of 18 billion baras were made by AEC and accepted by the BSDD, the contract was awarded primarily on capability. In any case it was recognised by all parties that with so many unknown variables present, precise costs were difficult to establish. That was five years ago.

The project was plagued from the beginning. As the unfriendly powers' missile technology became more sophisticated, the BSDD altered the specification. The special wing of the armed forces which would operate the system – the Space Defence Service (SDS) – declared that it doubted AEC's ability to meet even the original specification, and expressed a preference for the Grandian system. As always, the technological problems, which were greatly aggravated by alteration to the specification, proved harder to crack than was originally thought. So the project slipped further and further behind.

Now, in 1998, the project is at least two years behind schedule with a completion date of AD 2001 at the earliest. Expenditure to date has been over 40 billion baras. There has been a series of only partially successful tests. And there is still nothing to safeguard Barataria in space.

The patience of the Baratarian government has finally run out. AEC has asked for another 6 billion baras spread over the next eighteen months which will finance what it says is the final stage of research and development. Production costs, it maintains, will remain in line with estimates plus inflation. This request has met with outright rejection by the BSDD which has said, in a semi-public fashion, that it has lost faith in AEC's ability to crack the problem; hence there is no point in throwing good money after bad. It is therefore seriously considering buying the Grandian system which has now been in operation for two years with favourable reports of its capability, although it has never been tested in full warfare conditions. The cost would be in the region of 65 billion baras.

Faced with this very real threat, the AEC chairman has brought his negotiating team together. They are satisfied that the major problems have now been overcome, and that, providing there are no further changes to the specification, this request for an extension and additional funding will be the last. They have therefore decided to ask for a meeting direct with the government minister with responsibility for defence to discuss the position. He has agreed to this request, stating that he will be accompanied by senior officials of the Space Defence Department.

7
Identifying the issues and using them

Once the decision to negotiate has been taken, the process of formulating strategy can start in earnest. If the overall objective of negotiation is clear, so much the better. If, as is frequently the case, it lacks precision, so be it. It will gain clarity as preparation gets under way.

The need for techniques

Generating strategy from cold can be difficult. Where do you begin? What are the *real* issues? How do you set about handling them? What sort of negotiation will it be? Where are the sticking points? What are the arguments? These are just some of the problems.

But attempting to develop strategy without a system can be worse. At one extreme, half-formed ideas, random thoughts or vague pictures of strategy emerge that obstinately refuse to take on a clear form. Or at the other, a particular strategy, reached on an intuitive basis, immediately commends itself, and is then reinforced to the exclusion of all others. Both these situations are far from desirable. So how and where do we start?

When I wrote *The Effective Negotiator* fifteen years ago,[1] I introduced a technique which I called the 'expectation test'. 'Expectation' because negotiation is very much a matter for each side of dealing with the expectations of the other – the cynic would say, with apologies to Charles Dickens, of turning great expectations into little ones. 'Test' because it enables us to make a close examination of the expectations that are present and gives us a method for handling them in negotiation. In basic terms, then, this analysis starts from the point that parties come to the negotiating table as we say, with expectations – hopes, fears and arguments. They set out to satisfy their hopes, to allay their fears and to win their arguments. On occasion it turns out that expectations can be satisfied, so demands are met and assurances are speedily given. But more frequently it is a slower and more deliberate affair. Positions are further apart, common ground is harder to come by, persuasion takes longer, discussion ebbs and flows, there is give and take. But whatever happens, it all starts from the point that each side has its own way of looking at the topic under negotiation, and its own set of factors which it takes into account. From these, it generates its own set of demands or assurances with arguments to back them up.

Take change as an example: technological change, organisational change, virtually any change. For the initiators of change it is seen as an opportunity or a challenge. Hopes almost certainly exceed fears, and reasons are produced as to why change is essential. But for those affected by it, unless there are some very positive reasons given them to the contrary, change is often viewed as a threat. Fears exceed hopes, and as a consequence, arguments are produced as to why it should be challenged or rejected.

In short, expectations determine all. It is the expectations of the parties that determine the issues of negotiation. And it is the side that understands the issues and deliberately sets out to deal with them that is the side that is controlling the game.

The expectation test therefore is of great value. This is how it is used.

The expectation test

The expectation test starts with the issues of negotiation. An issue is a requirement that will be expressed or a reason that will be put forward in negotiation. Hence there are *substantive issues* that relate to what the parties want, and *justification issues* that relate to the means, most normally the arguments, that will be used to prove these needs as just or valid. While the issues you identify for yourself and for the other party are as many and varied as are present in the negotiation, it is best to state them generally and to keep the number to no more than seven or eight – and probably less – for each side.

With the issues identified, they can be put to work. We follow the development of how we handle two issues. The first is one of yours, the second one of the other party's. Figure 7.1 gives the overview. I will describe and then illustrate it.

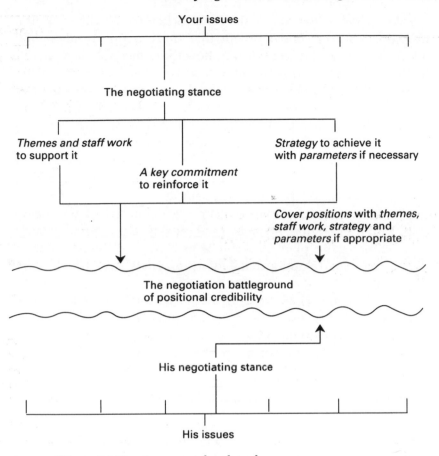

Figure 7.1 How issues are developed

For both, the issue can be a substantive issue, such as a price or wage increase, or a justification issue such as, for either of these, an increase in overheads or increase in inflation. Now, taking the issue for you, it is then developed into a *negotiating stance* which is quite simply the position on which you seek agreement. If it relates to a substantive issue, it probably has a figure on it. If it relates to a justification issue it will probably amount to an overall argument. Whichever it is, it constitutes what you are seeking to achieve on that particular issue. From now on, analysis concentrates on how to achieve it. So *themes* and *staff work* are developed to support it; a *key commitment* for each stance is created to reinforce it; and *strategies*, which will include *negotiating parameters* if the issue is substantive, are generated to achieve it.

Taking issues that you believe the other party will raise, the procedure is very similar except that there is one fundamental difference. Instead of considering how the stance will be achieved by the other party, you consider how you will handle it. So the *issues* are those you believe he will be discussing from his side. For each, the *negotiating stance* is that which you believe he will adopt. But the themes and staff work you identify constitute the *cover position* and its detail that you will adopt to handle each stance; the key commitment you create will reinforce it; and the strategy you will identify will enable you to deal with it, with *concessions* within your negotiating parameters as appropriate.

This approach constitutes a very useful means of getting to grips with preparation. It can be used quickly to give some general ideas about a game plan. Or it can be used in some depth as one of the means of developing detailed strategy. Its strength rests on two points.

First, it is comprehensive in that it deals with the issues of *both* sides. Second, because it is systematic, the best opportunity is created for developing insight in the areas given. For ease of discussion we will divide them into three groups:

1. Issues and stances.
2. Themes, staff work, key commitments and cover positions.
3. Strategies and parameters.

Before showing in detail how to use it in the context of the case study 'The space defence contract', we will say a little more on each of these.

Three uses of the expectation test

To identify issues and stances

There are two traps that are set right at the beginning of the preparation process. The first is that although you may be well aware that there are a number of issues involved, you only address yourself to some of them – probably yours! The second is that you tend to concentrate on the substantive issues – again yours rather than his – to the partial or even total exclusion of the rationale for them. The consequence of this is that the opportunity for developing the rich variety of themes that can be brought into play and that are an essential part of the persuasion process is lost.

Preparation, therefore, on the one hand is biased, and on the other, impoverished.

So the starting point is issues. Let us take an example. You have an antique you want to sell – to a local dealer would be your easiest option. Clearly there is one major substantive issue for both parties: *price*. But the outcome of that will be influenced by which of you handles the justification issues and stances to best effect. For you they are likely to include the *condition of the piece* with the stance that it is in excellent condition for its age; *verification* – the stance being that it is what you say it is; *saleability* – that there really is a keen market for such items; and *unique selling point* – that there is a feature about it that gives it that bit extra.

Issues such as these would be fairly standard. You hardly need an expectation analysis to identify them! But what are the dealer's justification issues and stances likely to be? They will probably include his own *superior expertise* – the stance being that since he knows more about antiques in general and your sort of item in particular, you should accept his advice on all points including price; *lack of interest of the market-place* which clearly affects the price it would be wise for him to offer you; and *verification* – the same issue as yours, but he could be expected to have a very different viewpoint.

There may well be other issues and stances for both parties. You would certainly have yours, but since you are only guessing at his, you may well miss one, such as the fact that unknown to you a *private collector's sale* of just your sort of item has recently taken place and the market is flooded with them. Which just goes to show that no analysis can cope with everything!

With your own issues and stances clearly identified and with your best estimate of his very much in mind, you are starting to get a real feeling for the negotiations that lie ahead, and useful preparation can now take place.

To develop themes, staff work, key commitments and cover positions

The inner game had much to tell us about the importance of all of these. So before we continue, a brief summary of the main points will be worth our while.

1. The importance of the motive base of expertise is immense. 'Demonstrate it', 'prove it', 'be logical', 'be rational' have

tremendous force. In addition, staff work matters enormously.

2. There is value in being able to talk in terms of benefits, opportunity and reward, although needs must be identified before benefits can be given; and in being able to use the desire to avoid punishment and fear if the other two motive bases need support.

3. It is useful to think and negotiate in terms of themes and of having a series of them rather than just one or two.

4. It is both efficient and productive to use pressure points – key commitments – which reinforce the themes.

5. There is always a need for cover positions to handle the themes that are likely to be used by the other side.

6. There is value in thinking about the desire of the other party to be seen to have status, to show power and authority, and to enhance self-esteem; and, more to the point, in considering how these needs can be met without weakening your own position.

So, returning to our discussion with the antique dealer, themes would include the excellent condition the piece is in, with a key commitment, 'Its excellence speaks for itself', the verification that was possible because 'The piece has been in the family for 200 years', the saleability of the item with the key commitment, 'I know there is a wide interest among collectors', and the fact that there are some unique features which give it a special attraction with a key commitment of 'There are a couple of features of particular interest'. And, checking back to the three main motive bases to see if there is another line that could be developed, you might use the avoidance of punishment and fear, by developing the theme of a lost opportunity for him if you were to take the item elsewhere. As far as cover positions are concerned, there would be a need to counter his superior expertise by demonstrating your own from a well-researched position, and at all points good staff work on your part would be essential. And it is worth noting that your ability to handle his 'bombshell' of the private collector's sale will be very much influenced by your success in the themes to that point.

Once again, as the thinking on all these progresses, insight into the discussions that lie ahead is increased, and strategy, which is the next step, begins to take shape.

To generate strategies and parameters

The expectation test is the starting point for specific strategy generation. From our study of the inner game there are some general pointers on strategy that we should keep in mind:

1. Personal credibility is important and should be established as soon in negotiation as possible.
2. The existence of a relationship of empathy and trust between the parties is usually of benefit to them both. Again, it should be established as early as possible and maintained, although it is prudent to ensure that there is true reciprocation.
3. Conditioning is important before proposals are made. Hence to create a platform from which to launch your proposal and to develop cognitive dissonance as it relates to his is essential.
4. Progressive summary of both conditioning and common ground as it develops is important.
5. Because of both the effects of pressure and the way in which cognitive dissonance occurs, phasing or the *progressive* development of themes is necessary.
6. Since the best way of getting movement is to be able to give it, it is wise to develop a range of positions within your overall negotiating parameters. They are your initial, realistic and fall-back positions. If you think they are necessary or justified, they should include concessions at the appropriate levels.
7. Rejection is an inevitable part of negotiation. The rejection pattern should be understood and its determinant period handled with skill. This may well include the use of signalling.
8. Movement should be offered only on a linked basis.
9. Negotiation has its own natural rhythm. This comprises the opening moves of conditioning and probing, proposing and signalling, the mid-game of movement and the end game of closure. To depart from this rhythm puts a successful outcome at risk.

With these points in mind, the final use of the expectation test is clear. Strategies and parameters are developed which then fit into an overall game plan. So in negotiating a sale with the antique dealer, opening move strategies would include demonstrating your own expertise and staff work, phasing your themes of the excellence of the piece, its verification and its saleability which is enhanced by the two unique selling points, probing for his reactions as you went along and generating as much common ground in your favour as possible (remember the three levels of 'agreed', 'acknowledged' or 'understood') before either asking him for an offer or stating your position on price. There would then be a need to handle the rejection pattern, and to use your parameters on price as you moved from your initial position on a linked basis to get movement from him. Finally it may be necessary to reinforce your realistic or fall-back position with the possibility of taking your business elsewhere.

This short example gives a very brief overview of how the expectation test is applied. It should have given an indication both of the general feel of the negotiations that lie ahead and a clearer view of how you can handle them. We will now apply it to the case study 'The space defence contract' so that the breadth and scope of the technique can be seen in full.

Detailed application

Identifying issues and stances

As we have seen, analysis and use of the test follow a natural sequence. First write down the topic on which you will be negotiating. State it in general terms since if it is too specific you may well miss some of the issues, particularly those the other party may raise. Then write down the substantive and the justification issues with their associated negotiating stances. There is no need to put them in a logical order – just try to home in on the important ones.

In this case we are applying the techniques from the point of view of the Advanced Electronics Corporation (AEC) in its negotiation with the Baratarian Space Defence Department (BSDD). The full format for this is given in Figure 7.2. The topic is 'Possible termination of AEC involvement in space defence project'. For the sake of clarity I have restricted my analysis to three issues only for each side: 'Cancellation now is the worst of all options' and 'Causes of delay' are obviously justification issues, while the third, 'Future investment by BSDD', is a substantive issue. There would certainly be others such as the following:

1. The effects of cancellation on AEC and other contractors involved.

Negotiating topic: possible termination of AEC involvement in space defence project.

The Advanced Electronics Corporation

Issue 1: Cancellation now is the worst of all options

Negotiating stance:
BSDD to accept that cancellation now:
(a)   yields nothing for the major expenditure undertaken;
(b)   requires substantial new expenditure to purchase an alternative system.

Themes
1.   Cancellation now will mean virtually no return of any sort for the major investment already made.
2.   Large *new* expenditure is required to purchase a foreign system. (Staff work to include examples of typical cost escalation.)
3.   A relatively small amount of new money is required to finish the job. (Staff work to give total amount and as a percentage of total expenditure in event of cancellation.)
   Key commitment: 'Cancellation gives you the worst of all worlds.'

Strategy
1.   Publicity and media coverage on 'How the taxpayer loses' through cancellation (pre-negotiation).
2.   Launch themes 1 and 2 in second stage of opening moves. Get agreement on the figures involved. Then contrast the expenditure of buying the Grandian system with the small amount of new investment required (theme 3).

Issue 2: Causes of delay

Negotiating stance
BSDD to accept that the delay, to which hi-tech research is prone in any case, was aggravated enormously by continual changes in specification.

Themes
1.   The uncertainty of leading-edge research. (Staff work to generate examples.)
2.   The effects which changes in specification had in terms of programme delay. (Staff work to demonstrate the effects of change on the critical path analysis.)
3.   The effects of change on costs. (Staff work to generate three major examples.)
   Key commitment: 'In hi-tech research the consequences of continual changes in specification are horrendous.'

Strategy
Wait for cost escalation or delay to be raised, then lead with theme 1. Attempt to make it into common ground, then launch themes 2 and 3 forcibly.

Issue 3: Future investment by BSDD

Negotiating stance
To achieve the best possible terms from the BSDD within the parameters given
for continued support of the project.

Themes
1. The relatively small amount of new money required. (Staff work to outline
    how it will be spent.)
2. The many benefits of completing the project. (Staff work to list and support
    them.)
    Key commitment: 'The long-awaited prize is within our grasp.'

Strategies
1. Delay launching the initial position until other conditioning themes have
    been developed. Then introduce theme 2 and develop it into common
    ground.
2. Always talk of the relatively small amount of new finance required
    (theme 1).
3. Move slowly from the initial position and trade on amount, funding and
    time-scale variables if required.

Parameters	Amount	Funding	Time-scale
Initial position:	6 bn	Full government funding	18 months
Realistic position:	6 bn	Shared funding: 75% BSDD 25% AEC	18 months
Fall-back position:	4 bn	Shared funding: 50% BSDD 50% AEC	12 months

The Baratarian Space Defence Department

Issue A: Availability of proven alternative

Negotiating stance
AEC to accept that in the light of all that has happened, the best BSDD
alternative is to buy the Grandian system.

AEC cover position
1. Question the ability of the Grandian system to meet Barataria's unique
    requirements. (Staff work to identify difficulties.)
2. Question clearly the operating record of the Grandian system. (Staff work
    to identify known or anticipated defects.)
3. Use themes from issues 1 and 3.

AEC strategies
1.   Question the assumption made about the Grandian system. Then introduce more information on difficulties and defects.
2.   Use own themes from issues 1 and 3 to regain initiative.

Issue B: Preference of SDS for Grandian system

Negotiating stance
AEC to accept that the views of the operator of the system – the Space Defence Service – are of paramount importance.

AEC cover position
1.   Stress some of the more abstruse technical requirements of the project and then question the SDS ability to pass an expert opinion on them. (Staff work to generate examples.)
2.   Give examples of how SDS opinions have changed in the past. (Staff work to generate examples.)
3.   Ask for SDS areas of concern and stress better liaison as a new joint requirement. (Staff work to generate positive proposals.)

Strategies
1.   Play 1 and 2 above lightly to start with but go into detail if opposition remains.
2.   When appropriate, accept that 'poor liaison' has been a shortcoming on both sides, and float proposals for improving it.

Issue C: Responsibility to get value for money for the taxpayer

Negotiating stance
Option A – To buy the Grandian system.
Option B – Give AEC a shortened time-scale and fixed budget within which to demonstrate capability.

AEC cover position – to deal with Option A
1.   Question to find the basis for the BSDD decision. Highlight points you know you can counter.
2.   Introduce mainstream conditioning strategy to move BSDD towards AEC position. (Staff work as previous.)

Strategies
1.   Attempt informal contact prior to negotiation to establish which negotiating positions the BSDD is likely to take. If clear indications are given, develop offer and movement strategies accordingly. If not, ensure an adjournment between receiving the first proposal from BSDD and responding to it.
2.   Notwithstanding 1 above, the most likely opening position of BSDD will consist of option A. This would be compromised by even intimating option B. The overall strategy of AEC will reflect this.

Figure 7.2 Strategy document

2. The effect of cancellation on the reputation of Baratarian technology in general.
3. The consequences of being dependent on a foreign supplier.

As far as the BSDD issues are concerned, AEC could reasonably assume that the first two justification issues of 'Availability of proven alternatives' and 'Preference of SDS for the Grandian system' would be present, with the third, 'Responsibility to get value for money for the taxpayer', being one of the substantive issues of the BSDD position. Other issues would include the following:

1. Failure by AEC to meet requirements.
2. Huge cost escalation and delay.
3. Strategic vulnerability.
4. Negotiations to terminate the project.

It is worth noting the greater proportion of justification to substantive issues for both sides. This is inevitable, and as mentioned earlier, the temptation to concentrate on demands should at this stage be resisted.

The negotiating stances follow logically from the issues. All speak for themselves, but it is worth making two general points about the process. First, it is when the stances are being decided that the die of negotiation is cast. The implications this has, particularly for the director with overall responsibility for negotiation, are immense. So, for example, the stance on the substantive issue 3 with its consequential negotiating parameters is obvious. Less dramatically, but on occasion of even greater importance, are the implications of stances on justification issues. So when, for example, the AEC team establishes the stance on issue 2 that 'BSDD to accept that delay, to which hi-tech research is prone in any case, was aggravated enormously by continued changes in specification', they do it in the knowledge that it will be a major source of contention, that they will have to be able to prove it, that it will probably antagonise the BSDD team considerably, and that this in turn could have adverse consequences for future business. But nevertheless they decide to pursue it. So if the director with overall responsibility for negotiation is involved at no other stage in preparation for negotiation, he should certainly be involved in or have knowledge of this one. It is only in this way that he can see not just the commitments that are being made on the substantive issues, but also the implications for the organisation of the main thrust of the negotiating survey. And it is only when he has agreed them that the lead negotiator can really believe that he has the full backing of his organisation with all that that means for his own self-confidence.

The second point, although obvious, is that the issues and stances of the other side are best guesses from which your strategies and the cover positions to handle them follow. Enough to say that if reality proves your insight wrong, the effects that this has on your overall game plan should be immediately taken into account.

Developing themes, key commitments, staff work and cover positions

The first point to note is that for each of the AEC stances, there is more than one theme. To have a number of ways of saying the same thing is important for all the good reasons given when we looked at the inner game of persuasion. For example, taking issue 1, the themes 'Cancellation now will mean virtually no return of any sort for the major investment already made', 'Large *new* expenditure is required to purchase a foreign system' and 'A relatively small amount of new money is required to finish the job' constitute various aspects of the same stance. But they progressively confirm it with something new to say.

Second, we know that there is a danger in that having a number of themes dilutes their intended effect. But equally this is where the key commitment comes in. So the second point to note is that each of the stances has a key commitment which is short, memorable and to the point. 'Cancellation gives you the worst of all worlds', 'In hi-tech research, the consequences of continual changes in specification are horrendous' and 'The long-awaited prize is within our grasp' all have impact. And each nicely brings together in one sentence the various aspects of the rationale on which it rests.

The third point relates to staff work. We need not dwell on it. Enough to say that *all* the stances and most of the themes require staff work. It is this which gives credibility. Regrettably it is also staff work that takes the time in preparation. But its full importance can now be clearly seen.

Finally, there are the cover positions. For the most part they are defensive. There are exceptions to this – when defence is seen to be the best form of attack. But mostly – and in the case of all three examples given – they constitute responses and the AEC team will use them only if it has to. Having said that, they all have strength, and rather than attempting to ignore a BSDD stance, each takes the point and handles it positively. Hence, far from the AEC lead negotiator dreading the issue being raised and then being caught with a dropping jaw when it is, he can acknowledge the point, counter it and, for example, in the third cover position for issue B, pave the way for a proposal which could de-fuse the issue.

Generating strategies and parameters

Strategy generation for each issue is no more than the answer to one of two questions:

1. For each of the stances that I adopt, what can I say or do either before or during negotiation that will enhance its credibility?
2. ·For each of the stances that I expect him to adopt, what can I say or do either before or during negotiation that will deal with it?

As will be noted, the second is not necessarily the opposite of the first. It may be that it is a good strategy for some of the stances of the other party to be accepted in total or in part. For example, as will be seen, the second strategy for the AEC cover position we have just mentioned acknowledges the stance taken by the BSDD team and makes a positive proposal on it.

By way of general comment, we can see that the strategies for the first AEC issue include a useful pre-negotiation move and also give an example of launching themes on a phased basis. There is also merit in the second strategy being launched as a second stage gambit in the opening moves.

The strategy for the second AEC issue is a reactive one dealing with a point that is bound to come up. But again it is an example of the phasing of themes and of the development of common ground. The same applies to the strategies for issue 3 which once more depend on developing other themes before launching the initial position.

Strategies for dealing with the first BSDD issue are mainly defensive. There is, however, quite a lot of potential in the second strategy for issue B which, particularly if negotiations are getting bogged down, might offer a new tack with an opportunity for progress. It is, however, on the strategies for issue C that much would depend. The informal approach is well worth trying. It may well be rejected given the fairly formal positions already established and the fact of ministerial involvement. But little is lost by attempting it, and any information about the BSDD attitude or even negotiating position will be of value. Even if there is a refusal to meet informally, it points to the fact that much time and effort will need to be put into conditioning to get the first movement started.

Three mainstream parameters are given. Of all items of preparation, they are the ones that, in the end, finally matter. As we have said, the director with responsibility for negotiation *must* be involved in developing them if he has not already set them – they are the product of a lot of bottom line analysis. The AEC parameters on 'Future investment by BSDD' speak for themselves with amount, funding and time-scale being the three variables. Obviously, the final agreement could be a different combination from those given, but they constitute an essential reference point for the AEC team both as positions to achieve and as the reference point of all major movement.

With the analysis of the major issues using these three aspects of the expectation test completed, much sound preparation work will have been done. There should now be a clear understanding of the negotiating stances that will be adopted by our side, some shrewd ideas about theirs and some very useful means on the one hand of developing and, on the other, of handling them. Though the strategies are not yet in the form of a game plan, and they may yet be changed, our preparation now has a strong base.

As we know, expectation analysis and use is only one of two techniques in strategy development. Certainly it can be used on its own, and this is far better than nothing at all. It generates a lot of insight. But as we have seen, for detailed and important negotiation where the outcome is of critical importance, it is only the first of four stages of preparation. The second is to do with power analysis and use. Is our realistic position attainable? What is our power base? How do we set about enhancing it? These are the questions which must be answered. It is to them that we now turn.

Summary

1. The first stage in systematic preparation is to identify the issues and to use them. The progressive use of the expectation test enables you to:
   (a) identify the issues and negotiating stances;
   (b) develop themes, staff work, key commitments and cover positions;
   (c) generate strategies and negotiating parameters.
2. It is here that the director and his lead negotiator should ensure that they are on the same wavelength. At the very least they should agree on negotiating stances and, where appropriate, parameters. At best the director should make the opportunity for either involvement in preparation or for discussion of its outcome.

Key question: How can this stage of preparation be implemented and monitored for the key negotiations undertaken by your organisation?

Reference

1. Atkinson, G. G. M. (1975) *The Effective Negotiator*, Negotiating Systems Publications, Newbury.

8

Assessing power and using it

To the negotiator, power is a factor of both interest and concern. So it should be. It is the crucial variable that determines the outcome. But what can be said about it?

A review of the research into negotiating power in practice finds that two main propositions hold good. First, that under 'conditions of unequal relative power among bargainers, the party with the higher power tends to behave exploitatively, while the less powerful party tends to behave submissively, unless certain special conditions prevail.' These certain special conditions include the ability of the less powerful party to leave the negotiation and take his business somewhere else or to find allies and to form a coalition.

Second, that equal power 'among bargainers tends to result in more effective bargaining than unequal power.'[1] In other words, because they realise they cannot exploit each other, they work harder with give and take to find a deal.

So far, so good. No negotiator wants to operate from a position of weakness, hence each strives to create a position at least of parity. And even when he has achieved this, there is still much work to be done. Truly the negotiator's lot is not a happy one!

But it gets worse. To be practical, if you want to achieve a position of parity, or better, how do you set about doing it? And what is negotiating power anyway? It is with the second question that we start our discussion.

The problems about power

In a nutshell, the problems about negotiating power start from the point that it is hard to define.

'Like the wind,' writes Gavin Kennedy, it is 'felt rather than seen. You have power over the other to the extent that you can

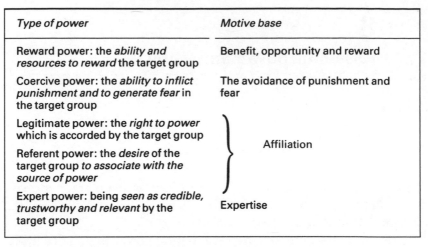

Type of power	Motive base
Reward power: the *ability and resources to reward* the target group	Benefit, opportunity and reward
Coercive power: the *ability to inflict punishment and to generate fear* in the target group	The avoidance of punishment and fear
Legitimate power: the *right to power* which is accorded by the target group	Affiliation
Referent power: the *desire* of the target group *to associate with the source of power*	
Expert power: being *seen as credible, trustworthy and relevant* by the target group	Expertise

Figure 8.1 Resources of power and the five motive bases

induce him to do something he would otherwise not do. And vice versa.'[2] As John Winkler[3] writes:

> Power is based upon the damage which will result if the parties do not agree. If one party is likely to suffer no effective damage, while the other will lose out badly, the first party is strong and the second is weak. The source of this question has to do with the quality and range of options available to each party in the event of the deal breaking down.

Thibaut and Kelley[4] state that it is the 'ability of an individual bargainer to move another through a range of outcomes.' And so they go on. But none of them in my view is wholly satisfactory. And when we look wider, for example to the contribution of the sociologist, we find that while the five types of power identified by French and Raven,[5] which are given in Figure 8.1, are useful as a check-list for identifying resources of power and relate closely to the five motive bases identified earlier, they take us no further in any detailed attempt to define or use it in negotiation.

With all the definitions that I have seen, we are still left with the same problem. It arises from lack of clarity. If you cannot define power, how can you use it? So for our purposes, all definitions are deficient – all, that is, except one.

A practical way of defining and using power

In the final analysis power is like beauty. It is in the eye of the beholder. Take military power as an example.

To be powerful I must have *resources* – tanks, guns, missiles and the like. I must also have the *skill and ability* among my troops at all levels to mobilise and use them. Without these two I do not even start. But they are as nothing if 'the enemy' believes that either I cannot or will not use them. Or, more fundamentally, if he does not fear the consequences of death and destruction. So in fact military strength is very much dependent on the way the other party sees both my position and the preferences that he has in relation to its consequences. My position of itself is neither strong nor weak. It is what it is – but only in his eyes.

So it is with negotiating power. The *resources* of power such as those given in Figure 8.1 – the power to reward, the power to punish, the power which being an expert gives and so on – are essential if you are to have negotiating power. So is the *personal skill and ability* of your lead negotiator and his team. But they are all dependent on how they are seen by the other party in the context of the third factor: *your proposal.* The key question is, looking at all aspects in the round, will he prefer to accept or to reject it? And, since you are facing him with your proposal – he is not thinking in terms of achieving his own – he will take whichever course of action he sees hurts him least.

Now this, I suggest, takes us much closer to both defining and understanding negotiating power. Following from it, an American economist, Neil Chamberlain, wrote 'We may define the bargaining power of A let us say [A is the proposer] as being the cost to B [the responder] of disagreement on A's terms relative to the cost of agreement on A's terms.'[6]

H. M. Levinson[7] then took the statement and converted it into a simple, practical and potentially very useful formula:

$$\text{The negotiating power of A} = \frac{\text{The costs to B of disagreement with A's terms}}{\text{The costs to B of agreement with A's terms}}$$

Relating to it, there are three points of explanation. First, it cannot be precise. The equals sign is not in the same league as two and two equalling four, rather it signifies 'is indicated by'. Second, the equation indicates a relationship: the costs for the other party of disagreement with my terms – the realistic position since that is the one I really want to firm up on – as against the costs for the other party of agreement. Third, by 'costs' we mean disadvantages or unpleasant consequences such as increased price, reduced flexibility, loss of face, difficulty in finding an alternative supplier and so on that are implicit in either disagreement or agreement. He will take whichever course of action he sees hurts him least.

This is now a starting point for specific analysis. As A, my power is a function of that ratio. And again, as A, if I want to get acceptance of my terms, my strategy is going to revolve round influencing the ratio in my favour.

But I would suggest that as it stands, the analysis is still too vague to be usefully applied. It could give a feeling for, but as yet no real indication of, power or of priority for strategy. So in *The Effective Negotiator*[8] I proposed that each element be rated twice. First for severity of cost to B using a 0–10 scale, and then for likelihood that B would view it as a cost that he would be forced to sustain using a weighting scale running from 1.0 for certainty down to 0.1 for unlikely. The cost rating would be multiplied by the likelihood weighting to give a figure for each element. Addition of the figures above the line and then below it would give a total for each course of action.

Working on the basis that the other party was in the business of reducing his costs, it could be predicted that he would take whichever course of action scored the lower. Hence if the costs of agreement were lower than those of disagreement, i.e. bottom was lower than top, he would on balance prefer to agree with you, and you had negotiating power. That was not to say that you were home and dry unless the balance was massively in your favour, but rather that, although there would almost certainly be further negotiation as he attempted to reduce his costs of disagreement, you had reached the point at which the tide began to flow in your favour. And conversely, if costs of disagreement were lower than those of agreement, i.e. bottom was greater than top, he would react against it – even to the point of rejecting it out of hand.[9]

The thinking works well. It is the only technique I have found that gives a real indication of where that 'crucial variable' rests. Certainly it has its limitations, most of which revolve round subjectivity. You need to be careful because you are both judge and jury; analysis can never be precise and never absolute; perceptions and circumstances change. But it does give you a means of getting to grips with what is otherwise a great imponderable that defies rational analysis. Such a technique has outstanding benefits which bear elaboration.

The benefits of systematic power analysis

A more accurate assessment of the negotiating objective

One of the tendencies that occurs when power is being discussed is for consensus to go to extremes, so that parties view themselves as all-powerful or pitifully weak, when the probability is that they have both strength and weakness. But this has been lost as the 'horn/halo' effect takes over. What systematic power analysis enables you to do is to consciously assess relative strengths and weaknesses – elements above the line tend to represent strengths while those below are weaknesses – and to emerge with a better-considered and quantified assessment with figures above and below the line. As a general rule if the ratio of top and bottom is greater then 1 : 3 (e.g. a total of ten 'cost units' of disagreement to greater than thirty 'cost units' of agreement), the proposal you consider making will be rejected – probably out of hand. Not even the best of strategies will be sufficient to bridge that gap. Anything less than 1 : 3 brings it into the area of 'negotiable'. The nearer to parity you get, the more attainable should be the proposal. Equally a ratio the other way round in which top exceeds bottom should really prompt the question 'Are we asking for enough?'

Major assistance in generating strategy is given

The first method for creating basic strategy is by using the expectation test; taking the elements of negotiating power and using them is the second. Clearly, the more you are able to alter the balance of power in your favour, the more likely you are to achieve your negotiating objective. While there is always a danger that excessive overt manipulation can develop a major hostile reaction, it is quite clear that since every element represents an aspect of negotiating power, it has potential for use. So since the aim is to achieve acceptance of your terms, basic strategy is generated by considering how to make it more unpleasant for the other party to reject your terms, i.e. to increase the figures above the line, and less unpleasant for him to accept them, i.e. to reduce those below. Not surprisingly these are known respectively as the strategies of the stick and of the carrot. If you want the other party to move forward to accept your terms there will have to be a subtle blend of both. All carrot and no stick requires an awful lot of carrot. All stick and no carrot creates tremendous resentment. So strategies which directly relate to the elements above and below the line lead to the desirable goal of achieving a *balanced* strategy.

A perceptive view of the strategies of competitors can be gained

Even if they were unsuccessful in their own negotiation last time round – you got the contract and they did not – competitors will not necessarily be idle in the period leading up to contract renewal. Whether they embark on it consciously or not, they will make some sort of analysis of why they failed, and they may decide to do something about it. Clearly identifying their likely moves is very desirable. It can be greatly assisted by looking again at the analysis you made of your negotiating power. In the end you got the contract by increasing your client's costs above the line and reducing those below. Your competitors have an interest in doing the reverse. If, before the contract is renewed next time, they can reduce the costs of disagreement for your client in placing the business with them rather than you, and increase his costs of dealing with you, they will have achieved a major strategic victory. The use of power analysis will help you to prevent this by enabling you to develop counter-measures.

These are three major benefits which I would suggest outweigh the undoubted dangers inherent in systematic power analysis. Perhaps power analysis in this way still looks pretty much like theory. Let us alter that by putting it to the test. Again using the negotiating case study 'The space defence contract' we will set about getting the most out of it by applying it in four different ways. The techniques we will use will enable us to

- assess negotiating power
- generate negotiating strategy
- identify competitors' proposals and strategies
- develop counter-measures

Applying power analysis

Assessing negotiating power: The technique described

I have already suggested a supplement to the original thinking of Chamberlain and Levinson in the proposition that the elements of negotiating power should be rated and totalled so that a clear indication is given. This, I think, is important. There are two other modifications which I suggest simply because I have found them helpful to my own mental process.

First both Chamberlain and Levinson talk in terms of costs of disagreement or agreement. Personally I find this too restrictive with its implication that only items which can be precisely measured are included in power analysis. This is patently not so, and was never intended by either Chamberlain or Levinson. So as indicated earlier I suggest that the word 'disadvantage' with its wider connotation of unfavourable consequences is more appropriate.

The second modification I suggest serves to put matters into starker relief. Again the original uses the terms 'disagreement' and 'agreement'. It is a small point, but I have found that what concentrates the mind more is to use the words 'rejection' and 'acceptance' instead.

So in its revised form, if I want to assess my power to achieve the terms of a certain level of settlement, the model runs as follows:

$$\text{My negotiating power} = \frac{\text{The disadvantages to the other party in rejecting the terms of my proposal}}{\text{The disadvantages to the other party in accepting the terms of my proposal}}$$

With the revised model given we can now look at the technique for assessing negotiating power and apply it to the negotiating case. The technique runs as follows:

1. Write down the position you wish to test. This is normally the realistic position, but it can be any position for which you want to identify your negotiating power base. The position should, however, be as specific as the terms you will propose.

2. List the disadvantages as you believe the other party will see them, first above the line and then below it. There is no limit to the number of elements; nor is there a requirement to 'balance' them by getting the same number below the line as above it. Indeed that would be rigging the model. But be on your guard for points that overlap or indeed repeat, since if you are not, when it comes to rating you will be in danger of double-counting and hence will give yourself a misleading result.

    The key requirement is always to try to think in terms of the factors that will be present in the mind of the negotiator on the other side and of his colleagues, at the negotiating table and away from it, as they decide on which alternative they take.

3. Rate each disadvantage on a 0–10 cost scale where 10 is the worst cost that the other party would have to sustain in that particular course of action. As you rate, take into account the effect which the strategies so far devised in the expectation test should have had. Clearly any element that was not included in the test can only be rated as you believe it would be seen without any strategy on your part. Again, clearly enough, strategies will be developed for all elements and the model re-rated in the light of them. But that comes later.

    One word of caution. Be honest with yourself! It is very easy to rate elements as you would like the other party to assess them, but this really defeats the purpose of the exercise. Rating is as you believe he would.

4. Weight each disadvantage, again through his eyes, for the probability that it will have to be borne. The probability scale I suggest is as follows:

    1.0 – the disadvantage is certain to occur
    0.7 – the disadvantage is likely to occur
    0.5 – the disadvantage has an even chance of occurring
    0.3 – the disadvantage is possible
    0.1 – the disadvantage is unlikely

5. Finally for each element, multiply the cost rating by the likelihood weighting to give you a total for that element. Then add them up to achieve a total for all elements above the line, and for all those below it. If top is greater than bottom, you have negotiating power. If it is the reverse – as is more normally the case before strategy is generated to change it –

The AEC power base
Position proposed

6 billion baras on a 75% : 25% funding basis spread over eighteen months.

Negotiating power of the AEC

			Cost	× Likelihood	= Total
	A.	Bad image for Baratarian technology	3	0.7	2.1
	B.	Loss of export potential	3	0.1	0.3
	C.	Loss of research capability	6	0.7	4.2
Disadvantages to BSDD of rejection of AEC proposal	D.	Additional cost of buying the Grandian system	7	1.0	7.0
	E.	Government shown to be unpatriotic	3	0.7	2.1
	F.	Loss of jobs – direct and indirect	2	0.7	1.4
	G.	Dependence on a foreign supplier	6	1.0	6.0
	H.	Large expenditure – little return	4	1.0	4.0
				Total:	27.1

			Cost	× Likelihood	= Total
	1.	Possible ultimate failure of project (good money thrown after bad)	8	0.7	5.6
	2.	Possible ultimate failure of project (defence capability impaired)	10	0.7	7.0
Disadvantages to BSDD of acceptance of AEC proposal	3.	Possible ultimate failure of project (major embarrassment for Baratarian government)	5	0.7	3.5
	4.	Signal of weakness to other government contractors	8	0.7	5.6
	5.	Precedent of weakness set for future negotiations with AEC	6	0.7	4.2
	6.	Hostile reaction from the SDS	4	1.0	4.0
				Total:	29.9

Figure 8.2 Analysing negotiating power

you do not. However, as mentioned earlier, do not despair. Good strategy generated from this analysis can frequently convert a ratio of 1 : 2 into better than parity, and may even make, on occasion, ratios approaching 1 : 3 into negotiating possibilities. But it is when you rise above 1 : 3 that a long hard look needs to be taken at the viability of the terms being proposed.

Assessing negotiating power: The technique applied

So much for description, now for application. An overview of the power assessment for the AEC position is given in Figure 8.2. Unlike the application of the expectation test given in the previous chapter which dealt with only six issues in all, this analysis is intended to be a complete one, since if it were not, the assessment would inevitably be misleading. The position proposed is derived from the parameters of issue 3 (future investment by BSDD) of the expectation test. As mentioned there, in reality it would be the result of much hard analysis by the AEC project team. There might well be other items included in the proposal, such as a method for involving the user in closer consultation, this arising out of the strategy for handling issue B (loss of confidence by the user). If this were so, these terms would be included in the position proposed and would be reflected in the elements and assessment of negotiating power.

Taking each element in turn, 'Bad image for Baratarian technology' is rated low on the basis that although cancellation of the project would hardly reflect well on Baratarian technology generally, this is just one branch of it with one company. But the likelihood of it having this adverse effect is high, and a weighting of 0.7 is therefore given. 'Loss of export potential' is included since this is clearly an element in the AEC 'pitch'. But given the somewhat jaundiced view of the project in BSDD eyes it is fair to assume it would be seen as a low and very unlikely cost. 'Loss of research capability' is another matter altogether. Once an organisation – or a country if it comes to that – opts out of leading-edge technology, it is very hard to get back into it. Key personnel are lost, and the gap gets more and more difficult to close. It is not a certainty that all momentum will be lost even with cancellation, but it is very likely, hence the weighting of 0.7. 'Additional cost of buying the Grandian system' is high and certain. The cash cost is stated – 65 billion baras. But it is the psychological effect which this has on the BSDD position, and indeed on government credibility, of being faced with the enormity of this sort of expenditure that must also be taken into account. Hence the high rating and weighting which are given. 'Government shown to be unpatriotic' is rated low on the basis that BSDD would undoubtedly play the 'must not jeopardise national security' card strongly to counter adverse publicity. But questions would still be asked.

'Loss of jobs' is a clear consequence. However, again in the light of the previous point and with relatively few people employed on the project at this stage, the cost is small. But 'Dependence on a foreign supplier' is a factor with implications on future costs (such as replacement parts, further modifications, etc.) and an ability to act independently in a crisis. It also has the consequence of giving greater monopolistic power to one foreign supplier. Hence the cost is relatively high and assessed as certain. Finally, 'Large expenditure – little return' is rated at 4 and 1. Since in the event of cancellation, expenditure on the project so far achieves virtually nothing, this could arguably attract a higher cost rating. But again BSDD would play this point down in the context that 'finding the best means of safeguarding national security' was paramount. All these give an above the line total of 27.1. Although the figure only has full meaning when seen in relation to the total below, it is possible to say even now that despite the strong line which BSDD has so far taken in advance of negotiation, the AEC team would appear to have a variety of themes that it could profitably bring into play.

The disadvantages to the BSDD team of accepting the AEC proposal are fewer in number, but constitute in total a greater cost. The first three are directly related to the failure of AEC to perform the single most important consideration for the BSDD team if they go down the line of the AEC proposal. Although the same effect is rated three times, this does not amount to double-counting since each relates to a very different aspect. The first is the simple point of good housekeeping. The second relates to the whole purpose of the exercise, national security, and therefore represents the highest cost of all. This being so, the rating becomes the bench-mark against which all others are made. The third is the purely political point which is rated perhaps surprisingly low, but on the basis of proven ability of most politicians to cover their tracks in a crisis. 'Signal of weakness to other government contractors' is a cost that would weigh heavily on the BSDD and, in view of the publicity that the concession would generate, on other departmental minds. The same would be true but to a lesser extent for any 'Future negotiations with AEC'. Finally, what of the user who has made it clear that he prefers the Grandian system? A low rating is given on the basis of 'he who pays the piper calls the tune'! In all, this amounts to a total of 29.9 unit costs of disadvantage.

So the final analysis shows that with the costs of acceptance exceeding those of rejection, the BSDD team, opting to take the line of lowest cost, will prefer to reject the proposal. The AEC team could either moderate its proposal or, more positively given the relatively small difference to make good, set about generating strategy which will develop their power base by changing the way in which BSDD views the various elements. The latter really should be the first option. We will turn to it in a moment.

First a final word about the technique. As mentioned before, it is imperfect. Indeed, since we are forced to make value judgements about the preferences of another party, it is bound to be. But I would suggest that if we are to get any real understanding of negotiating power, there is no viable alternative. You, the reader, might well disagree with my assessment, but at the very least you could tell me where and why. And hopefully, if we needed to, we could get closer to a truer assessment of our real power base. As a consequence, that crucial variable, instead of remaining just 'a feeling in the water' has now been evaluated. It can therefore be both controlled and used. In the section that follows we will show how.

Generating negotiating strategy: The technique described

Even those who feel uncomfortable with the assessment side of power analysis stand to gain much from using it for strategy generation. As mentioned earlier, the aim is simple. If you are trying to get acceptance of your proposal, the strategic requirement is to alter the balance of power in your favour. This therefore means generating strategies which make it more unpleasant for the other party to reject your terms, and less unpleasant for him to accept them. Hence above the line, strate-gies are based on varying degrees of coercion; below it, they are based on inducement. Strategy can be generated as follows:

1. Take each element in turn, and along the same lines as the expectation test, develop for it negotiating stances, themes, key commitments, strategies and, when appropriate, parameters and cover positions. Remember, the purpose of the exercise is

to make the disadvantages above the line greater, and those
below less. Where a strategy has already been given in the
expectation test and you can identify no other, let it be.

2. Now take each element for which you have developed a
   strategy (including those derived from the expectation test)
   and, on the assumption that that strategy has been successfully
   implemented, re-rate the element. Make no adjustments to
   those elements for which a viable strategy cannot be identified.

3. Add the figures for top and bottom. Total assessments should
   move very much closer to equality or into the position where
   top exceeds bottom. If, on the other hand, after this power
   reassessment the ratio is still worse than 1 : 2, very specific
   thought should be given to any attempt to achieve those terms
   through negotiation since it will almost certainly fail. On the
   other hand, if it is better than 2 : 1, very real consideration
   should be given to whether a more favourable settlement
   should be sought.

Generating negotiating strategy: The technique applied

Using the technique, the AEC team should be able to develop the
various aspects of their strategy to good effect as they set about
developing their negotiating power. Figure 8.3 gives full details of
this for each element and also a revised power rating that would
result from the strategy being successfully used. By way of brief
comment on each element, 'Bad image for Baratarian technology'
was originally rated low on the basis that cancellation would reflect
poorly on the technological expertise of one company. The
strategy widens this effect and hence increases the cost rating
somewhat. The strategy for 'Loss of export potential' is not a
strong one but if the staff work can make it convincing, the point
does have some value. This has the effect, in particular, of raising
the likelihood weighting, although the BSDD position is likely to
remain one of some scepticism. Again, although the themes for
'Loss of research capability' are worth using, the gist of the
position would probably already have been taken account of by the
BSDD team. They can therefore only have a small effect on the
power analysis. Strategies to make more of the 'Additional cost of
buying the Grandian system' have already been identified as part
of issue I of the expectation test. They are worth pursuing, but

since the element represents a major cost already, their effect can only be marginal. An adjustment to the power rating is made under element H since the strategies for both elements are the same.

'Government shown to be unpatriotic' is very much a matter to be handled with kid gloves – accusations of lack of patriotism rarely win friends in these circles! Nevertheless, the strategy with the lowest risk and highest pay-off potential is the first. If it is used in the pre-negotiation meeting it will be useful both for conditioning and for getting some sort of indication of the real strength of the BSDD feeling to buy the Grandian system. It can then be repeated towards the end of the opening moves. The third strategy would only be used if BSDD were clearly refusing to move from its 'Buy Grandian' position, in which case it would need to be preceded first by some fairly intensive lobbying, and then if absolutely necessary by a comprehensive media campaign. But

---

Strategies to enhance the AEC power base
Element A: Bad image for Baratarian technology

Negotiating stance:
BSDD to accept that loss of confidence in the project, publicly stated by a government body, will have a serious adverse affect on the international image of Baratarian technology generally.

Parameters
Not appropriate.

Themes
1. The importance of maintaining confidence in the country's technology – particularly in the cut-throat market of international competition.
2. The effects which public loss of confidence can have on other companies competing in the international market-place. (Staff work to generate examples.)
    Key commitment: 'International confidence is hard enough to gain without having your own government acting against you.'

Strategy
1. Lobby other companies who have a direct or indirect interest to encourage them to put pressure on the government (pre-negotiation).
2. Use themes 1 and 2 as ancillary arguments to support the initial position.
    Revised power rating: cost: 5; likelihood: 0.7; total: 3.5.

Element B: Loss of export potential

Negotiating stance
BSDD to accept that there is both direct and indirect export potential.

Parameters
Not appropriate.

Themes
1. The many other countries in the market-place who, given the opportunity, would tend to 'Buy Baratarian'. (Staff work to generate examples.)
2. The foothold this gives for future sales. (Staff work to generate examples.)
    Key commitment: 'There's a huge market out there. This is an investment for the future.'

Strategy
Use themes 1 and 2 in second stage.
    Revised power rating: cost: 4; likelihood: 0.5; total: 2.0.

Element C: Loss of research capability

Negotiating stance
BSDD to accept that once research is terminated, the difficulties and costs of re-entry are immense.

Parameters
Not appropriate.

Themes
1. The merits of having nationally based expertise and a nationally based contractor.
2. The near certainty of acquisition of key staff by competitors. (Staff work to generate relevant examples.)
3. The great difficulties and high costs of working or buying your way back in.
    Key commitment: 'Cancellation would be a loss to the nation.'

Strategy
Use to support opening move 1.

    Revised power rating: cost: 7; likelihood: 0.7; total: 4.9.

Element D: Additional cost of buying Grandian system

Already covered under issue 1 of expectation test analysis.
Power rating remains the same.

Element E: Government shown to be unpatriotic

Negotiating stance
To get BSDD to acknowledge that whenever possible it is the government's aim to 'Buy Baratarian' and that there would be a public outcry if this was not seen to be so.

Parameters
Not appropriate.

Themes
1.   The many damaging results of not 'Buying Baratarian'.
2.   The possible public outcry that could occur in switching to a foreign
     supplier. (Staff work to generate examples.)
     Key commitment: 'Baratarian needs need Baratarian solutions.'

Strategy
1.   Feed the many costly and damaging results for the country of cancellation
     into pre-meeting with the minister.
2.   Use theme 2 only if BSDD is refusing to move from its 'Buy Grandian'
     position. Reinforce it with lobbying and media coverage.
     Revised power rating: cost: 3; likelihood: 0.7; total: 2.1.

Element F: Loss of jobs – direct and indirect

Negotiating stance
BSDD to accept that cancellation would mean significant and increasing loss of
capability and jobs.

Parameters
Not appropriate.

Themes
1.   Immediate job loss in terms of both quantity and quality means the final
     loss of capability in this field. (Staff work to develop figures and profiles of
     jobs lost.)
2.   Job losses among suppliers.
3.   The loss of potential jobs that would otherwise be created if even
     moderate expert potential were to be achieved. (Staff work to develop
     scenario.)
     Key commitment: 'This is a nail in the nation's coffin.'

Strategy
1.   Encourage direct lobbying by employee groupings and related suppliers if
     cancellation becomes a real possibility.
2.   Introduce themes 1, 2 and 3 as *consequences which are avoided* if the
     initial position is accepted.
     Revised power rating: cost: 3; likelihood: 0.7; total: 2.1.

Element G: Dependence on foreign supplier

Negotiating stance
To demonstrate the risks and costs inherent in dependence.

Parameters
Not appropriate.

Themes
1. Control over the final product is adversely affected. (Staff work to illustrate effects.)
2. Cost escalation for modifications will be high. (Staff work to give illustrations from past experience.)
3. Dependent on a foreign supplier in times of national emergency. (Staff work to identify effects of key component shortages.)
4. In the hands of a foreign monopolistic supplier for future orders. (Staff work to illustrate consequences.)
   Key commitment: 'We are putting our national security into foreign hands.'

Strategy
Introduce themes in mid-game to support the realistic position and to cover the determinant period.
   Power rating: cost: 8; likelihood: 1; total: 8.0.

Element H: Large expenditure – little return

Negotiating stance themes, key commitment and strategies covered in issue 1 of the expectation test.
   Revised power rating: cost: 5; likelihood: 1; total: 5.0.

Elements 1, 2 and 3: Possible ultimate failure of the project

Negotiating stance
To convince BSDD that the project will now succeed.

Themes
1. The basic delaying factors (initiating leading-edge research, mobilising resources, the effects of changed specifications, etc.) are now behind us. (Staff work to develop examples of how these affected the project.)
2. The many areas of difficulty successfully handled and the few that remain. (Staff work to develop examples.)
3. The expertise now built up and the accelerating rate of success. (Staff work to develop examples.)
   Key commitment: 'The difficulties of the past are behind us now.'

Strategy
1. Use the pre-negotiation meeting to start the process of convincing BSDD that with additional finance and the revised time-frame, the requirements of the project as currently specified will be met.
2. Introduce the themes progressively in the second stage of the opening moves. Ensure that there is
   (a) total integrity in detail on past delays and the reasons for them;
   (b) precise detail on the project programme to completion, including time-scale, areas of possible delay, costings.
3. If necessary, blame the current loss of BSDD confidence on poor liaison between the company, BSDD and the SDS. If this line is accepted, make it into a joint problem solving issue.

Revised power ratings:	cost	likelihood	total
Element 1	6	0.5	3.0
Element 2	8	0.5	4.0
Element 3	4	0.5	2.0

Element 4: Signal of weakness to other government contractors

Negotiating stance
Acknowledge that BSDD control over the project should be greater.

Parameters
   Initial position: Project progress and expenditure review by BSDD on three-monthly basis.
   Realistic position: Project progress and expenditure review by BSDD on two-monthly basis.
   Fall-back position: Project progress and expenditure review by BSDD on monthly basis.

Themes and key commitments
Not appropriate.

Strategy
1.   If this element is quoted as a source of difficulty by BSDD, counter by identifying how the level of BSDD control will increase as a result of agreement already reached in discussion.
2.   If necessary, acknowledge the problem and negotiate round parameters given.
   Revised power rating: cost: 5; likelihood: 0.5; total: 2.5.

Element 5: Precedent of weakness set for future negotiations with AEC

Negotiating stance
To ensure that BSDD sees that the agreement made safeguards its position.

Parameters, themes and key commitments
Not appropriate.

Strategy
Do not make concessions too readily or too quickly. Negotiate toughly – and congratulate the BSDD team on doing the same.
   Revised power rating: cost: 5; likelihood: 0.5; total: 2.5.

Element 6: Hostile reaction from the SDS

Already covered in the expectation test analysis.
   Revised power rating: cost: 3.0; likelihood: 1.0; total: 3.0.

Figure 8.3 Strategy development

since the last of these very definitely introduces pressure border-ing on blackmail which can result in the win/lose of either major movement or of greater impasse, its effect on power analysis is difficult to predict. The revised power rating therefore only takes account of strategies 1 and 2.

For 'Loss of jobs' the argument that a government agency has a responsibility to keep jobs going even on a project which it considers ill-conceived is of doubtful value. On balance, if large numbers of jobs are involved, it may be worth mentioning and its effect can be increased by adding in job losses among suppliers and also the loss of potential jobs if further orders were to be achieved. A slightly stronger line is an extension of the loss of research capability argument and relates to the loss of direct skills and applied know-how. There is perhaps more mileage in this since it can reflect the loss of a national capability. All three themes can be used to take the initiative, but for the reasons given, it is doubtful that they would. It is therefore better to use them as suggested to support a position once the psychological momentum has been created.

'Dependence on foreign supplier' has considerable force as a pressure point, and the four themes could be used to good effect almost anywhere. They are, however, included in mid-game first to give additional support to the realistic position, and then to have something new to say during the determinant period. Strategy for 'Large expenditure – little return' has already been given in the expectation test, so as with additional cost of buying the Grandian system, its power ratio remains the same.

Below the line, the first three disadvantages all stem from the 'Possible ultimate failure of the project' because of AEC's failure to perform. In view of the past history between them and of BSDD's stated position, convincing the BSDD team will not be an easy matter. For this reason, two distinct opportunities are given. The first is in the pre-negotiation meeting when full confidence should be given that the project can be completed (the BSDD main concern) providing the time-scale can be extended, the finance increased and the specification unaltered (AEC's main concerns). So right from the beginning, linkage is firmly established.

The second occurs in the second stage of the opening moves after an attempt has been made to reduce the viability in BSDD eyes of the Grandian alternative. The risk of playing it that way round is less since the attractiveness of the AEC proposal will be greater if the other is less. Then in strategy 3, by casting the blame on an intangible, the opportunity for a way out with minimum loss of face is given. The success of these strategies is very much dependent on the view formed by the BSDD of the integrity both of the AEC lead negotiator and of his position. So his staff work in this area must be meticulous and his control of all the detail masterful. He must maintain consistency so that, for example, if he talks of a shorter time-scale to demonstrate capability he must also talk of different levels of capability. Or if he changes the level of funding sought, it must be to achieve a different outcome. With integrity, consistency and skill in the other areas of strategy, he may be gradually able to overcome scepticism. This is reflected in the revised power ratings with a reduction in both cost and likelihood for each element.

The parameters and strategies of 'Signal of weakness to other government contractors' are designed with the idea of showing movement in order to achieve success on the central item of funding. The initial position would only be put forward if greater control by BSDD over progress and expenditure were identified as a major problem. Then the proposal and, if necessary, movement from it, could be used as a means of maintaining whatever was the current position on amount, method and time-scale of future funding. By allowing BSDD to pin them down on this, AEC are reducing what amounts to the second most important cost element in BSDD's acceptance. Again loss of face in agreement is reduced. This is also the purpose of the strategy for 'Precedent of weakness set for future negotiations with AEC'. Although AEC are the supplicants, they must not be too eager to reach agreement. There is always the kudos of the other party to consider. If reactions are too quick, the minister will believe his points are not being given the attention they deserve; if movement is too speedy he will wonder why. So negotiation should be paced, each theme should be well developed and movement should not be squandered. 'Hostile reaction from SDS' has already been covered under issue B of the expectation test. Again these are good strategies, with the third constituting the basis of a concession. But since the SDS mind is probably made up, their effect on power rating is not all that great.

Strategies for each element have now been devised, and in the light of them the bargaining model re-rated. From Figure 8.4 we can see that even allowing for a fair margin of error, the realistic

			Cost ×	Likelihood =	Total
	A.	Bad image for Baratarian technology	5	0.7	3.5
	B.	Loss of export potential	4	0.5	2.0
	C.	Loss of research capability	7	0.7	4.9
Disadvantages to BSDD of rejection of AEC proposal	D.	Additional cost of buying the Grandian system	7	1.0	7.0
	E.	Government shown to be unpatriotic	3	0.7	2.1
	F.	Loss of jobs – direct and indirect	3	0.7	2.1
	G.	Dependence on a foreign supplier	8	1.0	8.0
	H.	Large expenditure – little return	5	1.0	5.0
				Total:	34.6

Revised AEC power base following strategy implementation

			Cost ×	Likelihood =	Total
	1.	Possible ultimate failure of project (good money thrown after bad)	6	0.5	3.0
	2.	Possible ultimate failure of project (defence capability impaired)	8	0.5	4.0
Disadvantages to BSDD of acceptance of AEC proposal	3.	Possible ultimate failure of project (major embarrassment for Baratarian government)	4	0.5	2.0
	4.	Signal of weakness to other government contractors	5	0.5	2.5
	5.	Precedent of weakness set for future negotiations with AEC	5	0.5	2.5
	6.	Hostile reaction from the SDS	3	1.0	3.0
				Total:	17.0

Figure 8.4 Reassessment of power base

position of AEC should be attainable. Indeed, as we see it at the moment, it might even be possible to maintain the initial position, thus saving for the company expenditure of up to 1.5 billion baras.

Identifying competitors' proposals and strategies: The technique described

Just as you are attempting to improve your own power base with your client, so an astute competitor will be trying to enhance his own. In this respect, his aim is twofold. First, to develop a proposal which eliminates the disadvantages for the client that are implicit in your own. Almost certainly it will be impossible for him to achieve this objective in full, but if he really means business a competitor will clearly pay much attention to developing and packaging his proposal in the most advantageous form for the client that is possible.

Second, to set about generating strategies which affect the client's costs as he chooses between the two proposals being made. Since a competitor's aim is to steer the client towards his own proposal and away from yours, this will be attempted in two ways. First by developing strategies which demonstrate how the client's costs of rejection are reduced if he accepts his, i.e. your competitor's, proposal. And second how they are increased if the client opts for your proposal rather than his.

As you look again at the original power analysis, you can get a useful indication of how to handle the first of these by considering the client's costs above the line which are implicit in your proposal, and then determining how your competitor will attempt to reduce them in his. For the second, you can get some idea of likely competitor strategies to sway the next round in his favour as you review the costs for your client below the line and as you consider how your competitors will attempt to make them greater.

But before we proceed, a strong word of caution must be given. Clearly as we compound the use of the power analysis we have made, we are in danger of compounding any error. As I said earlier, we should not expect too much from the technique. Inevitably analysis is subjective. First, we made a considered assessment of what we thought would be in the mind of the party with whom we were negotiating in relation to the proposal we were going to put. Now on the basis of that assessment we have gone one step further, assumed that our competitor will make a similar analysis and, on the basis of that, have now taken a view of what his proposal is likely to be, together with its supporting strategies. Anyone who felt mildly apprehensive about power analysis when we started can be forgiven for feeling distinctly twitchy now!

But I would say, 'relax' – somewhat. There is a safeguard. Any proposal your opponent may make will almost certainly be preceded by the implementation of strategy. At the very least you will get an indication of it, or you can probe to find out. Hence if the strategy you see is not consistent with your analysis, then it is unlikely that the proposal you thought would be made will in fact be put. Very well, you have got it wrong. You can think again and nothing is lost. But if the strategy you see developing is consistent with what you thought, you can reckon that you are on the right lines and can implement your counter-strategies and deal with it accordingly. So with this reassurance, I will describe the technique and then illustrate it.

1. From original power analysis take each element in turn and from what you know of the resources available to your competitor and of his normal approach and style, write down the most likely proposal you consider he would make that would reduce the cost of that element to the client. Not every element will yield an aspect of the possible proposal, but a number, particularly above the line, will. When you put them together you will get components, some of them key, that are likely to be in your competitor's proposal package.

2. For each element of the power analysis above the line, write down the strategy that you would expect your competitor to adopt in order to demonstrate that by accepting his proposal, that particular cost element for the client would be reduced.

3. For each element below the line write down the strategies that you would anticipate your competitor to use to increase the cost to the client of accepting your proposal.

Identifying competitors' proposals and strategies: The technique applied

So far the analysis made has indicated that for all their words, the Baratarian government is committed to completion of the project, perhaps more than it realised, and that with good strategy and a full and credible performance the AEC team might even achieve something above its realistic position. For them, so far, so good. But consideration of *possible competitor proposals* should make them less sanguine. In this case, there really is only one competitor – Communications Technology Ltd (CTL) – which has been out of the reckoning for the last seven years. It is now very much back in the picture and, as the summary in Figure 8.5 shows, could prove a very real threat.

If their package were to include the possibility of a *joint venture* say with Tirac Ltd (AEC's arch-rivals) in new high-technology

Possible proposals and strategies of Communications Technology Ltd		
Element	Possible competitor proposals	Possible competitor strategies
A. Bad image for Baratarian technology	Possible new *joint venture projects* with other Baratarian companies	1. *Develop possible joint venture relationships* with Baratarian companies e.g. Tirac Ltd (pre-negotiation) 2. Talk openly of the research capabilities of Communications Technology and that of certain Baratarian companies and how they complement each other
B. Loss of export potential	Selected joint venture partner to be given opportunity to *manufacture and compete in the international market*	Identify and talk of areas in which there could be *a market opportunity* for Baratarian partners
C. Loss of research capabilities	Baratarian research would be part of any joint venture arrangement	*Identify the research* that would be undertaken in Barataria
D. Additional cost of buying the Grandian system	*Offset arrangements* guaranteeing a level of CTL expenditure in Barataria in return for the contract	Indicate the possibility and use to clinch the deal
E. Government shown to be unpatriotic	Not appropriate	Identify how the proposal meets the *strategic and economic interests* of Barataria
F. Loss of jobs – direct and indirect	Anticipated numbers and types of jobs that joint venture projects would require	List the likely joint venture projects and identify numbers and types of employee required
G. Dependence on a foreign supplier	Not appropriate	Stress how joint ventures will strengthen the bonds between the two countries
1. Good money thrown after bad 2. Defence capability impaired 3. Major embarrassment for Baratarian government	Covered by proposals already generated	1. Stress repeatedly the difference: *the Grandian system is working – the Baratarian one is not* 2. *Demonstrate Communication Technology's wide operating experience – and the major*

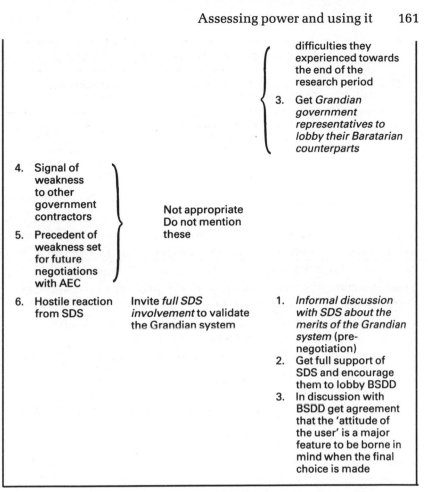

difficulties they
experienced towards
the end of the
research period

3. Get *Grandian
government
representatives to
lobby their Baratarian
counterparts*

4. Signal of
weakness
to other
government
contractors

5. Precedent of
weakness set
for future
negotiations
with AEC

Not appropriate
Do not mention
these

6. Hostile reaction
from SDS

Invite *full SDS
involvement* to validate
the Grandian system

1. *Informal discussion
with SDS about the
merits of the Grandian
system* (pre-
negotiation)

2. Get full support of
SDS and encourage
them to lobby BSDD

3. In discussion with
BSDD get agreement
that the 'attitude of
the user' is a major
feature to be borne in
mind when the final
choice is made

Figure 8.5 Identifying a competitor's proposal and strategies

ventures it would have the effect of reducing each of the BSDD cost elements above the line. If then CTL saw fit to erode AEC's position further, it could add proposals to the package that would reduce the costs of both the loss of export potential and additional cost of buying the Grandian system; their partners would be allowed to *manufacture and compete in the international market*, and through *offset arrangements* would guarantee a level of expenditure in Barataria. While it would be more likely that the last of these would be conceded in negotiation by CTL rather than offered up front, it is a fair enough guess that since they were pushing on an open door with the user, much would be made from the beginning of the desire for *full SDS involvement*.

If we turn to *possible competitor strategies*, we can see that there is much that Communications Technology can do. The key to any real success, however, lies in the pre-negotiation strategy of *developing possible joint venture relationships* with Tirac Ltd. If we exclude the possibility of acquisition of Tirac by CTL, this would necessarily have been a long-term strategy which would now come to fruition. Or alternatively it would need to be initiated immediately in talks with Tirac and/or other suitable Baratarian companies and any positive outcome made known to BSDD as soon as possible. The remaining strategies are all consequences of the first.

Other strategies that CTL might use can be identified from elements 1, 2, 3 and 6 and should cause the AEC team some real concern. CTL has a *success story* to tell, can *use its experience* to undermine the confidence of the BSDD team in anything that AEC says about having the major problems resolved, and can generate some *effective lobbying* at a very high level. In addition it can, and almost certainly will, work even harder to *make allies out of the SDS*, and then make much of the importance of any system having the full confidence of the user. It should also be said that once CTL felt the tide flowing its way, a media campaign would almost certainly be developed.

So when we use the third technique, what appeared to be a strong negotiating position for AEC begins to look distinctly weaker, unless, that is, AEC can develop some effective strategies to counter those of their competitor. And it is here that the final technique relating to power analysis can be useful for developing counter-measures. It is to this that we finally turn.

Developing counter-measures: The technique described

With some at least of the potential strategies of your competitor – or competitors if you extend the analysis further – identified, it is a short step to developing counter-measures to deal with them. The technique is obvious and amounts to an extension of the previous one. It consists of taking each of the major strategies you believe your competitor will use and then considering how you will counter it.

Developing counter-measures: The technique applied

As we see from the analysis in Figure 8.6 several counter-measures suggest themselves. Four are worth highlighting – three positive

Dealing with the Communications Technology strategies	
Possible Communications Technology strategies	**AEC counter-measures**
A. Develop joint venture relationships with other Baratarian companies	1. Close the negotiations with BSDD as swiftly as possible
	2. If a viable option within the corporate corporate plan, *initiate discussions on joint venture projects with other Baratarian companies*
B. Highlight areas in which there could be market opportunities for Baratarian partners	1. Dependent on 2 above, counter with alternative options
	2. Re-affirm the export potential that is available for other Baratarian companies (e.g. suppliers) once the system is in operation
C. Give the areas of research that would be undertaken in Barataria	Stress *known* research requirements and compare them with CTL 'promises'
D. Offset arrangements	Difficult to counter, but use the 'promises, promises' argument, *cast doubt on the validity of offset arrangements* and return to the strong arguments why the BSDD should stay with the project
E. Demonstrate how the proposal meets the strategic and economic interests of Barataria	Use strategies (developed previously) which highlight the many benefits of continued BSDD investment
F. Give manning requirements for likely joint venture projects	As for C above
G. Stress how joint venture projects will strengthen bonds between the two countries	Use strategies (developed previously) which highlight the vulnerability of dependence on a foreign supplier
1. Grandian system is working; Baratarian one is not	Talk of inadequacies of Grandian system using strategies already identified
2. CTL's wide experience – major difficulties arise at the end of the project	Ensure that the AEC position is extremely well supported
3. Lobbying of Baratarian government	Equivalent lobbying using strategies previously identified
4. and 5. Nil	Do not raise

6. Win the support of the SDS	1. *Improve existing relationships* with SDS 'link' personnel
	2. *Target and develop* new potential allies in the SDS
	3. *Raise the level of liaison*
	4. *Propose new liaison arrangements* (strategy previously identified)

Figure 8.6 Developing counter-measures

and one negative for the AEC position. Starting with the positive, the first, identified for elements A and B, is that providing it is consistent with the corporate plan, there is great merit in initiating discussions on the possibility of collaborative ventures with those Baratarian companies that might now be approached by CTL – in particular Tirac Ltd. If CTL has already taken the initiative it will probably even now be too late. But since establishing joint venture relationships with Baratarian companies is likely to play so important a part in the possible competitor strategies, they should be taken into account, even to the extent of AEC reviewing its corporate plan.

The second is as much a requirement in negotiation as a counter-measure. It has been identified earlier that the AEC team will have to do everything in its power to demonstrate its credibility in position and style – most of all with the minister. A major thrust of the CTL strategy is certain to be the fact that they have the greater experience which results from developing a system that is actually in operation (element 1). They will use that to downgrade the key AEC predictions relating to the problems in the project that still have to be dealt with (element 2). AEC's only counter to that is *total credibility*. This too will have an effect on how successful the 'promises, promises' counter-argument is in the various areas where it will be used – particularly elements C and D.

The final positive point that counter-strategy analysis yields is the considerable importance of developing and maintaining a *positive relationship* with the user – element 6. Again, any strategy here might be too late with the SDS having totally made up their mind. But now that there is a choice of systems, they emerge as major players in the game and their support could well be crucial.

The biggest, seemingly insoluble, difficulty for AEC that counter-strategy analysis demonstrates is the problem of how to deal with any really genuine CTL proposal on offset arrangements – element D. All that can be said is that if it emerges during negotiation, the triple strategy already suggested of first questioning its validity, second attacking its value, even its wisdom, and third returning to the strong arguments for continuing with the project should be placed on red alert.

One final comment

What the techniques have shown is this. While at first sight it seemed that the AEC position was weak, if not hopeless, power analysis showed that to be far from the truth. Also that when negotiating positions, themes, key commitments and strategies were generated, the basis of a viable and productive game plan was laid. It will be developed to completion in Chapter 9. But then the analysis of competitor proposals and strategies indicated that there were some powerful positions and ploys that CTL could use. Equally the counter-measure analysis demonstrated that there were key areas in which action taken by AEC both at the corporate and at the specific negotiation levels would exercise considerable influence over the outcome. In general terms it seems reasonable to state that if AEC is successful in these and pursues its overall negotiating plan with tenacity and credibility, the realistic position is still possible. If not, final analysis indicates that if CTL really mean business, AEC may be forced to modify.

So much for the specific case. On the wider front of application to all types of negotiation, subjective as the analysis is, and always will be since it rests on our assessment of the other party's views, it performs remarkably well. As we have seen, the four techniques relating to power analysis can give insight and analysis that take us to the heart of any specific set of negotiations and give some very useful guidance on strategy for conducting them. Yet again there are consequences in this not just for the all-important settlement which is achieved, but also for the relationships between the director and his negotiator and for the negotiator and his team. The main one is unity.

With the techniques for strategy development and power analysis now well and truly established, we will see how they finally fit together as we look at how to extend them into the optimum strategy or game plan.

Summary

1. Negotiating power is identified by considering two options that your realistic position gives to the other party. These are the disadvantages he sustains if he rejects it, and the disadvantages he sustains if he accepts it. He will take whichever course of action he sees hurts him least, and it is his choice which determines your power.

2. There will be a number of factors that he will take into account in each course of action. These are the elements of the power analysis. You list, note and weight them, *as you believe he would see them*. If the total units of disadvantage for disagreement exceed those of agreement you have negotiating power. If, however, the disadvantages of agreement exceed those of disagreement, you do not.

3. Any technique of power analysis is bound to be subjective. That is the warning. But when power is systematically addressed it enables:
   (a) a realistic negotiating objective to be established;
   (b) perceptive negotiating strategy to be generated;
   (c) likely competitor proposals and strategies to be identified;
   (d) counter-measures to be developed.

Key question: If power is indeed the crucial variable, how is it identified and then used in important negotiations undertaken by your organisation?

References

1. Rubin, J. Z. and Brown, B. R. (1975) *The Social Psychology of Bargaining and Negotiation*, Academic Press, London, p. 199.
2. Kennedy, G. (1987) *Pocket Negotiator*, Blackwell, Oxford, p. 184.
3. Winkler, J. (1981) *Bargaining for Results*, Pan, London, p. 97.
4. Thibaut, J. W. and Kelley, H. M. (1959) *The Social Psychology of Groups*, Wiley, New York.
5. French, J. R. P. and Raven, B. (1959) 'The bases of social power', in D. Cartwright (ed.), *Studies in Social Power*, Institute for Social Research, Ann Arbor, MI, pp. 183–205.

6. Chamberlain, N. W. (1951) *Collective Bargaining*, McGraw-Hill, New York, p. 220.
7. Levinson, H. M. (1966) *Wage Determination Under Collective Bargaining*, Wiley, New York, p. 8.
8. Atkinson, G. G. M. (1975) *The Effective Negotiator*, Negotiating Systems Publications, Newbury.
9. Ibid., pp. 13–15.

9
Creating the optimum game plan

So far in this part, I have suggested two techniques which carry the burden of preparation and strategy formulation. As we have seen they give considerable insight and they generate a lot of ideas. But it is the purpose of this chapter to take the final step of showing how to put them into an appropriate game plan, and also to look at a means of validating that game plan so that it can be identified and agreed by all who will use or are affected by it without it becoming the subject of negotiations in its own right.

When I talk to groups about negotiating strategy with its opening, mid- and end game moves, the comment that frequently comes back is that it looks to be rather like a game of chess. I think that this is a good parallel. No chess player am I, but I understand that if, for example, in the Ruy Lopez Opening you depart from the well-established moves, or if, in defending the pawnless end game of rook versus rook and bishop, you attempt originality, you are playing a high-risk game which you will probably lose. You will find that your pieces are wrongly positioned for either defence or attack and any initiative you may have had is lost.

Clearly the moves of negotiation are not as precise as those of chess, but the point holds good. As we will see if you respond to the standard strategy of, for example, the 'vague demand' with anything other than the question for clarification, or to 'the high demand' by making a realistic offer, you will find that you are at a disadvantage for the moves that follow. So we start this chapter by looking at what we call the *standard strategies* of mainstream negotiation – at what they are and at the implications they have for both parties. Next, I will suggest *four criteria* which are a very useful means of assessing the viability of any overall strategy. I have found them to be particularly useful for the strategy formulator, the lead negotiator and the director who has responsibility for negotiation.

168

Then, using the strategies from the expectation test and from power analysis for the case study 'The space defence contract', we look at how the optimum *game plan* can be created. And finally we conclude by assessing it against the criteria we have proposed.

The standard strategies of negotiation

Though most of them are straightforward enough, there is very real value in being familiar with all the standard strategies. As a brief glance at Figure 9.1 will show, some at least are likely to have a familiar ring to them. As we briefly discuss them, it is worth remembering that they would never all be used in any one set of

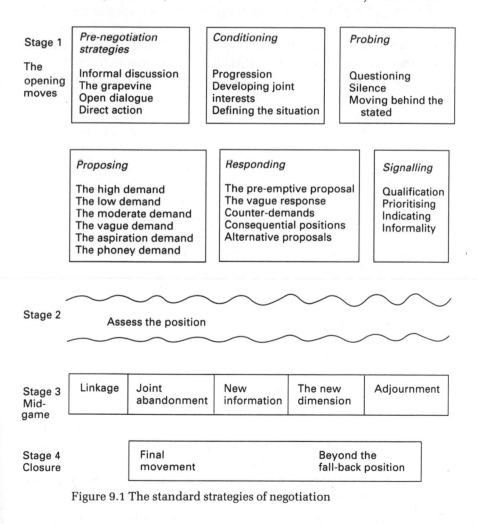

Figure 9.1 The standard strategies of negotiation

negotiations. Rather, success will rest in selecting the right combination.

Pre-negotiation strategies

As we know, the aim of pre-negotiation strategies is to influence perceptions, to set markers, to give indications, to get reactions and, perhaps, to discuss possibilities so that formal negotiating positions can more accurately reflect not just aspirations but also realities. If these strategies work, they tend to work well. Four strategies are now discussed.

Informal discussion

We have already seen the value of the lead negotiators meeting informally in advance of negotiation or of the two secretaries meeting to agree the agenda; indeed of informal contact generally. It can be immense. It allows empathy and trust to be developed and lays the basis for personal and therefore positional credibility; it enables information to be given and received before positions are established and formally stated; and influencing and persuasion can be at their most effective in the informal situation.

But there are two points that need to be made about this strategy. First, the convention that applies is an absolute one. It is that discussion is off the record and that unless there is mutual agreement to the contrary, it remains so. Break this, and not only are the negotiations put at risk, but also future use of this strategy will be denied. Second, informal and relaxed as the atmosphere may be, the parties should still view it as part of the negotiating process. So it pays to keep a clear head!

The grapevine

Using the grapevine is a well-established strategy for getting information about 'real' feelings and positions prior to negotiation. So for example the views of others who have contact with the organisation, such as suppliers, are sought; or the mood of the shop-floor as opposed to the negotiating position of the trade union leadership is identified. In short, insider information is sought. It is a strategy that works from the bottom up.

But this is only half of it. The other half is the use of the grapevine from the top down. So information that negotiators want to feed into the system prior to negotiation is given to selected individuals or groups on the assumption that it will structure the expectations of all who are involved in the negotiation that is to come. So individual contacts are fostered on the golf course and chance remarks are made; or opinion formulators on the shop-floor are targeted and information is fed to them.

Used either way, the grapevine can be a powerful strategy. But beware! Beware the intermediaries in the grapevine who will doctor the information as it passes through their hands to boost or protect their own position. Beware that you really are aiming at or using the right people. Beware that rumour does not get out of hand. And above all, beware that it does not generate more suspicion and distrust in negotiation than it is worth, since it may well be seen as an attempt to undermine the personal as well as the negotiating position of the lead negotiator opposite. In general terms, the closer the grapevine occurs in time to negotiation or the more overt it appears, the more it will be resented.

Open dialogue

By contrast with the grapevine, open dialogue is very much above board. It can take the form of discussion about problems or positions before they arise so that information is given, views are exchanged and expectations are gradually structured. In this form it is much used – and rightly so. It has few of the disadvantages of the previous strategy and more benefits, particularly in terms of the relationship of trust which it tends to create.

Another form of the strategy is that of *'talks about talks'*. So prior to negotiation one party will invite the other to a meeting 'just to set the scene'. Or junior diplomatic staff will pave the way for their seniors. As with informal discussion, it can be a very useful means of probing and conditioning, and again has the advantage that positions can be adjusted before they are formally put. But since the atmosphere is more formal and discussion is therefore on the record to a greater degree, it is more likely to be viewed directly as a part of the negotiation process with all that this implies.

Direct action

Action here is in the form of an event that 'occurs' prior to negotiation and which inevitably has its effect on the mood or outcome of the negotiations, although they still lie ahead. So employees vote on a 'survival plan' which clearly relates to job security prior to annual wage negotiation. Or major dissatisfaction is expressed to a supplier prior to contract renewal. Or media attention is aroused which focuses public attention on some of the issues. Or there is a diplomatic incident. Or, more privately, and I would suggest more productively, a letter is sent prior to negotiation outlining the 'intentions' or 'hopes' for the meeting, 'factors which cannot be ignored', 'pressures which are on the parties' and so forth. This particular strategy can set the climate for all that follows.

Strategies of the opening moves

The opening moves of formal negotiation are the important ones. If they are successful, they provide the basis on which movement towards adjustment and accommodation occurs. If they are not, negotiation degenerates into rejection, recrimination and breakdown. At this stage we are well aware of what is taking place. Each party is *conditioning* the other in an attempt to develop personal and positional credibility and to change the perceptions of the other in its favour. It is *probing* to identify positional and personal needs and to see how it is faring in the development of cognitive dissonance. It then moves on either to *propose a position* or to *respond to a position*, in both cases giving itself the room for manoeuvre it believes will be necessary. Finally, as the opening moves come to an end and the decisive phase is reached, each is involved in *signalling* to the other in an attempt to influence the mid-game stage.

The opening moves have the greatest variety of strategies of any of the stages of negotiation. We start with those of conditioning.

Strategies of conditioning

Conditioning to change perceptions featured strongly in each of the three dimensions of persuasion. I suggested then that the following strategic assignments were important:

- developing trust
- creating a positive image
- building the platform

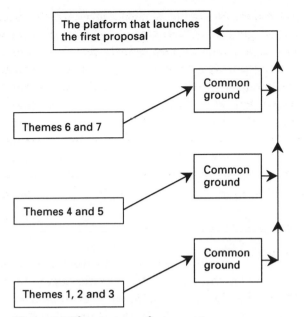

Figure 9.2 The strategy of progression

- developing cognitive dissonance
- creating common ground
- dealing with the other party's positional and personal needs

To these we can add three other specific strategies.

Progression

All that we have said so far has supported the view that negotiation is the progressive development of consensus. Rarely does willingness to change positions occur at a stroke: influencing and persuasion take time. Hence far and away the most important strategy of conditioning is the strategy of progression. Very simply this means that you progressively develop your platform rather than attempt to create it in a moment. So you start with the first two or three themes, which are probably the least contentious, and attempt to convert them into common ground. You then progress by introducing the next two, and once more attempt to make those into common ground – and so on, so that progressively a platform is built and cognitive dissonance is developed. Figure 9.2 illustrates this.

Obviously progress will not be as straightforward as this. The other party will also be attempting to develop a momentum of his own, so your cover positions will come into play. Inevitably there will be some thinking on your feet. Again it is unlikely that all the themes will be converted into common ground even though it is worth remembering the 'three levels' of common ground that we have already mentioned – at best that it is 'accepted', at 'worst' understood, with 'acknowledged' between the two. But the strategy of progression which as we have seen is based on sound insight, offers the best hope for successful conditioning in most mainstream negotiation.

Developing joint interest

We have spoken earlier of 'the lock-in effect' in negotiation whereby a cooperative opening tends to produce a cooperative response and a hostile opening makes for hostile negotiation. One of the ways in which a positive climate can be created is by the acknowledgement and then development of the interests that the parties are trying to resolve in negotiation. Some of these interests will be shared, for example the interest in a speedy settlement. Others will be different, for example one party looking for a front-loaded payment and the other end-loaded. But if the interests rather than the positions of both parties are stated and discussed, an even-handed and less antagonistic dimension is given to the conditioning. Clearly this strategy would tend to flow out of the previous one as needs and interests are identified and as common ground is progressively developed.

Defining the situation

This is a strategy for busy people! It has a higher risk than the strategy of progression in that its initiator gives a summary of the position as he sees it, during which he introduces his themes. He then progresses rapidly to suggesting positions or options that he believes to be reasonable. Clearly he is allowing little time for persuasion to work, but he is limiting his risk by suggesting, rather than demanding, positions and by obviously inferring that while he is clearly looking at them from his own viewpoint, there is indeed another. If it works and the other party responds in like manner, it can mean that the time spent in getting down to detail can be reduced. But the risk is that the initiator, having said so much, is rapidly put on the defensive.

Strategies of probing
    Questioning
We have already seen how important questioning is in negotiation particularly to clarify the positions and priorities of the other party and to see how successful you are at developing cognitive dissonance. 'Good negotiators ask many questions.' So the strategy of questioning for information and clarification is virtually an ongoing activity, and we have already discussed it in some detail.

But questioning has more uses than just information getting. It can be deliberately used to create unease – unease that you know more about his position than he thought you did; unease about the validity of his staff work. And used slightly differently it can demonstrate interest and concern. But however it is used, questioning, unless it is foolish, can develop psychological supremacy. So the strategy can be used for a variety of purposes: it may even form the basis of the strategy for a whole meeting.

    Silence
As we mentioned earlier, some negotiators find silence hard to handle. They go on talking to fill the vacuum. In so doing they modify their arguments, qualify positions, indicate movement and so on. So silence is always a tactic which is worth trying, since if it is sustained, it can become a powerful probing strategy. Unlike most other strategies, however, once its purpose has been identified by the other party, it can easily be countered by him.

    Moving behind the stated
A full picture of positions can only be gained if the needs, hopes and fears that give rise to them can be identified. Clearly whether this is possible depends on the level of trust and empathy that exists between the parties, and it is normally foolish to launch the strategy too soon in negotiation. But if as negotiations progress, a conscious and consistent attempt is made to go behind fixed positions and arguments to the concerns or aspirations that gave rise to them, a useful line for additional conditioning or for identifying alternative moves or concessions can be gained.

Strategies of proposing

Clearly it is up to the party who is seeking the change to make the first proposal, and in this respect it is he who, by the demand strategy he selects, uniquely determines the nature of the game that is played. Given that it is prudent for any party to establish a platform before making the first demand, there are then six possible strategies of proposing. All have important implications for both demander and responder.

The high demand

The high demand is only high when seen in the context of the negotiating spectrum of the other side. So the demand for a 20 per cent increase would be called high if the likely fall-back position of the other side was considered, for example, to be 5 per cent, in a way that it would not if his fall-back position were 15 per cent. So 'high', 'low' and 'moderate' are only such in the context of what is known about the parameters of the other side. As we have seen, one of the purposes of pre-negotiation discussion is to reduce the likelihood of either side misconstruing the parameters of the other and of making a confrontational proposal in ignorance or error.

So what is the demander signalling if he makes a proposal that gives the impression that his own fall-back position is nowhere near that of the responder? What is he indicating when he initiates the high demand? Some possibilities are the following:

1. 'I am strong, and if you want to avoid confrontation you had better revise your parameters in my favour.'
2. 'I am not looking for settlement but for an opportunity for confrontation.'
3. 'I am concerned at this stage at looking strong and powerful and/or raising the expectations of those that I represent.'

Now two at least of these signals point to a high-risk game, so for the demander the implications of the strategy are clear. First he should think long and hard before initiating it. Nothing is worse than playing a high-demand game if you do not have the cards to support it. He should either have a strong power base or have thought how he will abandon the extreme position without losing face when the requirement for him to move is made plain. Second, the demand must have at least some credibility at the time that it is put forward. If it does not, as Peter Warr writes

the opponent might well respond with disbelief and complete rejection, partly because the demand is excessive but also because it is so inconsistent with his view of the situation that the psychological effort attached to its serious consideration is just too great.[1]

But high demands are not all folly. For obvious reasons they increase the possibility of a high settlement and they can push the responder into making an error. So what are the implications for the responder? The critical decision he faces is whether or not to talk with the demander. His decision here will be a function of whether he feels that there is a requirement to keep the negotiation going. Clearly his best move is to refuse even to discuss the demand until it has been moderated. But this may well inflame an already tense situation. Certainly his worst move is to enter the game with an offer. If, for example, against a demand for 20 per cent and with a fall-back position of 5 per cent, he makes an offer of 3 per cent 'in good faith', he is giving the demander two winning options. Either the demander could match his offer by dropping his demand to 17 per cent and so require the responder to make the next move – a game the responder cannot afford to play. Or he can threaten to terminate negotiation because of the 'derisory offer' he has received, and cast the responder as the guilty party.

So if the responder feels he must keep negotiation going, yet he can see that it is foolish to enter the game, what should he do? I suggest there are five moves.

First, he should insist on the rationale for the demand in detail, and he should fight it wherever he feels he can. He should not at this stage widen his attack by introducing themes that relate to his own position. He should only fight the arguments given.

Second, on the basis of what has happened so far, he should ask for moderation of the demander's position. If none is given, this is the first point at which seriously to consider terminating negotiation – for one of two very different reasons. The first is to do with bluff. It could be that the high demand is a bluff. So particularly if the responder has regained the initiative, now is the time to call it. The demander will see little value in letting negotiation collapse and, maybe with some huffing and puffing, will prefer to moderate his position. And second, if the parties really are on a confrontational course, it may be best to break down now.

Assuming discussion is continuing, he should now as the third move introduce the pressures on him that affect his ability to respond, and he should make much of them.

Fourth, in the light of these pressures, which he can claim as 'new information' since they were not discussed when dealing with the demand initially, he should ask for further moderation, perhaps giving the incentive of putting an offer on the table if it is given. Again this is a possible termination point if the demander's position is not moderated.

Fifth, if moderation has been given, now is the time for the responder to enter the game with the lowest offer that is credible and probably a series of counter-demands which can be used to get further movement later on.

Dealing with the high demand is always difficult, but while the strategy suggested undoubtedly has risk, it is probably the optimum method for handling it. Any other will probably produce deadlock later in negotiation or will give an easy victory to the demander.

The low demand

This is a lower risk but a lower pay-off strategy for the demander. It normally results either from a weak negotiating position or a desire to avoid prolonged negotiation or possible breakdown. Clearly, responders tend to prefer low demands! This therefore points up the value for them of pre-negotiation conditioning, usually on a continuing basis or at least well in advance of negotiation so that extreme positions may be avoided.

The moderate demand

It is to reduce his risk but to achieve a good pay-off that the demander will usually engage in mainstream negotiation by initiating a demand which he believes will enable him to 'tweak' his opponent's fall-back position to the maximum. The demand will have a rationale that will give it particular credibility at the time that it is put. It will also allow room for manoeuvre between initial and fall-back positions. It will be high enough to preclude the possibility that it falls within the responder's own parameters. It will also be sufficient to act as a form of insurance against events during negotiation, and it will frequently have a number of elements to give greater opportunity for the trading process to occur. From the responder's point of view, it is therefore prudent for him to establish a position which enables him to operate in the same mode.

The vague demand

When the opening position of the demander is for 'a substantial increase' or 'an improvement in . . .', or when he just asks for an offer to be made to him even though he is the party looking for the change, it is called a vague demand. From the demander's point of view it has considerable merit. It exerts pressure on the responder to put the first proposal on the table which in turn gives the demander a number of winning options – to attack it, to reject it, or to ask for more. And his risk in doing any of these is low indeed. For the responder, there is really only one course of action: all others have an unnecessarily high risk. He should question for clarification. To make specific offers against a vague demand is, going back to chess, like falling for fool's mate! Certainly the fear in not making an offer may well be that to insist on clarity by the demander will meet with refusal, in which case negotiation may break down; or it may prompt him to make a very high demand. As far as the former is concerned I have *never* known negotiation to break down solely on a refusal to state a position – it simply is not in the demander's interests to allow this to happen. As for the latter I would suggest that it is better to know the sort of game you are in, even if it is a high one, and to act accordingly rather than to make offers and to hope for the best.

The aspiration demand

Similar in many ways to the vague demand, the aspiration demand is an attempt to get a firm commitment for the future in response to a vague position now. It is introduced by such phrases as 'Could you give me your thinking on . . .', or 'Of course I realise you can't give me a firm commitment on this now, but . . .' Again for the demander it is a low-risk strategy with a potentially high return. As with the vague demand, the response strategy is to ask the demander for clarification and then to treat it as though it were a specific request made now. Or the responder may be happy to give his thinking either to soften the blow or as a form of long-term conditioning. But he should always remember that even a vague response will tend to be viewed over the passage of time as a hard fact.

The phoney demand

It is here that some critics would say that negotiation enters the never-never land. Why ask for something you do not want? And what happens if you get landed with it?

These questions have validity, and if phoney demands are going to be put, the basis for them must be credible. Using them as no more than a very unsubtle ploy really is tantamount to playing silly games. But on the other hand the demand that you do not want, the 'throw away item' – particularly if it is not seen as that – can have considerable value especially when it comes to getting movement into what is otherwise a locked situation.

So the phoney demand should not be ignored. Used well, it should be respected.

Strategies of responding

As we have seen, the way the responder handles the various demand strategies can have a very significant effect on the outcome. But in addition there is a series of strategies that the responder can initiate in his own right.

The pre-emptive proposal

'Why not take the initiative? Before they can put their terms forward, get yours on the table. That way, you have got the high ground.'

Providing it is not seen as the substitute for negotiation, there are occasions when this sort of attack is indeed the best form of defence. It does mean that negotiation starts at any rate on your terms. And providing you can sustain them, your terms can remain the focal point of negotiation. There is great merit in that. But the risk is clear. The responder must indeed be able to sustain his position, for it gives the demander the option of acknowledging it and of immediately asking for more. Or of attacking it, rejecting it, perhaps even modifying his own parameters in his favour on the basis of it, and then tabling his own demand and treating the offer merely as a base point.

The vague response

The vague response, or in its extreme form the response of silence, is based on the thinking that if the responder gives little or no reaction as the demander attempts to build his platform, or he makes no comment as the demands are presented, the demander will lose momentum and will tend to moderate his own position.

Well, it happens. But in my experience, not a lot. What is more likely is that the demander, in the absence of any counter-attack, gains the psychological edge and becomes bolder. So although it is a response strategy that is employed, it is not one that in my view has much merit.

Counter-demands

Unlike the previous strategy, this has much to commend it. Indeed of all the response strategies, counter-demands is the most important for it generates for the responder room or additional room for manoeuvre. The basis for counter-demands should be the platform that has already been created so that when it is tabled it is seen as credible and not just as a perverse ploy. Just as with the phoney demand, counter-demands can include phoney elements – the same principles apply. But whatever the counter-demands are, providing they are seen as credible at the time they are put, they can be of real value to the responder. Ultimately, they enable him to get as well as to give.

Consequential positions

A version of the previous strategy, but one that deserves a mention in its own right, is the strategy of consequential positions. As its name implies, it is a strategy, open only to the responder, who on hearing the demand can then give a number of positions or demands which are tabled by him as a result or a consequence of the first demand. Clearly, these positions must be unpleasant to the original demander.

One of the great merits of the strategy is that it immediately introduces the basis for linkage and, providing the consequential positions can be held, offers the obvious starting point for getting movement by indicating their modification or abandonment when appropriate.

Alternative proposals

The last of the response strategies is one that falls into the category of high risk/high pay-off. It is based on the assumption that the responder is extremely successful in refuting the basis of the demander's proposal – so successful in fact that he is able to substitute a proposal or solution that he, the responder, would consider in its place. Clearly, this can radically alter the course of negotiation. But unless it is done skilfully and from the ruins of the demander's position, alternative proposals run the risk of being rejected out of hand.

Strategies of signalling

Signalling by its nature tends to be a fairly subtle business, To work, signals must be not only given but also received and understood. So much is obvious. But the danger is that in the heat of negotiation, both parties experience tunnel vision which exaggerates the mental set they have anyway. The net result is that there is so much 'noise' in the system that signals become hard to give and even more difficult to pick up.

The good negotiator is alert to this. There are therefore periods when on one side he chooses his words even more carefully, and on the other he listens even more attentively. The decisive phase of the determinant period is one of these; the adjustment and accommodation stage is another. With this in mind, therefore, there are four strategies of signalling to which both parties should be attuned.

Qualification

The strategy of qualification is the most obvious of all the strategies of signalling. Whenever a position is qualified, a signal – and not always a conscious one – is being given. So when 'never' becomes 'under most circumstances' and 'we have no interest in' changes to 'there is little interest for us in', there is something for the receiver which is worth exploring. To handle it he should first acknowledge the signal – 'I see' is usually good enough. Then, unless the situation is delicate indeed, the signal should be clarified – 'Under what circumstances would you . . .?' or 'What would then increase your interest?' are typical questions that would follow the two signals given.

In general terms, therefore, whenever a position is qualified by a subsequent comment, it is likely that the first indication of movement is being given. It is usually worth following up.

Prioritising

Giving varying priority levels to different items is another way of signalling. 'We view your long-term commitment to our product as being of prime importance' is a very useful indication, particularly when there are three other items outstanding. Or again in a summary prior to an adjournment, the statement ' . . . and while we take this recess we suggest that you give very careful consideration to our position on the new organisation structure' is the sort of signal of priority that can provide the basis for the next step forward.

Indicating

Another strategy which is simple but effective is that of indicating – for example the options you believe to be open and those that are closed; how you believe progress might be achieved; the areas which would appear are of greatest concern to each side or the sort of deal that might finally emerge; on a linkage that could be considered. In short, the indication of possibilities can be viewed as a signal and acted on accordingly.

Informality

Moving to the informal on a one-to-one basis provides a contact in which virtually all discussion can be viewed as a signal. Because the atmosphere is informal; because it is not bound by the conventions of commitment that surround formal negotiations; because, ideally, it is not the chief protagonists who are meeting, signalling can be direct and to the point but still not binding since it will only be ratified in formal negotiations after internal discussion by each side. So by way of a guideline, if the other strategies of signalling are not working and you believe that the other party is sincere in its desire to find a way forward, the strategy of informality may be of value.

The strategies of signalling are so important that before we leave them, there are three points I would like to reaffirm. First, signalling requires subtlety, sensitivity and probably the empathy of both parties if it is to be successful. Style in negotiation should reflect this.

Second, signals are for the most part dependent upon attentiveness – and a good memory. Attentiveness so that even in what might be a most boring or threatening phase of negotiation (when they are often given), they are not missed. A good memory is needed so that the signal is noticed as a change from a previous position. This is one of the areas when team members can be of value to their leader as they make sure, usually in an adjournment, that signals have been received. For the reasons given before of the stress of negotiation and of mental set, they may easily be missed by him.

Third, signals almost always require interpretation. So under most circumstances, unless the sensitivity of the subject is so great, a question aimed at clarification should be asked. If the answer takes you no further on, be on your guard. If it indicates a line of thinking you cannot entertain, say so. But if it offers the basis of a way forward, start to build on it.

Strategies of movement

When we looked at adjustment and accommodation, we identified ten 'facilitators of movement', and we saw how much movement relied on a perceptive use of the psychology of pressure. Each of these facilitators and the use of pressure can be developed into strategies in their own right. However, in addition there are a number of standard strategies which should be automatically considered when movement is being planned.

Linkage
Much has been said on this already. It is sufficient here to start by saying that linkage is the bringing together of two different items. Your opponent wants settlement of one, and you want settlement of the other. It leads to the proposal 'If you give us X, we might for our part be prepared to look at Y', and such proposals as these are usually the starting points for movement.

But what should now be added is that the implementation of this strategy starts earlier than that. Most linkages that finally carry the day would be rejected unless they were first preceded by conditioning and then by a sowing of the seeds of linkage. It therefore pays to work out in advance the linkages that you are planning to attempt. Having said that, some linkages can only really be identified when the priorities of the other party are more clearly known. So they are to a degree opportunistic. In this case, if the linkage is new to you, it is worth giving it further thought before you respond definitively to it.

There are some points about the strategy that are worth making, first for the party proposing the linkage. We have mentioned earlier that your only real hope of success lies in linking items of roughly equal preference value. You can try to link a minor concession by you with a major concession that you want from him, but it will almost certainly be rejected and will not do much for your own personal credibility. So in general terms, do not link a major with a minor.

The second point for the proposer is more a matter of tactics, and so we will encounter it again in Part III. But it is worth giving now what we call the 'three always'. First you *always* propose the linkage as hypothetical – 'if' is the first word. You *always* pose a specific position for the other party – you say what you want from him. And third, unless you are already committed on detail, you *always* offer a vague position by yourself in return. Playing it in any other way than this constitutes a higher risk than is necessary.

When responding to linkage, the key point is clarification. Since you are being asked for commitment to a specific position in response to a vague offer, you need to get more substance to what is being proposed before you make a meaningful response. So you ask for clarification. But the longer discussion of the linkage continues, the more you are committed to it. So the golden rule is 'Don't nibble at impossible proposals'. As one of the experienced negotiators said, 'If it's impossible, boot it into touch.'

Joint abandonment

While linkage provides the opportunity for both sides to get something, the strategy of joint abandonment enables them both to lose it! Since we have already seen how demands and counter-demands may include elements that are literally 'throwaways' and how consequential positions create pressure for the withdrawal of the original demand, this is not quite so silly a strategy as it might appear. It is not infrequently that the strategy of joint abandonment with the tactic 'If you will take A off the table, we might be able to look again at our position on B' is the way forward out of an impasse.

New information

New information comes in two versions. The standard low-risk but still high pay-off version is merely an extension of the strategy of progression so that new persuasion points are kept in reserve and then added in support, say, of the realistic position. In this way the pressure of persuasion is increased and an opportunity is given for the new information to be used by the other party as the basis for him to modify or abandon his existing position. The higher risk version can be called the strategy of 'the bombshell'. Here, as the name implies, rather than just being another persuasion point against his position, it constitutes radical information which positively demands that he changes it.

Clearly for either version to work, information must have been withheld earlier so that it can be used now. For the bombshell, because the change being demanded is more radical, the risk of it causing hostility rises. This adverse effect can be reduced if there is a legitimate reason as to why the information really is 'new'. So for example 'We took legal advice on this and have just been informed . . .' or 'Only today have we received the results of our tests on . . .' give a reason for the delay which may make the pressure point more acceptable.

The new dimension

There are times when negotiation cries out for a fresh proposal, for some form of repackaging, for a new perspective. It is here that lateral thinkers come into their own. But on occasion because positions and expectations are by now so fixed and options are so limited, even they can be at a loss. It is for this reason that the strategy of the new dimension can be so valuable. I suppose the hard-nosed realist would just call it contingency planning! But whichever, if a proposal can be kept in reserve which introduces a new dimension into negotiation, it can make the difference between agreement or breakdown. So for example the new dimension might consist of changing the time-scale of an agreement so that the last offer which was rejected for a one-year agreement becomes the offer for the first year of one which applies to two. Or again a different way of calculating compensation, or a completely new financing structure may serve to breathe life into dying negotiation.

Now this is not to say that the new dimension cannot be plucked out of the air if impasse seems to be the only alternative. But how much more effective and how much better if it is controlled and planned as a deliberate strategy.

Adjournment

Adjournment as a tactic is always useful, particularly to allow thinking time. But there are occasions when it is useful to elevate it to the status of a strategy by planning the adjournment. Then it will either reinforce a point or a position, allowing time for it to sink in and for cognitive dissonance to occur. Or it may allow time for reassessment of the situation and reconsideration of positions.

Adjournments may be a pause – say of up to an hour – within a meeting. Or they may mark the end of a meeting. Both types are governed by certain conventions, the most important of which is that although an adjournment need not be taken if it is offered, it is almost always granted if it is requested. It is recognised that it is too valuable to the negotiation process to treat in any other way.

Movement is of course crucial if negotiated agreement is to be reached. Pressure and the ten facilitators of movement are important. But the strategic burden does tend to fall on these five strategies. Fortunately, if well planned and implemented, they are usually well able to cope.

Strategies of closure

We finally arrive at the strategies of closure. Obviously the aim of closure is to finalise negotiation, and I suppose the gamesman would say if at all possible finally to 'tweak the agreement' in his favour. About closure I am certain, but I must say that for 'tweaking' at this stage I have my doubts. The 'one last point' may be a genuine matter which quite consistently with what has gone on before must now be cleared up. But if it, or anything like it, is seen as an attempt to reopen a closed package or to gain final advantage, it will be resented. It all depends on the longer-term relationship you wish to develop with the other party and the reputation you wish to create generally. If trust, fairness and goodwill for the future are important, the ill-effects of tweaking will be out of all proportion to the small gain it might achieve for the here and now. Since I have consistently stated that these qualities are important, tempting as it may sometimes be, tweaking in my view should be avoided.

But back to closure. If in fact negotiations have been handled well, the final moves tend to sort themselves out. Perceptions have been changed, movement from initial positions consistent with this has for the most part occurred, and what remains to be done to get an agreement is usually apparent to both parties. So negotiation at this stage is mainly a matter of tactics either to achieve final movement or to indicate finality. However, there are two strategies which are worth bearing in mind.

Final movement

The strategy of final movement can take two forms. The first, which amounts to meeting each other half way or *'splitting the difference'*, has the ring of fairness as well as finality about it. It is appealing and can be very hard to resist. Hence if it can be planned so that the concession pattern leading up to it makes it possible, so much the better. But even here a word of caution. I have suggested earlier that before proposing movement, it is prudent to probe for it. The same applies to this, and before actually suggesting that you split the difference or do a straight quid pro quo, it is worth testing it for its acceptability to the other party.

The second form that final movement can take is to *keep a concession in reserve* so that it can be added to the package and can finally tip it in favour of acceptance. Again the seeds of this strategy need to be sown much earlier in negotiation as agreement on an item is refused even though it could in fact be given, or a small area of difference is deliberately left hanging. Agreement or concession on these can then be used right at the end to tip the scales. But again a word of warning. If this final inducement is to be used, it should not be given in a way that looks as though a major item or even the whole agreement is up for revision. So an inducement which says 'if you give us the business we will give you another half per cent volume discount' is risky indeed – he might believe that if he says no he will get three-quarters of a per cent! Inducement then should not be on a major item and preferably it should not have substantive value. The safest is of the 'we can wrap this up by Christmas' or 'We can get these difficult negotiations out of the way' variety.

Beyond the fall-back

This strategy – BFB for short – normally represents the last move of negotiation and constitutes the position you will adopt if you cannot achieve your fall-back. In effect it is your last attempt to demonstrate that you have arrived at the non-bluff situation. It is well worth planning in advance and will save you from indecision if your fall-back position is rejected. Since BFB often represents something which is unpleasant to the other side, it also constitutes a threat which can be used to reinforce the fall-back position by giving a clear indication of the consequences its rejection will have.

Much, however, depends on your power base. If it is a strong one, BFB might be 'If these negotiations fail the next step for you is the Receiver' or 'If you can't agree this, we will impose it anyway'. But if you have a weak position, the BFB might be not to let the relationship break down completely and to propose an adjournment. To plan your BFB is valuable. It gives you your *final* step.

This concludes our survey of standard strategies. As we can see, there are a number. But they will never all be used in any one set of negotiations, and I hope that the brief discussion of each has served to reaffirm that although they are mainstream strategies, they need to be understood and handled with some insight. Then when they are used in conjunction with the strategies developed from expectation test and from negotiating power analysis, they serve to create the optimum overall game plan.

But what constitutes optimum? With so much to choose from, how do you know what is the right overall strategy before it is too late? Certainly with experience comes insight. But I would suggest that there are four criteria which can be of considerable value in developing and judging an overall strategy. It is to these that we now turn.

The four criteria of the optimum game plan

Our discussion of the inner game was designed to give insight into negotiation. One of the purposes of this was to enable the reader to get a real feel for what is right in strategy both in broad terms and then, as we looked at managing the inner game, in finer detail. It is the combination of both of these which in fact leads us to the four criteria.

For a game plan really to work it must first be *appropriate*, by which I mean it must satisfy the basic strategic requirements of the situation. Second, it must have *balance* so that credible platforms for proposing and for effective conditioning to develop cognitive dissonance are created. Third, it must facilitate *movement* so that the steps that you take from difference and opposition to joint agreement can be clearly seen. Let us take these three a stage further before we go on to the fourth. For each there is a check-list.

Appropriateness

1. Does the strategy enhance personal credibility?
2. Is it consistent with the long-term relationship I wish to maintain?
3. Does it have the appropriate sequence of strategies for:
    (a) pre-negotiation probing and conditioning;
    (b) the opening moves of conditioning, probing, proposing or responding, and signalling;
    (c) the mid-game of movement;
    (d) the end game of closure.
4. Does it have within it the staff work that will give personal and positional credibility?
5. Does it include the means of identifying and dealing with the positional needs of the other side? Does it take account of his negotiating style and personality?
6. Does it reflect and use negotiating power?

Balance

1. Does the strategy possess the themes needed to create the platform required to launch the initial position? Does it make use of the motive bases?
2. Does it include the obvious cover positions?
3. Does it attempt to develop cognitive dissonance by the progressive introduction of new themes? Does it make use of repetition of old ones?
4. Does it attempt to consolidate change in perception by summarising and building on common ground?
5. Does it allow time for cognitive dissonance to develop?

Movement

1. Is the strategy clear on how it is intended that the determinant period will be controlled?
2. Do the parameters allow what is considered to be sufficient room for manoeuvre? Do they include concessions at the appropriate levels?
3. Does it have the means for developing and sustaining productive movement? Does it take account of the ten facilitators of movement?

4. Is there a contingency plan to reinforce the final position or to withdraw from it?

Eureka

I have found these three criteria and their related check-lists to be invaluable both as a means of creating a comprehensive strategy and then of monitoring it. But one thing is lacking – life. Does it live? And this question takes us straight to the fourth criterion. I call it eureka!

Eureka is quite literally the inner feeling that tells you that you have discovered the optimum strategy, that it feels right. The other three criteria may be satisfied, but still you are not happy. Something is missing. The truth of the matter is that you may have to negotiate without eureka. But the search should go on for as long as possible, for what matters is that the lead negotiator has really found the strategy that satisfies him. More than understanding it, he really feels at one with it. It is this, the eureka factor, that will sustain him and give him the inner strength and panache that he will need.

With the techniques for deriving strategies from the expectation test and from power analysis behind us, with mainstream strategies and the four criteria understood, let us now see how it all fits together. We get down to specifics as we set about creating the optimum game plan for the case study 'The space defence contract'.

Creating the optimum game plan

Where appropriate, an overall game plan will start with the pre-negotiation phase. It will then move into the opening moves of conditioning, probing, proposing and, as the determinant period is reached, signalling. Then after assessing the position, when an unforeseen but major change may be required, it will progress to the mid-game stage of movement and finally to the end game stage of closure. For the case study 'The space defence contract', elements of strategy for each of these are taken from strategy development of the expectation tests (summarised on pages 129–31) and negotiating power analysis (pages 150–4). So that the reader can see this more easily, they are marked, for example,

ET1 if it is the strategy from the first issue of the expectation test, or NPA if it is the strategy from the first element of power analysis. Since the issues of the expectation test were not covered exhaustively, the strategy given is not fully complete. But I am sure it will be sufficient to illustrate the technique in full.

One final point before the strategy is given. As will be seen, certain of the original thoughts on strategies and their timing have now been altered. This is normal. When you are developing strategies for each of the issues and for the elements of negotiating power, although it is useful to consider generally the stage of negotiation when they would be used, it is only when you review them in overall terms and take account of the criteria of appropriateness, balance and movement that you get any real feeling for overall strategy and that eureka begins to happen. When this was done in this case, several factors became clear. First that too much store was being set on a pre-meeting with a senior civil servant which, since the meeting with his minister was now confirmed, almost certainly could not take place. So, as will be seen, some of the points have been incorporated into a letter which can certainly be referred to and used in the opening moves. Second, when it came down to it, the opening moves looked thin and some of the strategies were too negative. Third, the mid-game moves lacked impetus. Both of these have been rectified. Fourth, it should be noted that one strategic element – government shown to be unpatriotic (NPE) – was not used simply because it was too risky. So on the basis of 'if in doubt leave it out', it was omitted.

So here is the strategy. Certain moves might be queried by some readers. But I would ask that it be seen for what it is – an illustration of a technique. And I would add that if it was *our* strategy – the disagreeing reader and myself, that is – and was for real, we would have sorted out our differences before we started!

The space defence contract: AEC strategy document

Pre-negotiation strategy

1. Lobby Baratarian companies involved in exporting high-technology products and who are friendly to AEC to discuss with them the adverse effect that cancellation of the project would have on the image of Barataria technology generally. (BPA)

2. Develop independent publicity and media coverage on 'how the taxpayer loses through cancellation'. (ET1)
3. Send a letter to the minister thanking him for the meeting and saying that you are 'looking forward to this opportunity of satisfying him on several points'. Also that you hope that the outcome will be such 'that space defence will be safe in Baratarian hands' and that 'the future for Baratarian technology in this area will be secure'. (NPA, NPE)

Negotiation

The opening moves: First phase
1. Thank the minister for the opportunity of further discussion and confirm the purpose of the meeting by referring back to your letter.
2. Attempt to initiate discussion by introducing:
   (a) the uncertainty of leading-edge research;
   (b) the effects which changes in specification have had in terms of programme delay;
   (c) the effects of these changes on costs. (ET2)

Key commitment: 'In high-tech research, the consequences of change are colossal.' Probe for reactions, but gently convert the key commitment into common ground.
3. Move on to the fact that unless the specification is changed again, the difficulties that caused the delay are behind us and dwell on:
   (a) the many areas of difficulties successfully handled and the few that remain;
   (b) the expertise now built up and the accelerating rate of success. (NP1)

Key commitment: 'The difficulties of the past are now behind us.'
Handle scepticism with appropriate cover positions and detailed staff work, and attempt to develop the themes into common ground. Spend time on this.

NB If the minister starts the meeting by making allegations, acknowledge his 'concerns' and use appropriate cover positions to handle them. Then launch moves 2 and 3.

The opening moves: Second phase

4. Introduce the proposition that cancellation now is the most costly of all options by using the themes:
    (a) cancellation would mean virtually no return of any sort on major investment already made; (ET1)
    (b) the large *new* expenditure required to purchase a foreign system; (NPD)
    (c) only a relatively small injection of new money is required to finish the job. (ET3)

Key commitment: 'Cancellation gives you the worst of all worlds.' Battle strongly here and then reinforce it!

5. (i) Introduce the effects of the loss of research capability with themes:
    (a) the merits of having nationally based expertise and a national contractor in this field;
    (b) the near certainty of acquisition of key staff by competitors in the event of cancellation and the effects of this;
    (c) the great difficulties and high costs of working or buying your way back into a technology that you have lost. (NPC)

    Key commitment: 'Cancellation would be a loss to the nation.'

5. (ii) Develop the line that there is export potential by talking of:
    (a) the many other countries who have indicated that given the opportunity they would prefer to 'buy Baratarian';
    (b) the foothold this gives for future sales. (NPB)

    Key commitment: 'There is a huge market out there. This is an investment for the future.'

    Use moves 4 and 5 to develop the ground swell for (a) identifying in full the government's negotiating position and (b) launching your own initial position. If the general discussion is positive summarise the basis on which the initial position would be proposed and launch it. If negative:
    (a) express disappointment and probe to identify the priority of 'government concerns' – acknowledge them, but counter them with cover positions;
    (b) re-play the old themes as appropriate but with new staff work where possible – adjourn if necessary;
    (c) summarise common ground, government concerns and AEC contentions; then launch the initial position (only revise it

to take account of government's sticking points if it is considered *absolutely* necessary to keep negotiations going). Use the themes:
(i) the relatively small amount of new money that is required;
(ii) the many benefits of completing the project. (ET3)

Key commitment: 'The long-awaited prize is within our grasp.'
If adjournment is requested, agree it and summarise on a positive note.

The determinant period
6. If there is reaction or rejection:
    (a) go back to previous common ground;
    (b) reaffirm:
    (i) the costs and losses associated with cancellation;
    (ii) the benefits and opportunities of successful completion;
    (iii) the small amount of new money required.
7. Introduce the risks and difficulties inherent in being in the hands of a foreign supplier by launching themes:
    (a) control over the final product is adversely affected;
    (b) cost escalations for modifications will be high;
    (c) there is dependence on a foreign supplier in times of national emergency;
    (d) Barataria is in the hands of a foreign monopolist supplier for future orders. (NPG)

Key commitment: 'If we buy Grandian we put our national security in foreign hands.'
8. If there are still major objections, ask for the restraints that prevent full government funding to be prioritised. Handle them with empathy but use cover positions wherever possible. If appropriate, indicate the possibility of movement, but always link this to acceptance of the total amount asked for. Adjourn to consider positions but make the point that if the specification had not been changed the project would now be complete.

Mid-game: Movement
9. If all the indications are positive that a settlement is possible within determined parameters, negotiate using the parameter document. Use the themes at 10(c) below to support the realistic position.

10. If the indications are negative:
    (a) express disappointment;
    (b) contrast impasse now with the common ground achieved earlier;
    (c) introduce the 'bad image for Baratarian technology' angle with the themes:
    (i) the importance of maintaining confidence in the country's technology;
    (ii) the effects which public loss of confidence can have on other companies competing in the market-place. (NPA)

Key commitment: 'International confidence is hard enough to get without having your own government give a vote of no confidence.'

11. If it has not been discussed already probe to identify if the disadvantages of BSDD agreement of 'Signal of weakness to other government contractors' (NP4) or 'Precedent of weakness set for future negotiations with AEC' (NP5) are factors which affect the BSDD position. If so, table the 'Project progress and expenditure review' from the parameter document if this has not already been done or indicate the possibility of movement on this if it has.
12. Adjourn on the basis that either BSDD will consider the 'basis of an agreement' or AEC will 'consider where we go from here'.

End game: Closure
13. Ask BSDD for its thoughts on the position. *If positive,* negotiate to find settlement using the 'Retention of jobs' theme to support the fall-back position if required. *If negative*:
    (a) recap on previous themes identifying how a decision to 'buy Grandian' helps no one but Grandia;
    (b) introduce the loss of jobs angle by using themes:
    (i)   cancellation means the final loss of credibility in this field;
    (ii) the knock-on effect of job loss to suppliers;
    (iii) the loss of potential jobs that would otherwise be created if even moderate export potential were to be achieved. (NPF)

Key commitment: 'This is a nail in the nation's coffin.'
    (c) ask BSDD for final reconsideration of its position and propose that the meeting be adjourned for a week to allow time for reconsideration;

(d) if absolutely necessary, introduce (in sorrow, not anger) the inevitability of what will happen if negotiations fail, i.e. the AEC beyond fall-back position:

(i) the likelihood of action by the staff and unions affected; (NPF)

(ii) an inevitably hostile Press reaction which will cause embarrassment to the government; (NPS)

(iii) a loss of confidence in the government by other high-technology companies. (N/A)

AEC cover positions for additional BSDD themes

Cost escalation or delay (ET2)
1. The uncertainty of leading-edge research.
2. The effects which changes in specification had:
   (a) on the time-scale;
   (b) on costs.

Availability of proven alternative (ETA)
1. Identify Baratarian unique requirements and question ability of the Grandian system to meet them.
2. Concentrate discussion on the defects of the Grandian system.

Preference of SDS for Grandian system (ETB)
1. Question ability of SDS to pass expert opinion in certain highly complex but crucial areas.
2. Give examples of how SDS opinion has changed in the past.
3. Acknowledge SDS areas of concern that can be met and use them as the basis for enhancing liaison machinery.
4. Use 'the public outcry' argument if necessary.

Value for money for the taxpayer (ET1, NPE)
1. Talk of the many losses to the taxpayer of changing positions now.
2. Continually stress the small amount of new money required.

Signal of weakness to other government contractors (NP4)
1. Identify how discussions so far have increased the level of BSDD control over the project.
2. If necessary negotiate on parameters given round project progress and expenditure review time-scale.

Negotiating item	Initial position	Realistic position	Fall-back position
1. Amount	Baras: 6 Bn.	Baras: 6 Bn.	Baras: 4 Bn.
2. Funding	Full government funding	Shared funding: 75% BSDD 25% AEC	Shared: 50% BSDD 50% AEC
3. Time-scale	18 months	18 months	12 months
4. Project progress and expenditure review (table this only if BSDD identify it as one of their major concerns)	Every 3 months	Every 2 months	Monthly

Figure 9.3 The AEC parameter document

The parameters are given in Figure 9.3. Once specific items had been tabled by BSDD, they would be included on the document and parameters would be set.

Assessment of the game plan

Before we leave this game plan, it is only fair that it should be assessed against the criteria we have proposed. Here therefore are some comments under each.

Appropriateness

The power analysis prior to the implementation of strategy was adverse (27.1 : 29.9) but only just even before developing strategy. After strategies had been developed which increased the power base, a very favourable ratio of 34.6 : 17.0 was achieved. But as we have seen from the competitor analysis, this figure flatters to deceive if CTL are now making a serious attempt to sell their system and AEC have not developed the essential counter-measures particularly in relation to Tirac. But on the assumption that one way or another any CTL initiative is being blocked, and providing the AEC team can develop the positional credibility that should be possible, AEC should be able to settle above their realistic position by, for example, reducing their own funding requirement.

As far as the appropriateness of the strategies used is concerned, the opportunity for pre-negotiation play is fairly limited. Nevertheless the strategy of direct action to enhance the power base outside the meeting by lobbying other companies and by developing media coverage, and by sending the letter to develop a positive climate within it may well prove useful. For the meeting itself much is made of the strategy of progression leading towards developing joint interest. Probing will occur on an ongoing basis, but there are five occasions given when strategically it should occur. The demand strategy is that of the moderate demand which is consistent with the long-term relationship desired. Signalling is attempted by indicating, while movement rests heavily on the strategy of linkage supplemented by the introduction of new persuasion points which comprise the lowest risk version of new information. Closure is attempted using both final movement and beyond the fall-back.

Balance

Looking at the question of balance, proposition of the initial position is delayed for a considerable time while a platform is created, and in various ways the five motive bases are used. Together with the use of cover positions, the strategy of progression, the use of summaries and of adjournments, the chances of cognitive dissonance occurring are increased.

Movement

There is a clear indication of how the determinant period will be controlled, and although it is impossible to develop a full parameter document until the initial position of the BSDD team has been identified, there is room for manoeuvre on all four AEC items. Further concession patterns could well be developed once the BSDD position is on the table. Movement is sustained and made credible through linkage and new information, and there is opportunity to use most of the ten facilitators of movement. The strategies to signal closure look solid enough.

Eureka

Does this enable the lead negotiator on the AEC team to cry 'eureka'? Well, that is only for him to say, and he would certainly need to take into account the third dimension of persuasion and what he knows of the negotiating style, as well as the positional needs of the minister and his team. But there is considerable opportunity in the concession pattern for the minister to save face and, if negotiations are handled empathetically by the AEC team, for him to satisfy his likely personal needs of status, self-esteem and power. So 'eureka' is a distinct possibility.

This concludes our discussion of strategy. By most standards it has been a long one. But I hope it has achieved two purposes. First, to dispel the myth that the negotiator who breezes into difficult negotiations with little or no strategy in mind or staff work in his briefcase with the disclosed intention of 'playing it by ear' can be really successful. Good negotiators know that disaster lies that way. Second, to demonstrate how to create strategy and to develop it into a unique and relevant game plan. This can be as simple or as complex as the situation requires. In general terms, the more difficult the negotiation, the more detailed the strategy. And on the basis of meeting the higher need, we have shown how to develop a fairly elaborate game plan that would sustain pro-tracted negotiation. But at the other end of the scale, using the insight of the expectation test, a few key commitments put into a sequence using the strategy of progression, the most likely cover positions and the necessary staff work and parameters can make the difference between control of the negotiation and a good settlement, and embarrassment and failure.

With strategy and preparation now behind us, we will turn to what makes productive negotiation.

Summary

1. Creating the optimum game plan consists of bringing together the appropriate standard strategies and those derived from the expectation test and from power analysis.
2. The game plan should give you as much guidance as you believe you will need on how you will play:
    (a) any pre-negotiation moves;
    (b) the opening moves;
    (c) mid-game and closure.
    It should also include staff work and cover positions.

3. A game plan can be usefully assessed before it is implemented against the criteria of appropriateness, balance, movement and eureka. These have particular relevance for the director with overall responsibility for negotiation.

Key question: How does your organisation set about creating and monitoring an overall game plan for important negotiation?

Reference

1. Warr, P. (1973) *Psychology and Collective Bargaining*, Hutchinson, London, p. 30.

III
Productive negotiation

Introduction

We will start productive negotiation by looking at the rules of the game – at the 'conventions of negotiation' which, on the basis of enlightened and mutual self-interest, will tend to apply when negotiators meet to do business.

Then we look at the organisation and behaviour of the negotiating team. Here, usually in major set-piece negotiations, the team acts out its part. But its contribution is never neutral; it will be an asset or a liability. So we will try to identify the factors that make the difference.

In Chapter 12 we discuss tactics and behaviour for the lead negotiator. After looking back at the understanding that the inner game gives to him as he reads the process, we look in detail at the key tasks that he has to perform well if he is to succeed.

Our final chapter has the title of the book: 'Negotiate the best deal'. In it we show how the systematic approach that we have given can be applied to any type of negotiation. And we end with some of the common denominators that are frequently found in success.

10
The conventions of negotiation

One of the themes that has run through this book has been that it is in the negotiator's best interest to develop and sustain a positive image which embodies capability and strength, and that wherever appropriate this should be tempered by empathy. We have also maintained that mutual trust between the parties can be of enormous value, and that if it is to occur, it will be sustained by observance of the conventions of negotiation.

Conventions: The unwritten rules of the game

What then do we mean by 'conventions'? The *Concise Oxford Dictionary* is closest to hand. A convention is 'An agreement between two parties; general (often tacit) consent; a practice based on this; an accepted method of play.'

Two points arise from this. The first is a reaffirmation that conventions are most normally tacit agreements or understandings between those involved about what constitutes the recognised, accepted and approved procedure and method of negotiation. They are the unwritten web of understandings about negotiating practice which if embodied in the law cease to be conventions (which should be observed) and become legal requirements (which must be observed). In international negotiation the fine distinction between the two can be a minefield and the best insurance policy is to hire a good local commercial or labour lawyer!

The second is that conventions tend to be so much a part of negotiating practice that they are rarely directly mentioned: they are assumed. They receive scant if any attention in the literature of negotiation. But let one be broken and the possibility of finding settlement recedes; let the majority be disregarded and the negotiating relationship will almost certainly collapse.

So conventions come from the experience that negotiators have of the negotiating process and of each other. They are the tacitly agreed ground rules, the shared understandings about the process. They are therefore important for two reasons. First because they embody what is regarded as 'fair practice' in negotiation. And second because they are the bearings on which the wheels of negotiation spin freely. They are the great facilitators.

Besides playing a part in developing trust, with the many benefits that that gives, they serve to increase the effectiveness of those who negotiate for three reasons.

Conventions are the bedrock

As we know, negotiation involves bluff, particularly as conditioning is attempted and as positions are put. Now this is not to say that all conditioning is a try on or that every initial position can be improved. But bluff is certainly there.

However, if negotiation is to prosper, there must be certainty somewhere. And if there is not full certainty in the content of negotiation, then only process is left. It is therefore in the interests of both sides if they want agreement now and anything like an ongoing relationship in the future to have at least an understanding between them on the basis of the process that they are using. It is for this reason that they need conventions. They are the bedrock on which both stand.

Conventions give security

One of the great difficulties in negotiating with anyone for the first time arises from the question mark hanging over him as an individual. Does he have integrity? When you give information in confidence, will he use it openly to compromise your position? When the scope of negotiation has been agreed, will he try to add to it? When a proposal is made by him, will he stand by it? These and other such questions are foremost in your mind and probably in his. So you try to find answers in advance. You ask around. You see if there is a track record. You suggest that you meet informally and you make your assessment of how far you can trust each other. Here, and again in the early stages of negotiation proper, you are looking for clues that give some sort of security as far as process is concerned; you are looking for indications regarding the observance of conventions. If the right signals are given, you continue. If they are not, you are concerned. Conventions give security.

Conventions ease apprehension

Speaking for myself, one of the most comforting responses I got from the experienced negotiators was in their answer to the question 'Do you ever start negotiation *without* a degree of apprehension?' I am sure the purist would say that the question suggested the reply. Perhaps. But what surprised me was the speed and intensity of their response; it came from the heart. Anxiety and apprehension were indeed the norm – though I would guess they rarely showed. Indeed one negotiator, a very successful businessman who in his earlier days had been a major in the Paras, likened the sensation to his feelings as he jumped out of the aircraft: 'excitement and apprehension at overdose levels'.

Now the adrenalin has to be flowing, that is for sure. But is it in eager anticipation? Or because there is little but distrust? The difference is important.

I think we have said enough so far to be able to reaffirm the value of self-confidence and how apprehension can be eased by clear insight and good preparation. But if, in addition, it is known that the other negotiator does observe the conventions, that although 'he is tough, he is fair', at least one factor is taken out of the unknown. And if there is this confidence that conventions will be mutually observed, not only will both negotiators perform more effectively, but they are likely to find a quicker and, I would suggest, a better agreement as a result.

For these reasons, the benefits for both parties in observing conventions are considerable. But at this point, a very loud note of warning is given. The reason is obvious. If one party is indeed negotiating by rules which create fairness for both, but the other by devices that he hopes ensure full exploitation of the situation for himself alone, the 'fair rule' observer will almost certainly lose. So before giving the conventions of fair negotiation, I must turn to the point of factors that can limit their application.

The limiting factors

In negotiation, as in life, rules are broken for many reasons. But there are three that I would suggest are of particular relevance to us here. They are lack of knowledge, self-interest and cultural difference. They amount to the limiting factors that very much affect how we for our part are able to play the game.

Lack of knowledge

As I have mentioned, the amount of guidance given on conventions is small indeed. As for there being a 'code of negotiating practice' or a 'handbook of negotiating conventions' – they just do not exist. Other books are not much help either: the majority do not even mention conventions or anything like them. Neither does a lucid elaboration of them trip off the tongue of even the most experienced of negotiators. There appears to be something of a time-lag; codification has yet to catch up with practice. Small wonder then that those with limited experience of negotiation, those pushed in at the deep end, make mistakes. Even the smallest points confuse, such as which side is required to speak first after an adjournment – the side that requested it or the side that agreed to it? Or which side has to be prepared to put their position on the table first – the demander or the responder? These can produce an unnecessary wrangle if the appropriate convention is not known. And ignorance of the more important ones relating to conditioning or movement can lead to acrimonious breakdown.

Self-interest

The Machiavellian negotiator probably finds conventions too restrictive. Negotiation is for him a matter of using any and every trick in the book to get the most for himself for the here and now that he can. Lies are in order for the truth might not be found out; information given in confidence is a pressure point to be used; commitment can be given – and then said to be conditional on further gain. There is only one principle: 'Get the most that you can – the game is wild.'

In truth these are the temptations that face every negotiator, and I doubt that there is one alive who has not succumbed in part to at least one of them. But it is a question of degree. And should unprincipled negotiation ignoring all conventions become normal practice for an individual, an organisation or a country, they are on a path that can lead in one direction only. Their reputation is made and it precedes them. Then, with no device available to them other than coercion, they find fewer and fewer who will willingly deal with them, and every negotiation amounts to a shotgun lottery in which not even self-interest is well served.

Cultural difference

Probably the most obvious limiting factor in observance of conventions is that arising from cultural difference. But even here, such are the forces created by international barter exchange dealing that they exert similar pressure towards observance of the basic conventions of negotiation around the world. However, having said that, difficulties can and do arise with conventions that are more peripheral, and then misunderstandings that result can both sour relationships and prejudice settlement. Perhaps the most marked example of this is when East meets West.

In their most excellent book *Smart Bargaining*,[1] John Graham and Yoshihiro Sano take the most extreme of examples. They contrast the 'shoot first, ask questions later' up front style of the 'John Wayne' negotiator with the much more circumspect approach of the Japanese businessman. So the single American is not daunted by a number of adversaries – John Wayne never was! He uses familiar and informal terms; he has a mandate to settle and tends to distrust those who apparently do not; he goes straight to the point and dislikes anything less; he likes talking and shuns silence; he does not take no for an answer, and he believes that pressure will get him there in the end. In all these respects, they suggest, he is approaching the exact opposite of his Japanese counterpart. The implications of these differences are considerable.

The difference in the more peripheral conventions between East and West is probably the most publicised. But it is worth commenting that since conventions are a reflection of values in the culture in which they operate, a view can be taken of what they are likely to be by looking at the standards and values of the nation, organisation or even sub-culture such as the regional factory or office which provides the negotiators with whom you are dealing. And when you are on foreign ground, there is one convention that almost always applies. It is that 'unless there is overt understanding to the contrary, the conventions that are observed are those of the home team.' And you hope they will not try to confuse you!

These, then, are three limiting factors to bear in mind when considering the conventions that are, or are not, likely to apply. If you have good reason to suppose that for any reason they may not be observed by the other party, your own approach should be adjusted accordingly.

We will now identify seven conventions together with their implications that are at the heart of negotiation, and which the enlightened self-interest of the parties would suggest should be observed.

Seven key conventions

Convention 1: Information given in confidence will remain so until it is mutually agreed to the contrary

This first convention happens to be the most delicate. Arguably it is also the most valuable since as we have seen much negotiation is launched by informal and confidential discussion.

For the convention to work, parties must have confidence: confidence in themselves and their own ability to sustain the testing of each other that takes place in what can amount to very pertinent discussion; and confidence in each other that neither will overtly break confidentiality. From these two points come some very simple guidelines for operating it:

1. Do not embark on informal discussions unless you are sure you can sustain them. They are in effect part of the negotiating process of probing, conditioning and signalling; and they are taking place in what, in more ways than one, can be a very seductive atmosphere.

2. Do not reveal anything of real value until you have good grounds to believe that confidentiality will be maintained. A good indication that it will be is when *both* parties are indicating or committing themselves beyond what would be expected at that stage. So it is best to let the level of confidentiality increase on a joint basis incrementally rather than in substantial revelations. Indeed if there is a departure from this by the other party you should view the process with suspicion and stick to small talk.

3. Remember the point that whoever initiates the meeting should make the running, and should be the first to speak 'off the record'.

4. Above all, maintain confidentiality afterwards. This will be both during negotiation and outside it. It means that during negotiation you *never* quote verbatim indications that have been given outside it.

Convention 2: Once the requirement to negotiate has been acknowledged, parties must come to the meeting 'willing and able' to negotiate

Little has a more damaging effect on the conduct of negotiation than one side being patently unable to keep up with the other. Here everything has to do with the stage of negotiation you have reached and with having the resources available to handle it. So, for example, in the opening moves, the party that wants the change must be able to specify what he wants, and why. As a matter of strategy he may try to get the other to make an offer first. But the set convention is that since it is he who wants the change, he must be prepared to state what he is looking for. Again, when building their respective platforms, both parties must have the necessary facts, detail, projections and information so that they can use them as negotiation progresses. And when the movement stage is reached, both must be clear on what they can give and the concessions they require in exchange, and be prepared to embark on the process with a will.

Clearly the likelihood of there being complete harmony between the two sides on speed of negotiation is slight. There will always be delay and impatience somewhere. One party will want to dwell on the conditioning, believing it to be to his benefit. For the same reason the other will want a proposal if only so that it gives him something he can attack. Progress, or lack of it, has very definite strategic implications. But a rhythm of negotiation does develop, and if one side cannot satisfy the general expectations of the other in this respect and is very obviously just stalling, great frustration results.

There are a number of points relating to the convention which are useful to bear in mind. The first I have already mentioned – it really is incumbent on the party that is looking for the change (the demander) to make the first proposal. The other (the responder) is entitled to wait and see.

There are five others:

1. If the scope and purpose of a meeting are made known in

advance, negotiation is more likely to be productive. If they can be *agreed*, it will be.

2. When positions are established, or arguments used, the full rationale for them should be ready for use. Staff work should be in place.

3. If there is a major area in which a position has not been thought out and there is a definite requirement to do so, it is normally best either to delay the meeting or, if the point comes up during it, to say that you need time to consider it and you will come back to him on it later. True, this may be seen as a sign of weakness. If it occurs too often it will, for the reasons given, provoke a very hostile reaction. But occasionally and with good reason, if it is handled as suggested, it should not be a stumbling block.

4. Once indications of movement have been given, they should be handled firmly. They should be explored and, if necessary, time out should be taken to assess the position. But when the stage for negotiating terms has been reached, movement should be handled decisively.

5. There should be no denial of what has been unambiguously said. To the negotiator, there is a world of difference between saying, 'This is so' and 'I understand that this is so'. The first represents a non-bluff statement on which the other party is entitled to build. The second does not. If the other negotiator finds that he has been misled, he will react not against the statement, but against you.

In almost all cases, the most orderly negotiation is the most productive. If you spring too many surprises on the other party, you will, as one of the experienced negotiators put it, 'provoke him into turning wrecker'.

Convention 3: It is normal in negotiation for each side to establish a position from which it can move

This convention embodies one of the fundamental principles of negotiation which we have discussed at some length earlier. But from a practical standpoint there are four points relating to it which are worth making here.

1. It is conventional for the demander to allow himself more room for manoeuvre between his first position and his last

than the responder. The reason for this is that it is tacitly understood that the demander is to a degree whistling in the dark when he puts his first position and therefore can be somewhat more flamboyant in it than the responder can in his.

2.   The corollary, however, to this is that movement does not have to be of equal value to each side. By convention, the demander can be expected to move further than the responder. However it should be stressed that once final or near final positions are given and the gap is small – for example you are at 5 and he is at 3 – the convention of equal movement does tend to apply. It seems that this particular notion of 'fairness' does creep in.

3.   There will be issues that arise in negotiation in which it would appear that there is no movement available. If this really is the case, then it should be signalled up loud, clear and early. As we have said before, just because negotiation is about movement, it does not mean that you are required to move on everything.

4.   Since movement is the most precious commodity available in negotiation, it should not be squandered. Linkage, trading and joint abandonment all work on the basis that movement will only be given if movement is gained. 'If you . . . then we . . .' are the four key words if settlement is to be reached.

In general terms this convention is so strong that most negotiators work on the basis that unless there are the strongest of signals to the contrary, if the other party is talking, then somewhere, sometime he will move.

Convention 4: Movement is towards rather than away from the other party

Perhaps this is the most obvious of the conventions. Yet it in part also tends to be the one broken with greatest frequency. There are two sub-conventions which are most at risk.

1.   'The first positions of each side cannot be made more onerous for the other as negotiation progresses.' In other words, it is unconventional to increase demands; they can only be reduced. Yet the desire to add on can be great, particularly if negotiation is going well and in the light of it you believe that you have underbid your hand. So an additional demand is put after the first substantive position has been established; or the 'one last point' turns out to be a major one.

The temptation to add may be hard to resist, but it should be since nothing will stall negotiation or undermine personal credibility faster than what is rightly regarded as devious dealing.

2. 'An offer once made cannot be withdrawn unless it was conditional at the time of making and the condition has not been met, or the circumstances surrounding it have radically and demonstrably changed.' The all-important point to remember here is that when you make an offer you are bound by it. It should therefore not be made lightly. It should be well researched and carefully tabled. On the other hand if the other party rejects it or refuses to accept the linkage you propose as it affects him, then you are also released from it. It is important to note that in this situation, the onus for making a fresh proposal passes to him.

Convention 5: The means of achieving movement should not be abused

When we look at the tactics of negotiation in Chapter 12, we will see that a number of them are to do with creating an effect. For example, some of those concerning conditioning and reinforcement are used for the impact they have. They are used to heighten effect. But there is a group associated with achieving movement to which this very definitely does *not* apply. If you use them, you mean them. You want them to be taken at their face value. Their credibility must therefore be maintained. They include the following:

1. The *invited proposal* in which you indicate the sort of proposal from the other side that you would seriously consider.
2. The *tentative proposal* which is an outline of the sort of proposal you might make. It is floated in order to get a reaction.
3. The *hypothetical linked concession* which is a rather long way of describing 'If you give us x then we might look at y'. It is the most useful of all tactics.
4. The *option* when you offer choice to him of concessions you might make.
5. '*Possible and impossible*' when you outline what you can talk about or consider, and what you cannot.

6. The *suggested adjournment* to consider a proposal or to think about making one along prescribed lines.
7. *Tactics to indicate finality.* Into this group would go any tactic which indicates finality or closure.

These and other devices for achieving movement or closure are not to be used lightly. They are the means of moving from general conditioning to final settlement. They should therefore only be initiated to introduce a position you really do mean. If they are abused or diluted, the signal given becomes a confusing one.

Convention 6: Adjournments are part of the negotiating process

The handling of adjournments and other breaks in negotiations we discuss later. But there are some additional conventions relating to adjournment that should be known:

1. Adjournments are taken by mutual agreement – otherwise they amount to a walk-out.
2. Requests for adjournment are normally granted, particularly if they constitute 'time for consideration'.
3. The duration of an adjournment needs to be established and is by mutual agreement.
4. The party that requests the adjournment can be required to speak first after it.
5. Unless the meeting is in neutral territory it is normal either for the 'home team' to leave the room or to make one available for the 'visitors'.

It is perhaps worth remembering that adjournments are a very valuable part of the negotiating process, but they are no substitute for it.

Convention 7: A means of saving face should be permitted in defeat

Very little needs to be added to this. If a long-term relationship of any value is required, it is quite obviously in the interests of neither party to exploit a current position to the maximum or to make concession unduly difficult for the other. So unless there are some very good reasons to the contrary, the means of maintaining personal credibility, most of all in defeat, should be made available.

These are seven conventions which I suggest, for reasons of the self-interest of the parties, rise above national culture. If they are abused or ignored, negotiation, certainly over the longer term, becomes difficult, if not impossible. Rarely are they overtly stated. But nevertheless they are deeply felt. They embody the fairness side of the 'tough but fair' reputation to which most negotiators aspire. But more than that, they are the firm bedrock on which successful negotiation can be built.

Summary

1. Conventions are the 'unwritten rules of the game'. If parties wish to create and maintain a long-term relationship, it is in their mutual interest to observe them.
2. Conventions, however, are fragile and can easily be broken – through ignorance, self-interest and because of cultural difference. Hence it is prudent never to assume that they will be automatically observed.
3. Seven key conventions which tend to apply regardless of cultural values were given and their implications discussed.

Key question: If the non-observance of conventions is hindering negotiation by or within your organisation, what steps can be taken to put the matter right?

Reference

1. Graham, J. L. and Sano, Y. (1984) *Smart Bargaining*, Ballinger Publishing, Cambridge, MA, pp. 7–31.

11
The negotiating team

When any of us negotiates, we are undertaking three main tasks at the same time. Obviously we are talking as we set up the basis of our conditioning and then as we move towards settlement. We are also listening to, filtering and selectively remembering what the other party is saying to us. And finally we are considering – our strategy and how it is working, his strategy and how we should handle it and, as we read the game, our next move and how we should initiate it. I would suggest that these are three very different tasks which can exact a heavy toll on us both mentally and physically. In addition there is the potential that all this will take place in a tense and emotionally charged atmosphere. Small wonder that after three hours of negotiation – or even one – we can feel completely drained.

Some negotiations only justify the time of one person on each side. Others, by tradition, are handled by single negotiators even though they may warrant more. But for the reasons given, when the outcome is important and the stakes are high, I suggest that it is asking a lot of one person to cover efficiently and productively the three main activities. In these circumstances, a team is not just necessary, it is a good investment too.

Our starting point in this chapter is a discussion of the three key players who are at the heart of any team involved in major negotiation. We will look at them in turn and make some observations on the different personality types which may be suited to each of the roles. Finally we will end the chapter by giving some indications of how the good team shows itself and what makes the difference between a team being an asset or a liability.

Tasks, roles and types in team negotiation

The three key members of the team

The key task of course is a talking one. Despite all that our body language friends tell us about the ineffectiveness of the spoken word, old positions can only be changed and new ones created by talking. So the *lead negotiator* probes, conditions, proposes, summarises and generally manoeuvres to find settlement. As I have suggested, this alone is taxing enough which is why in difficult or important negotiation he needs help. If for any reason he cannot get it, there is one rule for him and one alone: 'Keep the negotiating sessions short and sharp'.

The second key task in the team falls to the *recorder*. What does he record? Unless his shorthand is good he cannot get down every word. And even if he does, there still has to be some sifting. So what is important?

Well obviously the themes, arguments and positions of both sides as they are actually stated. And again, equally obviously, the movement which occurs by each side and the final agreement which is reached. Most recorders, however new to negotiation, will probably manage this without too much difficulty. They are like the slices of bread of a sandwich: the trouble is that unless they know what they are looking for, recorders tend to miss the meat in the middle. It can take many forms – signals that are given, indications of movement, 'possibilities' which are outlined, options that are open and those that are closed, statements of 'what it will take' to get an agreement and so forth. In short, anything that indicates movement even though it has not yet occurred. These are often the outcome of a lot of hard work by the lead negotiator and the irony is that recorders, certainly those who are new to the game, tend to miss them.

The third basic task falls to the *analyst*. His task is to monitor strategy and to think ahead so that the lead negotiator is never at a loss for his next move. He is not groping for the detail of staff work, or giving unnecessary or unlinked movement.

These three, negotiator, recorder and analyst, are key players in the game. Where the ability to field a team of three is restricted, two, with the recorder doubling up as analyst, will do. But the tasks to be performed do indicate that the optimum size of a basic team is three. And the situation to avoid at all costs is the John Wayne one of the last chapter where you alone take on the rest.

Personality types of the key members

Before we look at the larger team it may be useful to comment on the personality types best suited to these three roles. While there are no absolute rules on this, there are, I think, some useful indications. As far as the negotiator is concerned, the conclusions reached when we discussed the influence of innate sociability and motivational orientation in Chapter 4 must hold good. The message there was a clear one – wherever possible to match type with type. Where this is not possible, take account of the style of the other negotiator.

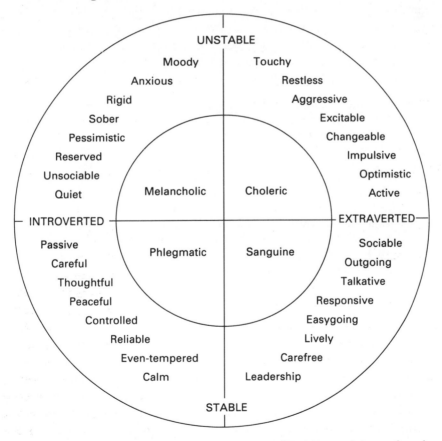

Figure 11.1 The four personality types of H. J. Eysenck (reproduced from *Know Your Own Personality* by permission of H. J. Eysenck)

Having said that, I think we can see a further dimension in respect of the difference in personality types that it is useful to have, particularly between negotiator and analyst, if we look at the general model produced by H. J. Eysenck, given in Figure 11.1 It is certainly interesting in its own right. What Eysenck has done is to take two main 'dimensions' of personality which are first on what he calls the extroversion–introversion axis and second on the stable–unstable axis. Then putting them together so that four quadrants are formed, he has identified a series of behaviour characteristics or 'traits' that have a high correlation with each type. So we can see, for example that the unstable extrovert has traits that include being 'touchy, restless, aggressive and excitable', and that the stable introvert is characterised by being 'controlled, reliable, even-tempered and calm'. For good measure and to demonstrate that astute observers of their fellow men have been around for a long time, he relates it to the four temperaments identified by the Ancient Greeks. He then goes on to suggest that the personality type of a quadrant will also gravitate to a certain sort of work or social group. So he writes

If these personality types are of any importance, we would expect that people in the four quadrants would be found with unequal frequency in various groups differentiated on social, or work criteria. This is in fact so. Thus for instance sportsmen, parachutists and commandos in the army are almost entirely found in the sanguine quadrant; they combine emotional stability with extroversion. This connection can be found even among children; those who learn to swim quickly are precisely those children who are in the sanguine quadrant. Criminals tend to be found in the choleric quadrant, neurotics in the melancholic quadrant. These two groups are apparently almost equally unstable emotionally, but for the most part the criminals are extroverted, the neurotics introverted. Scientists, mathematicians and successful businessmen are frequently found in the phlegmatic quadrant; clearly their phlegmatic behaviour does not extend to their work![1]

Now if we attempt to apply this to the personalities of our negotiating team, I think there are two main conclusions that can be drawn. First that, taking the Greek terms, the melancholic and choleric types look as though they would be a positive liability to have in a team for negotiation of any substance, with he of choleric temperament the man you would least like as a colleague. Negotiation is not the place for neurotics or criminals! More positively, I would suggest that the one element that is vital is stability. Hence negotiating teams should comprise the phlegmatic and sanguine types. I know this a broad generalisation, but when I look at the experienced negotiators and at the many negotiators whom I have learned to respect over the last thirty years, I find it hard to think of any who fall outside this generalisation. Second, and now getting down to specific roles, for the negotiating team to be well balanced, the negotiator and the analyst should be different types so that they can truly complement each other. So if, for example, the negotiator tends to be sanguine and is 'sociable, outgoing, talkative and responsive', his analyst puts the brakes on by being 'careful, thoughtful, controlled and reliable'. Once they have discovered each other's qualities and how to use them and their shortcomings and how to work together to offset them, they will provide the core of a good team.

Shared and additional tasks

Before we leave the tasks and roles of team members it is worth commenting on other tasks, one shared and the rest additional, that may be required.

The first task is one of *protection and support*. Very few negotiators are not in need of protection when quite clearly they are under pressure or when the words simply are not flowing. It is on occasions such as these – particularly if the empathy of the team is such that the wingmen are aware of it before the other side – that the question for clarification by the analyst or the summary by the recorder gives just the sort of protection to the negotiator that he needs. The general guideline here seems to be that when the leader is in trouble, protect him; but when he is clearly on top, let him be. Again, if it is a wingman who comes under attack, he should also be protected, preferably by his leader. Giving support runs along the same lines, but in addition, for the wingmen, it extends to demonstrating an active interest in what their leader is saying – particularly when he makes a proposal. Unprofessional team members tend to look uninterested and unenthusiastic most of the time, expressions which are only relieved by the odd gesture of alarm as their chief handles an issue in a way they would not!

As far as additional tasks are concerned, the first is that of *supplementary negotiator* to the lead negotiator. It probably means the creation of a 'negotiator number 2'. This device is much loved both in theory and in practice. The role can take the form of hard man, conciliator or just plain support negotiator. Obviously the 'hard man' role requires the use of pressure so that when it is relaxed and the 'soft man' comes in, he stands a better chance of getting movement on the rebound. I would suggest, however, that it should rarely be the lead negotiator who takes the hard line since this might put both his credibility and his empathy with the other party in jeopardy, would tend to tar him with the adversarial brush and would mean that it was another member of the team who made the key proposals for movement. However, played with the right blend of sensitivity and panache, it can work well. Well that is, until it is rumbled by the other side and seen as the tactic that it is, in which case it withers away.

'Conciliator' works in much the same way except in reverse, in that when the conflict level is rising too high or impasse is just around the corner, he breaks the build-up by summarising either common ground, the positions of both parties, or movement or signals that have been given so that both negotiators can have time to think, and with that to create the opportunity to take a different line. This particular role can be given to either recorder or analyst.

I must say that contrary to most written advice and to the views of a number of the experienced negotiators, I think there is considerable value in having a supplementary negotiator who has the fairly loose brief of support negotiator. He can then carry out any of the additional roles mentioned together with whatever else might be appropriate: 'sympathiser', 'humourist', 'rubbisher' and so on. To have him there takes the pressure off the lead negotiator and generally adds weight and variety to attack. Obviously if the two negotiators get out of step or tune with each other, that can be bad. And one of them must clearly both be and be seen to be the leader. But I have seen the double negotiator combination used too frequently and too well to believe that, providing it is handled well, it does not increase effectiveness.

The other additional role which normally does mean supplementing the negotiating team is that of 'expert'. It speaks for itself – and accountants, lawyers and other specialist personnel can contribute much. They need to preserve their credibility by keeping to their specialist role and out of negotiating exchanges unless it is with their opposite number. But they should be sensitive to the negotiation that is going on, and should be aware that any information they give has the potential to be used by the other side to gain a negotiating advantage. They should therefore view themselves as active members of the team, and should behave accordingly.

With these roles now clearly established, the basis of team membership fits into place.

Team organisation

Team size

The first point to be made about team organisation relates to the number of members. From what I have said so far, it does seem that the optimum team will consist of the three key members plus others, depending on the tasks to be covered. But the key message has got to be 'three – plus as few as possible'. In fact the experienced negotiators were quite emphatic on this. 'Don't have hangers on – there should be a purpose for everyone being there' and 'Don't have additional members – they only get attacked' seemed to sum up the general consensus. The difficulty is that there are occasions when individuals feel that they should be there because they believe their status in the organisation requires it or because they feel that their interests will lose out if they are not. Both these are legitimate reasons. But I would suggest that systematic strategy and parameter formulation into which they could make an input or of which they could have sight or approve before negotiation could reassure them, together with briefing during negotiation and after it.

One final point on size. There is, in my view, no special merit in matching numbers on a one-for-one basis. For the reasons given, a team of three would tend to have the edge over a team of two. But providing the two know what they are doing, this need not be critical. And, going the other way, providing the tasks are covered (and physical intimidation is not likely!), a team of four can take on a team twice its size and prove considerably more effective.

Team preparation

I have already indicated how valuable I believe team preparation to be. With the systematic approach I have suggested, it not only makes for the creation of a better strategy, but it also generates a high degree of team understanding and unity. However, some of the experienced negotiators took this a step further. They spoke of the 'strength and courage [for the lead negotiator] that come from knowing that you represent an agreed position' and of 'the extra energy that comes from working as a team'. Indeed team preparation does wonderful things to a team. It does wonders for the organisation of staff work too!

Seating

There are some interesting theories about seating plans for negotiation. For example, 'use a round table because it looks less confrontational', and 'because territorial space is harder to define, it won't be seen as a barrier'. Well, King Arthur had his Round Table! Here is another comment: 'Since you don't want to appear as a power block and you don't want to give the other team the opportunity to do so either, choose a round table and put your team members at every other position round the table. That way power blocks are broken up.'

Before commenting on these, let us return to first principles. What *must* a negotiating team be able to do? First, it must be capable of being controlled by its leader. Second, its members must be able to support their leader and each other. Third, its members must be able to communicate efficiently with each other. Fourth, its members must be able to guard the confidentiality of their material.

In the light of these, the Arthurian and dispersal of power block theories of seating stand condemned. There is only one seating layout that permits control, supports internal communication and allows confidentiality, and that is with the lead negotiator and the second negotiator, if there is one, sitting side by side and in the middle of their team, with, probably, the analyst sitting next to the lead negotiator. Experts are as close to the lead negotiator as their importance to the negotiation requires. The recorder, being the third key member, is seated as close to the lead negotiator as is possible given the other circumstances. And as far as the shape of the table is concerned, there is only one, excluding the exotic, that is *not* compatible with the four requirements and that is circular!

So a normal seating plan is given in Figure 11.2. As will be seen, both teams have chosen to 'cocoon' their expert who has the least experience of negotiation and is probably the most vulnerable. The slight difference in the positioning of expert and analyst is interesting, as is the decision of one lead negotiator not to sit directly opposite his counterpart. To retain confidentiality of information you need a distance of at least 1.5 metres between

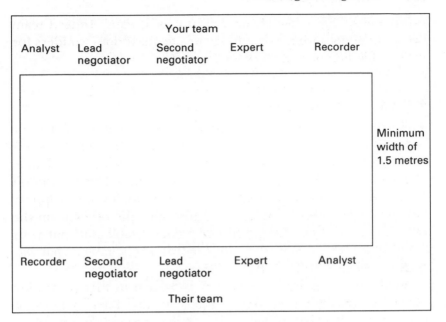

Figure 11.2 A typical seating plan for major negotiations

your own side and the other team. But too much, say more than 2.5 metres, really does have an adverse effect; it makes it feel as though there is a real gap between the two sides. Put the other team on a separate table and it feels like a gulf!

One final point. There is little purpose served in tinkering with the props. Putting the light in their eyes, giving them lower seats, no ashtrays or water when you have and so on amounts to playing games and will be resented.

Internal communication

The point has already been made that for a team to function effectively, its members must be able to communicate conveniently with each other during negotiation. This may be on the detail of negotiation as it arises, on what to do next in response to new positions, on how to handle an unexpected impasse, on whether to adjourn, and so on. If a team cannot do this, it will tend to become unnerved so that it will not confer when clearly it should, or it will adjourn excessively and so break the flow of negotiation.

But internal communication can be a touchy matter. Communication such as prompting by the analyst or expert on detail, or the cueing in of a team member to handle a particular topic is looked upon as being normal at any stage of negotiation. However, internal discussion on how to handle a point in the early stages or anything that smacks of lack of preparation or division within the team is likely to be exploited by the other side. So in general terms, internal discussion in the opening stages should be kept to the essential minimum. If something comes up which is so important to a member that he feels he should bring it to the attention of his leader, probably the best option is a note. Indeed it is his only option if he is sitting a distance away. The note should be short and legible since the lead negotiator probably cannot afford to lose too much eye contact with his opposite number in reading it. If it fails on either of these two counts, he will probably ignore it.

But later in negotiation, internal discussion is a different matter. As the basis of a deal begins to emerge, both sides are well aware that they will need to confer, and so internal discussion is seen as necessary and normal. True, it may well indicate something to the other side, for example that the offer they have made has something of interest even though initially anyway it has been rejected. But by and large internal discussion in the later stages is generally accepted. However in this instance it is still courtesy for the leader of the side wanting it to ask for the agreement of his counterpart. Odds are that they will use the opportunity also.

A second aspect of internal communication is the ability of team members to read each other's body language. Hence wingmen can follow the cue of their leader or, perhaps more importantly, be aware of when they need to protect or support him. Extreme examples they may be, but the team leader who signals finality by boxing his papers only to become aware that the rest of his team is looking with great interest at the other negotiator as he is elaborating on a proposal, and the one who rises to walk out of negotiation only to find that team members down the line have not picked up the cue and remain firmly in their seats, nicely illustrate the point. Having pre-arranged signals whereby the team leader indicates he wants support is another more positive example.

Internal communication is important. Again it points to fewer rather than more team members. But when the channels are really open between members, communication gives the coordination which converts a group of individuals into a team.

The team in adjournment

If the outsider is permitted, he can find out as much about the quality of a team by looking at how it behaves during an adjournment as he can by watching how it performs in negotiation. The good team behaves like this.

First they *review*. The lead negotiator stops talking and asks the recorder to re-cap on the key points of the last session, and especially on 'the meat in the middle of the sandwich'. Then they *analyse* what new information they have got and *determine* together what their objective and strategy are for the next meeting.

Finally, realising that their leader must have time to marshall his thoughts, with at least five minutes to go, the wingmen stop bombarding him with ideas and they leave him alone. These five minutes are golden for him.

Asset or liability: What makes the difference

Most of the characteristics of the effective team are already visible. So I will end this chapter by giving seven factors which I suggest make the difference between a team that is an asset in achieving a favourable settlement, and one that is little but a liability.

Unity of effort in preparation

This point has to be the first in the discussion of those that make the difference. If a team really does come together with a common understanding of how to set about preparing for the negotiations ahead using the techniques we have discussed, they are giving themselves an impetus that will sustain them from beginning to end. More than that, they will make the best use possible of that scarcest commodity of all, time, as together they swiftly gain insight and develop their negotiating plan. And they will find that in so doing they rapidly develop a sense of common purpose and unity.

A clear understanding of roles

When I asked the experienced negotiators for their views on the most important aspects of team organisation and behaviour, the most frequently mentioned of all was 'identification of roles'. It is such an obvious point and yet so often it is clarified only at the last minute, particularly if the status of the team members makes it ambiguous. It may be part of the great tradition of amateurism not to appear to be preparing too strenuously for the Big Event, but as we have seen, negotiation is no place for amateurs. Roles must be identified well in advance so that team members have time to think themselves into them. They can then prepare themselves mentally for the negotiations that lie ahead. If they do not, the shock just might be too great!

Discipline and perseverence

At one stage when I was doing a lot of training of some very senior managers spread across a number of industries in two countries, I thought it would be interesting to keep a record of the various 'learning points' that came out of their role play. Now I know role play is not quite reality, but what people do in a game situation, they will tend to do in the real thing. This particular sequence of records extends to thirty groups – some 300 intelligent and well-motivated people in all, so I would suggest that it is statistically significant. My records show that the point that I most frequently felt justified in making was 'lack of team discipline'. Now rarely was this caused by, for example, team members openly disagreeing with each other. But it was a more subtle indiscipline such as one of the wingmen elaborating on a point his leader had made which merely served to dilute it and to give the other side greater thinking time. Or a team member undermining the power of silence. Or occasionally a wingman being unable to contain his desire for progress any longer and changing his team's position with a new offer – a prerogative that *only* the leader has. These are the points of indiscipline which can cost a team dear.

The same applies to lack of perseverance. The truth of the matter is that most negotiations are at times boring. Nothing much seems to be happening, so the great temptation for the wingmen is to free-wheel. So the recorder misses a signal and does not make a note of a marginally changed position. Or the analyst does not pick up a flutter of body language that would tell him that a particular theme had the other side at a disadvantage.

Support for the leader

Overt disagreement within a team, such as heads shaking when they should be nodding, is in fact a fairly infrequent occurrence. But lesser indications such as lack of interest or poor professionalism do occur: for example, apparent disinterest by the wingmen even when their leader is making a significant offer. Rather, like him, they should sit forward and look alert. And if he is looking keen, they should look keen; if he shows disdain for a proposal, so should they. True, it is possible to overdo this. But it will make a more positive impact on the other side and, perhaps more importantly, it will transmit a sense of unity to the leader which will give him the feeling of support he needs.

Taking full responsibility for the negotiation

When negotiation is going well, everyone wants to get in on the act! But in times of stress and failure when the leader needs all the active support he can get from his team, it may be in short supply. If the team has developed its strategy together, it will probably keep going. But the involvement that comes from each team member taking full responsibility for the negotiation, not just for his part of it, and acting accordingly, can mark the transition from failure to success.

Using adjournments to the full

I have written my piece on this already. But in my view the way a team behaves in adjournment has a significant effect on what happens after, and is a key ingredient of team success. The sequence of review the last meeting, analyse ongoing strategy, determine the aim and strategy of the next meeting – and then give the leader some thinking time – is the best way I know of making productive use of an adjournment.

Developing together

When negotiations are over, the great temptation is to breathe a sigh of relief – and get on with the next job. Very understandable, but it misses the opportunity for real development. Far and away the best course of action is for the team to get together again two or three days after meeting when the full negotiation starts to fall into perspective and to review what happened. Here I would suggest they focus their attention on the 'turning points' of the negotiation. Most negotiations have not one, but a number of critical stages which, when you look back at them, really are the turning points. After them, the negotiations took a different course for better or worse. So if the team can first identify them, and then look at what led up to them and at what happened next, they will get a good insight into the viability of the strategy they developed and into their performance as individuals and as a team. The experience can sometimes be somewhat chastening and much depends on the attitude of the senior member of the team. Also it is probably better not to let the discussion drag on or to have it in front of others – that can happen later if it is necessary. But if the team can review its performance together, its strength as a team will grow.

These seven factors suggest two final thoughts. The first is that a team of any quality always has a level of effectiveness which is greater than the sum of its parts; I hope that readers who have not had much experience of negotiating as a member of a team can now see why. The second is that to the two characteristics that mark out an effective team, discipline and empathy, I think we should now add a third – a sense of professionalism. These three are the winning combination.

Summary

1. The effectiveness of the negotiating team depends on its three key members: the lead negotiator, the recorder and the analyst. They should be clear on what is required of them.
2. For difficult or protracted negotiations, there may be value in having a support negotiator. When specialist information is required, a specialist member should be included.
3. The team needs to be organised so that such matters as coordination, seating, internal communication and adjournment work smoothly.
4. It should have as its aim discipline, empathy and professionalism.

Seven suggestions on what makes the difference between a team that is an asset or a liability were given.

Key question: Do the negotiating teams that represent your organisation perform to their full potential?

Reference

1. Eysenck, H. J. and Wilson, G. (1976) *Know Your Own Personality*, Penguin, London, pp. 16–17.

12
Leading negotiation

What does it take to lead in negotiation? A large question indeed, but we have already gone a considerable way towards answering it. When we looked at personal credibility, we saw that self-confidence plays a large part. It gives panache and an inner strength, it enables pressure to be handled more positively; it means that the necessary risks are more likely to be taken.

It also takes an understanding of the inner game. 'Before you can lead negotiation, you must read negotiation' is not a bad maxim. So in this chapter we refer back to the insight of the inner game as we apply it direct to reading negotiation so that our lead negotiator can be that pace ahead of the other party. We then take the key tasks of negotiation on which good performance depends and give some guidance on behaviour and tactics for each.

Reading negotiation

There is much for the lead negotiator to read as negotiation unfolds. So much in fact that if he is to make anything of it, he will be well advised to concentrate on five areas:

- The negotiating sequence.
- The use and effects of pressure.
- The mandate and behaviour of the other party.
- Rejection and the determinant period.

And all of these in the context of the fifth which is:

- His game plan.

We will look at each of these in turn.

The negotiating sequence

If there is one point of understanding that is at the heart of reading negotiation, it is an awareness that there is a natural sequence that should be observed. From my own experience, from watching others negotiate, and from all that the experienced negotiators said, many of the problems that are encountered arise from a failure to work with this natural sequence. 'Not allowing time for the conditioning to take effect'; 'not creating a rational base'; 'insufficient time in probing'; 'making an offer too soon'; 'over-eagerness'; 'a desire to get it over with' were all described by the experienced negotiators as pitfalls in negotiation. And they all arise from a lack of awareness of sequence. This natural sequence was given in the first chapter and has been sustained throughout the book. Let us briefly restate it.

The *opening moves* start with the development of personal and positional credibility. Personal credibility begins with the body language you use, and from then on the image of capability, strength and empathy gradually takes shape for better or worse until a clear picture exists in the mind of the other party. Consciously or not, he then filters all that follows in the light of it.

Creating the platform, managing the themes and gradually developing cognitive dissonance take time. Here we have suggested that a key strategy is that of progression as themes are progressively brought into play, and we have stressed how important staff work and cover positions are. Whether creating the platform is the first major exercise or whether it consists of probing and responding is very much a function of which side is seeking the change. In this context, we have stressed the value of observing the convention that it is the side that wants the change that will be expected to make the running.

Proposing a position should only occur when the platform is strong enough to bear it. So common ground – at best agreed, at worst understood – and cognitive dissonance should be present before the initial position is put. It will be followed by the determinant period when signalling may well be required to control it. And we have suggested that it is in the interests of both parties that the opening moves should end with a break in negotiation, an adjournment so that positions can be evaluated in the light of all that has happened so far.

Although we call them the opening moves, they account for anything up to 70 per cent of negotiating time. Rush, handle or read them wrongly, and what follows after will be flawed.

Mid-game negotiation comprises progression by both parties on a mutual movement basis in an attempt to find the foundations of the deal. It is here that signals are exchanged so that the basis of a settlement is developed. Movement, as far as possible, is on a linked, though not necessarily an equal, basis. So it is here that the strategies of linkage, joint abandonment, new information, the new dimension and adjournment come into play. The spirit as well as the substance is one of movement, and if either side comes to the negotiating table without that factor in mind, negotiation is almost bound to break down.

End game negotiation is to do with finalising discussions so that agreement is reached. There should now be little left to do. If negotiations up to this point have been both measured and purposeful, the final movement required will commend itself. If not, both parties will have difficulty in demonstrating that they have reached the 'non-bluff' position. Success in closure is wholly dependent on success in all that leads up to it.

Reading negotiation for the lead negotiator therefore is very much a matter of understanding the natural sequence and of knowing where he is within it. But let him initiate strategy, tactics or behaviour which are at odds with sequence, and he puts a successful outcome in jeopardy.

The use and effects of pressure

We have seen how important pressure is in negotiation. Without pressure on the other side's position, without the platform with its emphasis on themes demonstrating expertise, benefits, opportunity and reward, and the avoidance of punishment and fear, cognitive dissonance is hardly likely to be created.

But we have also seen that pressure in negotiation can be counter-productive. It stimulates the other party to defend himself and gives rise to defence mechanisms, most of which obstruct progress towards agreement. So too much pressure is counter-productive. We saw that the secret of pressure in fact lies in taking it off. As pressure is reduced, movement is more likely to occur. So for the lead negotiator, reading negotiation is very much a matter of reading the pressure gauge and of adjusting to it as appropriate. Regrettably, other than with the extreme reactions of too much pressure, leading to the walk-out, or too little, producing sublime indifference, there are no right answers on how much or how little to apply. The hawk in negotiation applies more than the dove, and trusts that when its adverse effect has worked its way through and out of the system, he will achieve greater movement. The dove applies less and trusts that empathy will produce results. As we have seen, much depends upon the personality of the negotiators involved and on other pressures such as the tightness of the mandate that they are under. But in general terms two of the conclusions that we reached earlier are worth repeating:

- Pressure must be present, but must be controlled.
- The secret lies in alternating pressure with relaxation.

So for the lead negotiator as he reads negotiation, let him also keep an eye on the pressure gauge.

The mandate and behaviour of the other party

A difficult area, yet a most important one. It is for this reason that the experienced negotiators made much of thinking in terms of the likely 'bottom line' positional needs of the other party and of incorporating movement towards them into their own parameters and negotiating strategy. It is for this reason that when we discussed the inner game of opponent management, we made much of developing positional control by anticipating needs, clarifying positions and priorities, shaping and signalling. To prepare him for what might be required on these, the lead negotiator can use the expectation test and negotiating power analysis so that a strategy is developed which ensures a minimum of surprises.

As far as the negotiating style and behaviour of the other party are concerned, we looked at the matrix and saw that there is a typical personality profile of the good negotiator. But, more importantly I suggest, we also saw that different negotiating types are innately better in their own negotiating environments with Peter the Positive doing well in a cooperative environment, and Competitive Clive thriving on tough negotiations. So the ideal situation is 'horses for courses'.

However, the reality is that negotiators and their teams tend to be fixed and cannot, even should not, change according to the negotiating climate or the opposition they face. So although our advice was wherever you can to match like negotiator with like, it was followed by 'if there is a mismatch, exercise strong self-control'. What this means is that there will be times when the lead negotiator will not be just reading negotiation or indeed acting out a role. He will be gritting his teeth and sticking to his game plan not because he *feels* that it is right, but because he *knows* it to be prudent.

Rejection and the determinant period

We have seen that negotiation has much to do with the handling of rejection, that rejection of themes, positions and proposals can come at any time, and that when it occurs there is a cycle of behaviour which we called the rejection pattern that comes into operation. Reactions to the pattern by those who do not read negotiation tend to be over-dramatic and merely serve to aggravate the situation. The lead negotiator should therefore expect rejection at any stage and on anything, and should view it with all the equanimity he can muster. He should set out to control the transactional hostility that is likely and should concentrate on handling the determinant period well.

We saw that while rejection could occur at any time, the rejection pattern of greatest overall significance is likely to occur after the initial position has been put. Everything that has happened in the opening moves that precede the initial position affects both its length and intensity. If it is handled skilfully, with empathy and, as the decisive phase is reached, with the inclusion of signals if they are necessary, then there is the real prospect of negotiation moving into adjustment and accommodation, and then to final agreement. If it is not, then rejection, recrimination and final breakdown become a real possibility.

The game plan

We have said much of strategy and of the development of the game plan. I hope that the techniques for doing this are now clear. For the lead negotiator his game plan is crucial. It is his map, his plan of negotiation. It tells him his next move, it keeps him on track. When he has it, the lead negotiator can not only read negotiation; he can control it.

Leading negotiation

The variety of negotiating tactics and behaviour is immense. Most writers on negotiation record at least some. Indeed in *The Effective Negotiator*[1] I list over eighty, and I have to say that familiarity with as many as possible is an asset. On the one hand it means that the negotiator can incorporate them selectively to enrich his own style, and on the other he can learn to recognise them and to deal with them accordingly. But having gone down the broad road once, I have come to the conclusion that there are ten areas, ten key tasks of negotiation on which it pays a negotiator to concentrate. If he is fluent in them, they will see him through all negotiations and enable him to do well in most. Though all can be called on at any point in negotiation, they are given now in the order in which it is most likely that they will first be used. For each, some relevant aspects of negotiating behaviour and then a series of tactics are given. Some general points for each stage are also given.

The opening moves

As we have seen, the way you handle the opening moves depends on whether it is you or the other party who is looking for the change. If it is you, the pattern will be first to condition and then to probe before you propose your initial position. If it is he who wants the change, your pattern is more likely to be to probe for his arguments and positions, to respond to them by countering and initiating conditioning of your own, and then in your turn, if appropriate, to propose your own initial position which may or may not take account of his. Either way, therefore, you will be involved in conditioning and proposing, and since one develops from the other, we will take them together.

Key task I: Conditioning and proposing

Much of Chapter 3 was devoted to creating positional credibility with its emphasis on platform building and the development of cognitive dissonance. Certain of the points coming out of this are worth highlighting:

1. The importance of pre-negotiation conditioning cannot be overstated. Anything you can say or do in advance of negotia-

tion which will structure expectations or positions in your favour is almost certain to have a pay-off later.

2. To think in terms of arguments in negotiation is too narrow and is unnecessarily divisive. To work on themes tends to be considerably more productive.

3. Of the five motive bases to which themes could appeal, three are of particular importance: *expertise* which contributes to the rational base of your proposal; *benefits, opportunities and reward* which are of value since they initiate and sustain the positive lock-in of negotiating behaviour; and the *avoidance of punishment and fear* which if used from a base of legitimacy can have major persuasive force.

4. All themes are heavily dependent on the staff work that supports them.

5. It is useful to have a slogan or key commitment as we have called it to reinforce and summarise each theme.

6. Themes, progressively used, create the platform from which the initial position can be launched.

7. Persuasion is very much dependent on the number of themes that can be brought into play – but not all at once.

8. Strategies for conditioning include progression, developing joint interests and defining the situation.

Building the platform is only one of the aspects of conditioning. The other is the development of cognitive dissonance. For this we have seen the following:

1. The development of cognitive dissonance is a progressive affair. It takes time. It will therefore be important to reinforce old themes – usually best done by the introduction of new examples and staff work – and to introduce new ones.

3. The possession of cover positions to handle the most likely arguments you will face is important.

3. Involving the other party in anything that develops his own cognitive dissonance is useful.

Finally we suggested that the aim of conditioning is progressively to create common ground. This is better done if you can do the following:

1. Introduce the least contentious themes first.

2. Summarise common ground as you progress.

3. Keep clearly in mind that there are three levels of common

ground. At best it is fully accepted by both parties; second best, it is marked by an acknowledgement; at worst it is understood.

With these points in mind, you can consider using the following tactics as you develop a pattern of conditioning which then leads on to your proposal.

Give the history which has led you to want to talk now and introduce your themes as you do so.

Develop a scenario of what could happen if no action were taken or the opportunity to meet to discuss the topic were lost. Again introduce your themes as you do so. The scenario can be gloomy and harsh or bright and cheerful; or a mixture of both.

Introduce constraints: as you talk of 'the situation we are in', introduce 'constraints' or 'difficulties' which relate to it, so narrowing the options in your favour.

Explore opportunities: pose possibilities or identify opportunities. As you do so, introduce themes or positions which are attractive or challenging.

'My truth': a good low-risk tactic, which entirely complements the strategy of defining the situation, is to give the situation saying quite openly that it is as you see it. It very clearly offers the other party the opportunity to then give 'his truth'. But it does enable you to introduce themes and positions quite openly and frankly, and for the latter, providing you allow room for manoeuvre between initial and fall-back positions, enables you to set up your stall without prejudice.

Interpret your position: appeal to the experience or interests of the other side by saying what your conditioning or proposals mean for them as individuals. With examples and illustrations, paint personal pictures.

Key task II: Probing

As we have said before 'good negotiators ask many questions'. The only question they try to avoid is the one to which they already know or suspect an answer that does not help them. Apart from that, questions, particularly as they relate to clarifying the other party's position and to testing him in how he supports it, almost invariably give good value. The strategies of using silence and, at the appropriate moment, of moving behind the stated are worth planning.

So far, however, we have said little about questioning technique itself. For this it is worth remembering the following:

1. When you want to get more information, use an open question of the 'Could you explain/tell me more about . . .?' variety.
2. When you want to question for commitment, use the closed question such as 'Are you telling me then/Are we agreed . . .?'
3. Have a long build-up to a question if you like. But when you ask it, ask it briefly – and *wait for the reply*. Any elaboration after the question only gives the other party thinking time.
4. Do not ask more than one question at once.
5. Keep good eye contact when you question.
6. Do not answer your own question.
7. If you are in any doubt, before you respond to an argument or position, question to make sure you understand it and to see if there is anything of significance that lies behind it.
8. If you have a number of questions or you intend to question closely, indicate your intention to do so. If you do not, he will stand it for so long and then complain that your questioning amounts to an inquisition.

With these points in mind, here are some tactics for probing.

Ask for their rationale: if you are faced with an argument or position that does not make sense to you, ask for the reasoning behind it.

Question assumptions, facts and conclusions: if any of these are put forward and you feel you can challenge them, first ask for evidence. Remember, the burden of proof rests on the proposer, not the responder.

Ask for concerns, hopes and fears: particularly if you are faced with an intransigent position, ask for what has given rise to it.

Question the wingmen if you have reason to believe that their contribution would be productive. But never appear to be trying to 'divide and rule' – it almost invariably backfires.

Question for priority: if you are faced with a series of arguments or positions, ask him to prioritise them for you. He may refuse. But nevertheless, it is a very good question to ask.

Key task III: Responding

There will always be an element of thinking on your feet. But for negotiation, the old maxim of 'forewarned is forearmed' really does hold good, and for this we have suggested the preparation device of the expectation test. To supplement it, and to sharpen the lead negotiator prior to negotiation, it can be worth using a devil's advocate – if you can find one! I have also discussed the value of the following:

1. Developing cover positions.
2. Maintaining an empathic style and manner.
3. Being tenacious, particularly on points where he is evasive. But nevertheless on the basis that, like pressure, excessive tenacity is counter-productive, to moderate it when necessary with temperance.
4. Wherever you can, rather than deny or denigrate his arguments, reinforce or build your own themes on them. Building is a vastly more productive activity than fighting to demolish.

Some specific tactics for this key activity include the following.

Talk of the difficulties or *unpleasant consequences* for you in accepting his argument or position. Paint a gloomy picture of what it could mean.

Identify and use his weak points: if you have sustained your questioning, you may well have found the inconsistencies or weaknesses in his position. Attack them first.

Identify and use omissions: there are two sides to most arguments – particularly his! A fruitful line of responding is often to identify what he has not said and to discuss it extensively. Or failing that, to put an alternative viewpoint or position which amounts to the downside of what he has said.

'You've got a problem and so have I': rather like 'my truth', this tactic smacks of evenhandedness. It might even prejudice your overall position. But rarely will your own themes or proposals be shouted down if they are prefaced by an acknowledgement of his.

Likes and dislikes: in short, tell him what you like and what you do not like about what he is saying. True, this assumes that what he has said is not all totally unacceptable, but if you can launch this tactic, you will probably find that negotiations move rapidly forward.

Key task IV: Summarising

The importance of summarising as a key task is often understated – even ignored. But without summaries, nothing is confirmed. And without confirmation, every move forward amounts to a leap in the dark.

We have already seen how important summarising is in the progressive development of common ground, during the decisive phase, and immediately prior to an adjournment. But it should also be added that summarising to demonstrate that you have heard the point or position that is being put to you is also a useful aspect of negotiating technique.

I would suggest that if the summary is to be regarded as the springboard for the next move, it really should be accurate. I know that tactics such as the false summary or the selective summary – both of which speak for themselves – are employed as a means of trying to gain advantage. But when dealing with an experienced negotiator, they will almost certainly backfire. So for a summary to be an effective tool of negotiation, let it be relevant and balanced; and let it depict the true state of affairs.

Key task V: Handling rejection

Looking at rejection so far, particularly in the context of the determinant period, we have already seen how a lack of skills in handling it can rapidly transform a difficult situation into an appalling one. General guidelines we have suggested have included the following:

1. To be aware of the rejection pattern and of the need for the shock and defensive retreat phases to be lived through before progress can be made.
2. Successful conditioning prior to the position or proposal giving rise to the rejection pattern will reduce both the level of transactional hostility and the length of the determinant period.
3. The existence of empathy and common ground is also beneficial.
4. Acknowledgement of his reactions and the reasons for them will often reduce their intensity and can be a good springboard for reassertion of your own position.

These are some good points. But despite them, dealing with rejection can be a problem. Here then is a series of devices which good negotiators keep in their armoury.

Do not accept the blanket rejection: ask why the point or position is being rejected and use the reply to identify his particular needs; where possible set out to build these needs into the deal; where you cannot, attempt to modify them.

Go back to previous key commitments and, better still, common ground and ask how in the light of these he can give a flat rejection.

Talk of the benefits of continued discussion and of the adverse consequences of breakdown.

Summarise your pressure points and ask for a reaction.

Move on to another issue or point.

Ask for an indication or a priority on the points of objection. If that does not open a useful line, deal with what you believe to be the lowest priority point first.

Lift the veil: if there has been a veil over your position, lift it. Indicate an area or areas in which you can move, and what you will be looking for in return.

Key task VI: Signalling

The last key task that we discuss under the opening moves is the difficult one of giving and receiving messages which in fact fall short of plain statements. In the United States they call it 'meta talk'. In the United Kingdom we call it 'signalling'. Whatever it is called, it is important since it usually represents the first sign of movement in a so far implacable position. And when it is sustained, it defines the basis of further movement that may follow. The tactics of signalling are well worth knowing.

Qualifying: as we saw earlier it is the qualification of a previous position that is the most widely used tactic of signalling. 'Won't' bcomes 'might', 'never' becomes 'under certain circumstances', 'it is impossible' becomes 'there might be some hope if . . .' Listen for qualifications – they are normally worth pursuing.

Priorities are signals. Once a priority is given to a series of themes or positions, it is as clear a signal as any that there is a possibility that the lower levels may be dropped if the higher ones are agreed.

The possibility of progress: outline how progress might be achieved particularly if you are at a sticking point. As you do so, indicate how positions might change in the process.

Selective summary: by persistently repeating certain themes or positions you are highlighting their importance to you. By dropping them out of a summary or appearing to add them as an afterthought, you are indicating that they have less value.

The opening moves of negotiation do take time. As we have suggested, anything up to 70 per cent of the total negotiating time can be spent on them. It is almost certain that the lead negotiator will be required to perform in each of the key tasks that we have mentioned. But he should not lose sight of certain patterns of mainstream negotiating behaviour. So before we leave the opening moves, there are a number of general guides to productive negotiating behaviour that he might consider.

Take the initiative

Be the first to extend the hand of welcome. Be the first to engage in eye contact. Be the first to introduce small talk. But also be the first to get down to business.

Make notes

Even if you have a recorder with you, make notes of the themes the other party is using, the positions he is adopting and the questions, points or cover positions you will introduce when he has stopped talking. This serves as a very useful lead in to the move that follows next; it regains the initiative; and it is likely to bring a sense of order into negotiation. But before you start, check with him that he agrees that you can take notes. He might prefer to say no – but he will always say yes!

Establish facts early

If you are doubtful about his facts, say so. If they affect an area of discussion, defer it until they can be verified. But *never* accuse him of lying or attempting to mislead you. Just say that what he has said does not quite tally with what you thought, and that you would like to check your own information.

Identify and use common ground

This is back to the lock-in effect. So if you can get 'yes, we agree' going early, it will create a positive climate. However, one point of caution. Do not use all the points of obvious common ground in the opening moves. It is good to keep some in reserve to introduce when the going gets tough.

Fight the effects of frustration

It is very easy to introduce or get locked into the defence mechanisms that occur when you or the other party are feeling frustrated. Scoring 'Brownie points', aggression and rigidity of response are the most likely. So try to relax. Do not get personally involved. Team members should take the pressure off the lead negotiator if they feel he needs time to recover his poise.

Do not get cornered in silly positions

If your theme or position really does turn out to be a non-starter, abandon it with good grace.

Get a reaction

When you have used a theme, get a reaction. A nil response from the other party does not necessarily mean that he agrees with it – that may be far from the reality. And, although we have said it before, do not be shy of repetition, particularly of your key commitments. They are an important means of persuasion.

Look for signals

And when you believe you are being given one, explore it.

Stay positive

The opening moves might be long-winded. They might be tedious. They might be frustrating. But try to stay positive in your belief that a settlement will be found – it will certainly help your own feeling of well-being!

And do not forget – summarise

Mid-game

If it is going to happen, movement will start in earnest after the determinant period that occurred when the initial positions were put. If they were wise, both parties will have adjourned to assess their strategies and positions in the light of all that has gone before. But now they have come back to the negotiating table, and movement is in the air.

Key task VII: Getting movement

There is a whole series of tactics that can help here. But first, a quick summary of the main points about movement that we have already seen:

1. Movement begets movement. The best way of getting movement is to be able to give it.
2. A proposal that can be said to be 'fair', for example one that follows from agreed common ground or one which proposes movement by both sides, often provides the basis for settlement.
3. An irregular movement pattern is more likely to generate movement than a regular one.
4. The value of having new proposals to put, which have their starting point in common ground, is immense.
5. The expiry of a time-scale or the emergence of a deadline will accelerate the process of movement.
6, The strategies of linkage, joint abandonment, new information and the new dimension almost certainly hold the key.

Now for tactics. They are pure gold. There is nothing phoney about them. If you use them, you must mean them because once the other party has responded positively to them, you are committed. It is for this reason that in most circumstances, it is *only* the lead negotiator who can use them.

Using the signal: having got the clarification of the signal that was given, having now thought about it and decided to use it, play it back with an indication that you would like to build on it. 'The point you made on X was an interesting one. We would like to pursue it . . .'

The new departure: having got a clearer idea of the possibilities in negotiation, make a proposal designed to meet the needs of both sides. It is not a compromise. It is something new. Such a proposal can be like a breath of fresh air. If it can be planned in advance – following the strategy of the new dimension – so much the better. But a word of caution. It may indeed be a useful position that you propose, but since it is new to negotiation, it runs a number of risks. First it adds another dimension which can complicate the handling of previous positions. Second, it runs the risk of rejection by the other side simply because it is novel, and it was 'not invented here'. Third, it might be used merely as a fresh negotiating position for the other side to manipulate, rather than a possible solution. It is therefore perhaps best to delay it until the other lower-risk tactics which we will discuss next have been tried.

Options open – options closed amounts to saying what you can talk about and what you cannot. Clearly the options that you say you can consider must have the seed of an incentive for the other party, or the proposal that follows them will fail.

The hypothetical linked concession is the best tactic of them all, and has certainly been mentioned before. But it is worth repeating. Bring together two items of roughly equal settlement value; he wants one, you want the other. Then make the linked proposal. It starts with the word 'if'. It is then highly specific about what you want from the other party, and in return the offer is vague. So it runs 'If you give us X, we might be prepared to look at Y'. If the linkage you offer is not totally unacceptable, the other party will want to explore it and, providing he acknowledges that X is not impossible, you will agree to this.

The tactic can be played the other way round where you offer a specific in return for the vague request that he 'considers his position'. But put in this way it is weaker since it indicates that firm movement by you is available without any sort of indication by him.

One other point. Never try to link a major concession by him with a minor one by you. It is almost certain to be seen as the shallow device that it is, and your credibility will suffer.

The invited proposal is a very straightforward tactic in which you state a position you would be prepared to consider, even prepared to accept, and then suggest he makes this proposal to you.

The jump move is otherwise known as 'the major concession'. If you are using the strategy of the high demand, the jump move is its perfect partner. So, for example, both parties are locked. The jump move is a major move towards the other party by you. It is unlinked. There are no strings – except that since it was a major move by you, the onus is now on him to match it. For this reason it is a hard tactic for the other party to ignore. But it has a risk since because the offer was unlinked, it is difficult to withdraw it from the table. If you do use this tactic, the one point to remember is that you do *not* move twice. You have moved and it is now his turn.

Key task VIII: Face-saving

To the outside observer, and particularly for the cerebral outside observer, face-saving may appear trivial. But for those involved, it can be very important. Indeed for the experienced negotiators, who were not at their hottest when describing conventions, it was the one they mentioned most frequently: 'To allow the other side to save face in concession' was in fact the convention they most frequently mentioned. As we saw when we looked in Chapter 4 at negotiating personalities and styles, face-saving is more important for some than for others. But even the Positive Peters of this world, for whom face-saving is of least importance, have boards, colleagues, superiors and subordinates whom they will need to satisfy. So tactics which help them sell concessions to themselves and then to those they represent will be of value.

Mutuality: the normal pattern of concession is on a linked and mutual basis anyway. So if the other party is quibbling about the movement he is giving, it may be well worthwhile reminding him what you have already given or will give in return.

Misunderstanding is a tactic that is frequently used. The party looking for a way out goes back to first themes or positions, claims that he misunderstood them and that if he had not, he would not have contested them in the first place. The reality is that almost certainly he did understand them and that he consciously decided to oppose them. But a misunderstanding is happily accepted as the reason now for his abandonment of them.

Weight of argument is the cleanest of abandonment tactics and the one which is most likely to gain respect in the other party's eyes – providing it is not used too often. It acknowledges that the weight of argument is such that concession by you is now justified. It is a good tactic, yet it is infrequently used because of an excessive sensitivity about the maintenance of personal credibility and the image of capability and strength. A minor version which does not have this overtone is the acknowledgement of *changed positions* in which the party using it infers that what was a major concern is now a minor one.

For progress's sake is a tactic which enables concession to be seen as a positive, even statesmanlike, effort to get mainstream negotiation back on course.

Changed circumstances is the tactic that partners the strategy of new information. He can now claim that since the circumstances surrounding his position or the information relating to it have altered, it is now consistent for his position to change also.

Getting movement and face-saving are the two key activities of the mid-game which, if negotiation is to progress, must be performed well. But again, as with the previous group, there is a danger for the lead negotiator in myopia – in getting the tactics right but in missing some mainstream behaviour. So here are some more general behaviour guides that are useful for him to keep in mind.

Do not just keep adding to concessions

A common failing of inexperienced negotiators is that instead of getting movement as they give it on a linked basis, they offer concessions in the hope that as they mount them up, at some point there will be enough to gain overall agreement from the other side. The risk inherent in this is obvious and almost invariably means that more is conceded than need be.

Probe to get a reaction to a new position before you actually put it

The danger implicit in most of the movement tactics is that since they propose something new, they give indications which are useful to the other party even if the tactic is turned down. This risk, which in most circumstances is a small one anyway, can be further reduced by probing to get an initial reaction to a proposed linkage before it is put.

Keep linkage as simple as possible

The ideal is the single 'item for item' or 'movement for movement' linkage. The more items that are made dependent on each other, the greater is the risk of complexity confounding the deal. If there are a number of items, the best way to handle them is to use the *package approach* in which all are discussed but none is considered to be finally settled until all are agreed. It is then possible to agree some provisionally, leave others hanging, move on to agree others and then return to the outstanding ones. In this way progress is maintained, linkage is kept simple, and complex negotiation is gradually completed.

Take the easier items first

There is always a temptation to attack the biggest issue first, on the basis that if it falls, the rest will follow. So they probably would. But reality is that because it is the major issue it is the most difficult to settle. So negotiations get bogged down, the momentum of movement is lost and frustration rises. Better therefore, if it is at all possible, to sandwich the difficult items with easier ones on either side. Those in front give the negotiation momentum, and those behind can restore the feeling of movement if negotiation on the major item is locked and is therefore put temporarily to one side.

Do not be afraid to leave items hanging

Following on from the previous two points – and particularly in the context of the package approach – if an item is indeed proving difficult to settle, there is usually great merit in leaving it in abeyance and in moving on. This restores a sense of progress, and enables the parties to get settlement or indications of settlement on other items which then affect the way they are able to view the item which is locked. The main danger of this procedure occurs, however, if it is done too frequently so that too many items are shelved, and difficult issues are not tackled when they should be.

Give a graded response

One of the most valuable means of encouraging progress is to give a graded response. Rather than give a blanket rejection because you do not like 90 per cent of what you hear, be more precise: 'While X is impossible, I believe that your proposal on Y is worth further discussion. As it stands Z is a non-starter. But if you were prepared to give us A we could look at Z again.' How much more fruitful this could be than just plain 'no!'

Do not reject a different form of settlement only because it was outside your mandate

It might indeed be outside your mandate, and it might in fact be impossible. But it could be at least worth considering as a new point of departure on which you could then build.

Which brings us to the next point.

Where you can, take elements of their proposal and build on them

As with the graded response, there is a world of difference between saying 'I like the principle. We will have to look very closely at the figures, but what you suggest is, in our view, well worth further discussion' and saying 'We reject your repayment schedule entirely' when it is really only the figures that upset you.

Use rejection constructively

This has been mentioned earlier in the context of the jump move, but it is worth repeating. Very simply it is that if you have put a proposal on the table and he has rejected it, you can by convention ask him to make a proposal for your consideration. In this way even rejection can be used constructively.

Handle adjournments positively

We have already spoken of the value of adjournments, of how they are governed by convention, and of the part that the negotiating team plays during them. But so far we have said little about managing them. Here are some points for the lead negotiator to bear in mind:

1. It is normal to agree to a request for an adjournment at any time in negotiation. Adjournments tend to be requested either when a team needs to take stock of its position or its arguments, or when movement is in the air. However, an excessive number of adjournments can be queried.
2. Ensure that the adjournment's duration is agreed before it is taken; then observe it. If the other side returns before the agreed time has elapsed and you are not ready to continue negotiation, you are perfectly entitled to require that the

agreed time be given. If the other side extends the time-scale and does not reappear at the appointed hour, you are entitled to contact them to find out what has happened. Equally if you require an extension, you should inform them and get their agreement.

From this it can be seen that it is important to exercise some discipline over the time-scale of adjournment.

3. Because of the convention that the side that requests the adjournment speaks first on return, there is sometimes some jockeying as to who is actually seeking it. Therefore be clear on this before you part company.

4. Also be clear about the basis on which an adjournment is taken. It should usually be preceded by a summary.

5. When it is you who request the adjournment, always give the other side something to think about during it. For example, it can be a theme or a consequence that you wish to highlight, or a position or a proposal that you would like them to consider.

Adjournments are a very valuable part of the negotiating process. Hence, manage them in a way so that they work for you.

Do not nibble at impossible proposals

If for example a linkage is impossible for you, say so. The longer it remains under discussion, the more difficult it will be to move away from it.

If you have to concede, do not make a meal of it

If an unlinked concession has to be made, make it willingly and get some personal mileage out of it.

Beware the seduction of movement

Once you have started even a linked concession pattern, it can be difficult to stop. Movement develops its own momentum. So keep a close eye on your parameters. And if you have a team member acting as analyst, make sure that he monitors the movement of both sides. Be careful that you do not give more than you get.

End game

As one of the experienced negotiators said, 'If the end game doesn't look after itself, you shouldn't be there.' This is not a cry of desperation, but rather a statement that reflects the fact that now there are few cards in your hand left to play. If parties are still far from each other, then almost certainly negotiation will not be the means of achieving final settlement. Indeed if this is so, they should have seen the impasse coming much earlier and adjusted their strategy accordingly.

The inducement to settle, or the 'cherry on the cake' as it is sometimes called, is at its lowest risk when it has no real money value. So the inducement to 'wrap these negotiations up quickly and get back to business' or to 'get in the Christmas week pay packet' will cost no more, but does have some intrinsic value.

Key task IX: Demonstrating finality

As with getting movement, which was heavily dependent on the conditioning, proposing and signalling that had preceded it, so it is with closure. Most movement should already have occurred so that here all you are left with is either closing the final gap or demonstrating that you have now reached the non-bluff situation. Both will only be credible in the context of what has gone before although use of the strategies of final movement or beyond the fall-back will help. There are also some tactics.

Equal movement: there is no requirement for movement on substantive items to be equal. Indeed in movement from initial to realistic positions the demander would expect to undertake more movement than the responder. But at end game, equal movement is more normal. 'Splitting the difference' has the ring both of fairness and finality since it involves both sides in equal loss and equal gain. Hence when the parties are close to each other, they can usually reckon that the final small haggle will end with equal movement.

The inducement to settle, or the 'cherry on the cake' as it is sometimes called, is at its lowest risk when it has no real money value. So the inducement to 'wrap these negotiations up quickly and get back to business' or to 'get in the Christmas week pay packet' will cost no more, but does have some intrinsic value.

The inducement becomes more risky when it does have real value since the inference the other party can draw is that if he rejects it, he might end up with more. But usually a feeling for the negotiation so far will tell you how the inducement will be viewed. And if the one small additional concession will get you there, it should be offered – but still on a linked basis, to 'clinch the deal'.

Repetition of the last offer, particularly if it is accompanied by the standard body language cluster of boxing of papers, leaning back, putting pens away, folding arms, etc., will usually be sufficient to indicate finality.

Reference to past experience: when parties have done business with each other before, a reference to the context surrounding finality in the previous negotiation and drawing a parallel with this one will normally be enough to demonstrate that the end of the road has been reached here.

Consequences: it is always possible to indicate finality by talking of the consequences that rejection of the 'final offer' will have. These can include how one or both sides will lose if the offer is turned down, or how 'the failure' will be made public. It may also include reference to the beyond the fall-back position. If this holds unpleasant consequences such as 'having to take our business elsewhere' or 'worsening the firm's reputation in the City', then it can be a powerful end game motivator on the other party to settle.

Key task X: Handling deadlock

Clearly there are similarities between handling rejection and handling deadlock. But while rejection is often by its nature more spontaneous, transient and amenable to change, deadlock is measured, deliberate and not far short of final. But even then it is worth remembering that parties can deadlock for various reasons: for example, if the level of frustration is so great that the response is to 'leave the field'; or the will to find settlement is for some external reason undermined; or, more practically, the parties literally cannot think of anything else to say; or the safest option is 'no deal'. In these circumstances, one last effort might be called for. Here then are some possible tactics.

Ask for an indication of priorities either on items of settlement or on points of objection.

Ask for the one most important factor which is obstructing progress.

Try to move away from fixed positions and progress to the hopes, fears and opportunities that lie behind them.

Give thinking time by adjourning to consider 'where we go from here'.

Adjourn formal negotiations and meet on an informal basis

Finally there are just three behaviour guides for the end game which the lead negotiator should bear in mind.

Do not re-open a closed item

It may be a temptation, particularly if the end game is so easy that you believe you have underplayed your hand. But the convention is a clear one: items which have been settled are closed. Any attempt to re-trade will undermine your personal credibility.

The 'last small point'

Beware 'the last small point' raised as negotiations have virtually if not entirely finished. It may be genuinely small, and it may really be part of the tidying up operation. But equally it may not, and it is well worth while to probe a little further before agreeing to discuss it.

Recap on the agreement

This may be tedious. It may even seem risky after long and hard negotiations to do so since it may show that full agreement has not yet been reached. But in 99 per cent of cases, ambiguity and lack of clarity are in the interests of neither side. And so a final summary is required. Make it; shake hands; and thank the other side!

I hope that this brief discussion of tactics and behaviour has been of value not just to those for whom leading negotiation is something of an ordeal, but also for those who already negotiate with ease and panache. For all, I trust there is something new that they can incorporate into their style as they handle the key tasks on which success in face-to-face negotiations will depend.

Others can benefit too. Perhaps in the light of all this the director can now discuss the cut and thrust of negotiation with more empathy. Perhaps he will be more able to give the support to his lead negotiator that we have seen is so vital in their relationship. Certainly, the negotiating team will benefit. They will understand more clearly what their leader is doing, they will be able to play their part with more confidence. And particularly in times of difficulty when their leader is under pressure, they will be able to read negotiation in such a way that they can actively come to his aid.

Summary

1. To read negotiation it is useful to concentrate on five areas:
   (a) the negotiating sequence;
   (b) the use and effects of pressure;
   (c) the mandate and behaviour of the other party;
   (d) the rejection pattern and the determinant period;
   (e) your own game plan.
2. Effective negotiation entails performing well in ten key areas. They are:
   a) For the opening moves
       (i) conditioning and proposing
       (ii) probing
       (iii) responding
       (iv) summarising
       (v) handling rejection
       (vi) signalling
   (b) mid-game
       (vii) getting movement
       (viii) face-saving
   (c) For end game
       (ix) demonstrating finality
       (x) handling deadlock

In all, forty-seven tactics and twenty-six behaviour guides were given.

Key question: How can your own performance be improved in these key task areas?

Reference

1. Atkinson, G. G. M. (1975) *The Effective Negotiator*, Negotiating Systems Publications, Newbury.

13
'Negotiate the best deal'

As I said in the Introduction, this has been a book designed to take the mystique out of negotiation. I have attempted to do it in two ways: first by giving insight into what I have called the inner game, and second by giving a systematic approach and sound technique.

I have suggested that insight is all-important since only when you understand the processes that are at work, can you use those that favour you and manage those that do not. Hence, this understanding is an intrinsic part of successful strategy generation and of effective negotiation, as are system and technique.

I have suggested that while what happens in negotiation and its outcome can never be fully predicted, method, system and technique in both preparing for and in conducting negotiation are possible and offer the best chance of success. It is for this reason that I devised the techniques of systematic negotiation. The four-stage approach to preparation is unique. Its method and associated techniques are the key to successful preparation. And the four stages of negotiation provide a very useful framework with which to understand and control negotiation.

The main case that we used to illustrate preparation techniques related to major contract negotiation. For negotiating techniques, we tended to look to general experience. But to demonstrate that the techniques are relevant to any negotiation anywhere, we will now, as we summarise them, apply them to two other types of negotiation. Then as we finally look at systematic negotiation, we will end almost where we began, with some comments of the experienced negotiators.

Systematic preparation

The example that we will take to illustrate Stage 1 is the acquiring of a company. To illustrate Stage 2 we will look at power analysis

257

and its development in labour negotiation. Neither will be detailed, but both will be covered sufficiently to demonstrate that the four-stage approach we have given can be applied to negotiation on any topic.

Stage I: Identify the issues of negotiation and use them

The issues are identified for both sides. They are the substantive issues that relate to what the parties want to get out of negotiation, and the justification issues that relate to the means they will use to demonstrate that what they ask for is just or valid. From the issues, negotiating stances are developed. While they are certain for you, they can only be inferred for those of the other side. Now, from your stances you can set about developing the themes that you will use, and the staff work that will support them; the key commitments that will reinforce them; and the strategies, and where appropriate, the negotiating parameters that will achieve them. For the stances that you believe will be his, you develop the cover positions, strategies and, where appropriate, the concessions that you will use to deal with them.

Applying this to acquiring a company, your issues as the prospective purchaser will include the substantive issues of *valuation, method of payment* and *confidentiality*. The justification issues will include the *reasons for your interest, benefits for the prospective vendor*, the *need for further information* and the fact that you have *other options*. From these, negotiating stances are established which accurately reflect your position in the context of both your aspirations as they relate to that issue and to the company policy on it.

So, taking the first justification issue – reasons for your interest – themes that you might develop could include the fact that you were 'looking for an opportunity to expand', that 'the products of his company nicely complemented your own product range', and that 'geographically he is stronger where you are weaker'. The staff work such as his market profile would support them, and they would be reinforced with a key commitment such as 'In this case two into one certainly goes'. All this would probably be played in the first stage of the opening moves to demonstrate the credibility of your company and of your interest in his.

His substantive issues would not be dissimilar to yours, although the stances he would take on the first two anyway would probably be very different. He could also be looking for 'guarantees for the future' relating to his existing company and to his 'own position' in the new one. Justification issues could include the fact that he has 'no immediate need or desire to sell', his company has 'strength in the market-place', that the 'future for the company' looks particularly bright, and so on. Again taking the first justification issue, his stance could well be that your offer would therefore have to be tempting indeed. Your cover position and strategy would probably be to avoid the point by saying that both of you hope for a beneficial outcome, that further discussion and negotiation would enable you both to get a clearer picture of what was possible, and that if at the end of it he did not like what he saw, he could still walk away from the deal. Since it is a justification issue, parameters are unlikely to apply. But it should be added that as the substantive issues of both sides are reviewed, so your own negotiating parameters may become more specific and richer in negotiating terms as possible concessions are identified.

We have seen how the expectation test is progressively used and so the basis of strategy and its associated detail is laid. This applies to any type of negotiation.

Stage II: Assess and develop negotiating power

To illustrate this stage, I have taken an extreme case. It relates to the power analysis that turned out to be crucial for the future of the coal-mining industry in the United Kingdom in the mid-1980s.

In March 1984 the National Coal Board (NCB) told the Executive of the National Union of Mineworkers (NUM) that it intended to cut capacity the following year by a further 4 per cent. This meant a reduction of 4 million tonnes of deep-mined coal which would involve the closure of twenty pits and the loss of 20,000 jobs. Although there would be no compulsory redundancy, pits, it was stated, would be closed 'at the discretion of management'. In reply the NUM made a series of demands which included an end to pit closures and redundancies, an increase in subsidies, a write-off of NCB debts by the government and a freeze on the nuclear power electricity generation programme. These the Board rejected. In response the NUM balloted its members for all-out official strike action, but failed to get the 55 per cent majority required, thus repeating the two failures on the same issue the previous year. Nevertheless one colliery (Cortonwood) struck and was immediately supported by the Scotland and Yorkshire Regions with South Wales and Kent declaring strong sympathy. The Leicestershire and the Nottinghamshire miners, however, made it clear that they had little sympathy with their colleagues.

So as *The Economist* wrote of the two sides at the time, 'They're in the ring, but how hard will they fight?' In fact the outcome, which was a settlement on NCB terms, took over a year to be decided, during which period there was widespread industrial action. The outcome was, however, determined by an accurate prediction and use of negotiating power by the NCB before its position was formally put. In this case power analysis determined all.

So taking the power analysis model with which we are familiar, the negotiating power of the Coal Board would be indicated by the disadvantages to the NUM of disagreeing with the NCB position relative to those of agreeing it. The NUM would then take whichever course of action it perceived hurt it least.

Taking the disadvantages of disagreement for the NUM first, elements would include *difficulties in achieving full disruption* of supply since if the strike were not official, certain regions would probably maintain production, and reduce its impact; *difficulties in making the sanction bite* since the main user, the Central Electricity Generating Board, had coal stocks in the power stations which would act as a buffer against immediate loss of supply; and *consequences of legal action* since if the NUM did not actively dissuade its members from taking industrial action, it could legally be held to be liable for them. Initially, at any rate, the NCB could predict that the NUM would rate these elements as of some importance and would therefore attempt to reduce them.

On the other hand, disadvantages that the NUM Executive would be likely to consider if it agreed with the NCB proposal would include *further closures in the future* without any limit; *loss of the jobs of NUM members*, and with that a *reduction in union power*; *major loss of face for the Executive* as it was seen to back down (in fact for the third time) not just to the NCB, but also to the Conservative government to whom the Board was answerable; and a *hostile reaction* from a large and vociferous section of its membership. All of these would be elements that the NUM Executive could be expected to regard as very serious and hence they would rate them highly.

So power analysis before the proposal was made would indicate that the NUM would reject the proposal. Indeed closer analysis revealed that the disadvantages to the NUM of agreement were more than three times greater than those of disagreement, in which case it could be firmly anticipated that the proposal would be rejected outright.

So as far as the Board was concerned, there was a major imbalance between its negotiating objective and its power base.

In the light of this the NCB had, as would any other party faced with such an analysis, one of three options. Either it could moderate its negotiating position massively to one that the NUM would at least see as meriting discussion; or it could abandon its position completely; or if it elected to maintain it, it must set about improving its power base and planning to win the confrontation that would certainly occur. The last of these was its chosen option.

In this case power analysis has indicated the near certainty of a failure in mainstream negotiation at least over the short term. But it has also indicated to the NCB the areas in which strategy to develop its power base will be required. Here its overall aim is twofold. First, to increase the disadvantages to the NUM of disagreement. So before the proposal is put, the Board must set about attempting to ensure as far as possible that the strike will not be a total one and that sufficient supplies from inside and if necessary from outside the country can be maintained. It will delay making the proposal which will initiate the strike until the main users, the power stations, are as well equipped to deal with the disruption in their coal supply as they can be. So the proposal will be made at the end of the major coal-burning season rather than at the beginning of it; nuclear and oil-fired stations will be made ready to operate at peak load; measures will have been taken to ensure that the coal that is produced together with other necessary supplies will get into the power stations; and steps must have been taken to handle the NUM's most likely means of reducing their disadvantages of disagreement – in other words to neutralise the 'flying pickets'. As far as legal sanctions are concerned, these can be kept in reserve and used if and when they are necessary as a further pressure point. These are all 'strategies of the stick' and with the exception of the last will be initiated before the proposal which will start the trial of strength is put.

On the other hand, the 'strategies of the carrot' which reduce the disadvantages to the NUM and its members in agreeing with the proposal will for the most part be used in negotiation after the trial of strength has taken place. They will be dependent on what has happened during the battle, but will include favourable redundancy and job creation packages to reduce the hostile reaction factor and minor modifications to the original proposal which will have the effect of reducing the disadvantage levels of all the other elements.

In this way power is analysed. Through strategy it is developed and used. The technique is applicable to all negotiation.

Stage III: Create the optimum game plan

Strategies that have been identified from use of the expectation test and from power analysis are now merged with the standard strategies of negotiation to develop an overall game plan. As we have seen, this has its pre-negotiation strategies which were of particular importance in the last case. It then has its opening moves as conditioning on a progressive basis to develop the credible platform occurs, and as probing takes place to identify the needs and priorities of the other party as well as to get a reaction to your own conditioning. The case of acquiring a company showed just how important these two assignments of the opening moves are. The opening moves then continue into proposing and responding and into the decisive phase, with its associated signalling, as the basis for subsequent movement is laid. Negotiation then proceeds to the mid-game of movement and the end game of closure.

It is a sequence, and how it is managed is a function of the game plan. Its opening moves can be well defined. The mid- and end game moves will be generally prepared but will need to be made more specific or amended as the negotiations develop.

A game plan for any negotiation can always be developed by thinking in terms of the unique strategies derived from expectation and power analysis, and from the standard strategies of negotiation and by then putting them into a sequence relating to the four stages of negotiation that will almost invariably apply.

Stage IV: Check the detail

The final stage of preparation is very much a safety net. It is a review of all that you are likely to need for the negotiations that lie ahead.

The negotiating parameters

Are they clear? And agreed? Do they include concessions? Do they give me the room for manoeuvre I think I will need?

The negotiating strategy

Is it in place? Does it satisfy the three criteria of appropriateness, balance and movement? Has it got the fourth – eureka? Am I comfortable with it? And are the negotiating stances agreed?

The staff work

Is it now ready for me to use so that I can support my own stances and themes and deal with his?

My negotiating team

Are we, at best, in full accord on strategy? And at worse do they understand it? Will they abide by it? Are the roles clearly understood? And will the team act with empathy and discipline?

And finally, me!

Am I at ease with myself, my position and my strategy? Have I got the confidence and support of the director with overall responsibility for negotiation and of those who matter in the organisation? Do I approach these negotiations with the eager anticipation of eustress? Am I now ready to perform?

If the answer to all these is yes, you are ready indeed. These negotiations are an opportunity!

Systematic negotiation

Rather than go again through the four stages of negotiation, I think there is more to be gained by finally giving the general consensus of the experienced negotiators in two of the areas that relate to them.

We have said much about how to succeed. But the first of these areas concerns the weaknesses in negotiation shown by the inex-

264 Productive negotiation

perienced. They are salutary, to the point, and in some cases surprising! I give them in the order of frequency they were mentioned. Though many were given, here are the top eight.

First, *a desire to get it over with*. On the face of it, this is a surprising comment. But in fact most of the other reasons for poor performance can be traced back to having a sense of unease in negotiation; or worse, of being down-right unhappy with the process, the strategy and the position.

Second, *a failure to really 'play the themes'*. By this is meant a reluctance to embark on conditioning and to sustain it with tenacity on the one hand and with empathy on the other.

Third, *poor timing of offers* which usually means putting them on the table too soon before either a platform has been firmly built on which they can be made, or cognitive dissonance has been created that prepares the ground. And into this went also a failure to observe the natural rhythm and sequence of negotiation, and a failure to use and to respond to signals.

Fourth, *failing to build*. Rather than using, wherever possible, the themes and positions that are being presented there is a tendency to ignore or reject them outright. As one of the experienced negotiators remarked, negotiation is then rather like the sea battles of old when ships would sail past each other firing a broadside as they did so. They would then turn round and repeat the performance until one was destroyed. Negotiation, he said, can be like that. But it need not be.

Fifth, *making unlinked concessions*, and hence failing to preface them with the magic word 'if' in the hope that to go on heaping benefits on the other party will finally make him say yes. It probably will, but at what a cost!

Sixth, *feeling that you have to dominate*. We have mentioned the stereotyped view of the negotiator which often includes this aura of total psychological supremacy. However, good negotiators understand pressure and know that while they must apply it, movement from the other party tends to occur as pressure is withdrawn.

Seventh, *superficial treatment of arguments and positions* on the basis that the more you ignore them, the faster they will go away!

Eighth, *appearing nervous or embarrassed*. This starts with poor self-confidence, which in turn leads to a sense of insecurity. So panache in negotiating style is absent, posturing is defensive, necessary risks are not taken, the defence mechanisms are frequently shown, and opportunities for productive negotiation are all too often lost.

These are the weaknesses of the inexperienced. And which of us can claim to be immune from them?

But this book is about success. One of the questions I asked the experienced negotiators was this: 'Looking back on negotiations that went particularly well for you, what were the common denominators in success?' So we were not talking of good strategy, tactics and behaviour alone; I was asking them to tell me what for them had been the 'plus factors'.

I have to report that the runaway winner was *effective preparation and planning*', 'overkill in preparation', 'being so well prepared and organised that I knew I couldn't be beaten'. So preparation and planning have it!

Moving on from that to face-to-face negotiation, what were the plus points that made the difference? These were the eight points most frequently mentioned. First, *good conditioning* before formal negotiations started and then during it so that the first proposal made 'came as no surprise'. I know we have laboured the point – but so did they. And with it was the emphasis of 'versatility in conditioning' of having 'many ways of giving the same message'; 'a hundred and one ways of saying the same thing – and even then it might not be enough' were comments that were typical. But not for them dilution. Rather versatility lay in the 'rich variety of examples' and 'in the detail of the staff work' that was progressively used as themes were developed.

Second, *tenacity and clarity of purpose*. I have made much of the value of keeping negotiation moving, of avoiding impasse if that is possible, and of relaxing as well as applying pressure. So did they. But they also spoke in this context of 'determination and guts' and of 'strength and courage' which for them were key features in sustaining positional credibility and in the drive to a successful conclusion. The point is well made.

But with tenacity they mentioned clarity of purpose. 'Being quite clear on what you want from negotiation' and 'keeping your eye on the main purpose of why you are there' were comments that summarised their general thinking. So tenacity, yes; but on the right issue. As one of them said, quoting the salesman's dictum 'I never change the price, but I will change the package'.

Third, *the personality opposite*. 'Good chemistry'; 'a feeling that we could do business'; 'we were always in sync with each other'. And although I did not press them on it, I would be pretty sure that when 'the chemistry was right', they were negotiating with their own type and they shared the same values and understandings relating to negotiation and its processes. So Competitive Clive met his namesake. And although they would never have dreamed of rattling off the conventions even if they could formally state them (which would be very doubtful), they implicitly accepted the same set of rules and shared the same understanding of negotiation and its processes. So the mainstream approach was accepted – even welcomed; needs and positions were positively stated; signalling was skilfully given and received; and movement was not far short of an art form!

Fourth, *being ahead of the game*. 'A function of preparation' they insisted. But they went on to say how much in the negotiations that went really well they 'read the game like an open book'; they 'didn't seem to put a foot wrong'; 'I didn't make a move I regretted'. And more than one acknowledged the stroke of luck! But we need labour the point no further. It was that on the day their insight was particularly acute, and perhaps the next factor was present too.

Fifth, *psychological and physical well-being*. As one of them said 'just feeling strong in every way'. And another 'feeling larger than life'. We have said quite a lot about the psychological well-being of self-confidence, and how important it is. But the need to feel physically fit and mentally alert so that you know that you can 'take on whatever they throw at you' – that is a point well made.

Sixth, a *good team*. For these particular negotiations, the team 'just clicked'. The roles were firmly established, the approach was fully understood and there was discipline, empathy and consultation between the team members: 'We all knew what we were there for, and we did it well'; 'There was the distinct feeling that each of us was a professional and we just worked together.'

Seventh, *the development of trust* between the negotiators. As we have seen, this springs out of shared values and understandings. But significant store was set on 'relationships and values', on 'respect and a code of ethics', and on 'integrity and honesty'. And it came as no surprise when they commented that 'getting to know the other man' had been of prime importance.

And lastly, *knowing when to close*. I could not agree more!

These then are the eight plus factors which convert good strategy, tactics and behaviour into real success.

In this book we have looked at insight and at the techniques of systematic negotiation. But in the end, it is the blend of experience, insight and technique that carries the day. Experience I cannot give here, but I hope that our discussion of the other two has already added to it, and that you now feel that you are equipped as never before to 'negotiate the best deal'.

Summary

The eight stages of systematic negotiation from the beginning of negotiation to conclusion of the deal have been summarised.

Key question: How do you set about developing the people in your organisation who will indeed 'negotiate the best deal'?

Index